Epistemic Justification and the Skeptical Challenge

Epistemic Justification and the Skeptical Challenge

Hamid Vahid
Professor of Philosophy
Institute for Fundamental Sciences (IPM)

First published in 2005 by
PALGRAVE MACMILLAN
Houndmills, Basingstoke, Hampshire RG21 6XS and
175 Fifth Avenue, New York, N.Y. 10010
Companies and representatives throughout the world.

PALGRAVE MACMILLAN is the global academic imprint of the Palgrave
Macmillan division of St. Martin's Press, LLC and of Palgrave Macmillan Ltd.
Macmillan® is a registered trademark in the United States, United Kingdom
and other countries. Palgrave is a registered trademark in the European
Union and other countries.

ISBN-13: 978–1–4039–9354–0
ISBN-10: 1–4039–9354–8

This book is printed on paper suitable for recycling and made from fully
managed and sustained forest sources.

A catalogue record for this book is available from the British Library.

Library of Congress Cataloging-in-Publication Data

Vahid, Hamid, 1959–
    Epistemic justification and the skeptical challenge / Hamid Vahid.
        p. cm.
    Includes bibliographical references (p.) and index.
    ISBN 1–4039–9354–8 (cloth)
        1. Justification (Theory of knowledge) I. Title.

BD212.V34 2005
121'.6—dc22   2005043138

10 9 8 7 6 5 4 3 2 1
14 13 12 11 10 09 08 07 06 05

Printed and bound in Great Britain by
Antony Rowe Ltd, Chippenham and Eastbourne

For my parents

Contents

Acknowledgments

The project undertaken in this book is meant to be a contribution to contemporary discussions in epistemology. It is primarily concerned with the nature and importance of the concept of epistemic justification and also our understanding of the problem of skepticism against the background of certain prominent responses to it. In thinking about the issues discussed in this work, I have been helped by many people who have provided me with ideas, criticism, discussion, and encouragement.

My first exposure to epistemology was through Susan Haack's lectures on this subject when I was an undergraduate. Later, as a graduate student in Oxford, I got to know many philosophers who through their lectures and conversation helped shape my thinking on many important issues; in particular, David Bostock, John Campbell, Quassim Cassam, Bill Child, Hugh Rice, Christopher Peacocke, Stephen Williams, and Tim Williamson. Among those who particularly influenced my thinking at various points through their written works and correspondence, I should mention William Alston, Laurence BonJour, Anthony Breuckner, Alvin Goldman, Elliot Sober, and Brian McLaughlin. The late Yousuf Aliabadi and Muhammad Legenhausen deserve special mention for their helpful comments and criticisms. I also owe a substantial debt to Youcef Nedjadi whose unflagging support and encouragement throughout many years of friendship have been invaluable. Special thanks are due to my wife who had to put up with me while I was preoccupied with working on this project. Finally, I give thanks to the Institute for Fundamental Sciences and, in particular, to Javad Larijani for their enduring support and encouragement in my research projects.

I am also grateful to the editors and publishers of *Synthese*, *Erkenntnis*, *Dialogue*, *Kant-Studien*, *Metaphilosophy*, *Ratio*, *European Journal of Philosophy*, and *Journal of Philosophical Research* for permission to reuse and rework material from my papers in those journals.

Introduction

Beliefs can be evaluated from a number of perspectives. Depending on our choice of the standards and goals (moral, practical, etc.) the evaluation will yield different results. Epistemic evaluation, however, involves epistemic standards and appropriate epistemic goals. A theory of epistemic justification must therefore address the question of the aim and objective of epistemic justification, that is, what is the point of epistemic justification and why we value it. Although it is fair to say that the concept of epistemic justification has occupied the center stage in contemporary epistemological thought, the questions involving its own nature and characteristics are still very much matters of dispute. The situation has further been aggravated by the recent controversy over the internalist/externalist character of justification with both sides of the debate taking their cues from what they consider to be the nature of that concept. The increasing sophistication of current theories of epistemic justification and the ensuing disarray have prompted some theorists to deny its privileged place in epistemology, and redefine the debate in different terms.

Another central concern in contemporary epistemology has been skepticism. Recent discussions of skepticism usually take their departure from Descartes's skeptical hypothesis according to which instead of the world one normally supposes to exist, we can imagine a world consisting of an evil genius causing an agent to have just those beliefs that she would have were she to be situated in a world consisting of familiar objects. The fact that these two situations are phenomenologically indistinguishable, Descartes concludes, undermines much of what we ordinarily claim to know. Concerned about the skeptical consequences of this feature of our cognitive situation, defenders of commonsense have made a number of attempts to construct theories of knowledge and justification in order to refute Cartesian skeptical arguments by rebutting some of their underlying assumptions.

This book comprises three parts. The first part is concerned with providing a comprehensive account of epistemic justification by high-lighting certain desiderata on that notion. I begin, in Chapter 1, by discerning two elements that any successful theory of justification should incorporate. The idea being that every epistemic situation involving a cognizer forming a belief can be diagnosed along two dimensions: perspective and the objective. The perspective dimension is characterized in terms of the phenomenology of the cognizer's epistemic situation, in terms of how things appear from his perspective (this is usually highlighted by referring to our intuitions regarding the epistemic status of beliefs in the so-called skeptical demon scenarios). The objective dimension, however, is characterized in terms of how things actually are independently of the cognizer (this is what underlies our intuitions regarding the truth-conducive nature of epistemic justification). Commensurate with the two dimensions, justification will be both a function of how things appear from the cognizer's perspective as well as how things in actual fact are. It will be argued that it is not only the de facto reliability of our cognitive processes that renders them the source of justification of the beliefs they produce but our recognizing them to be so. To give an example, I shall explain how the deontological conception of epistemic justification aptly accommodates the perspective constraint. It will also be emphasized that to gain insight into the nature of epistemic justification one need not be able to solve the problem of skepticism as such insights may also be gained by seeing why the problem resists a resolution.

After elaborating on both the perspective and truth conducivity concerns, I shall go on to criticize certain well-known attempts to accommodate them. These include Foley's subjective theory of justification, Goldman's reliabilist account and Sosa's virtue perspectivism. I will also take issue with Alston's recent position which involves abandoning epistemic justification altogether. The bulk of the second chapter is taken up with discussing how the contours of the deontological conception of justification should be drawn. And, having defended it against some well-known objections, I argue that it offers the best hope of presenting a theory that is accountable to the concerns highlighted earlier. Next, I turn to the internalism/externalism debate in Chapter 3 and go between the horns of the dilemma. This is in accord with the position I have already taken on how the perspective constraint should be understood. It will also be emphasized that the deontological approach to the question of epistemic justification does not impose any internalist constraint on justification. Not being content with the current attempts to resolve the internalism/externalism debate, I try to open a new angle on the controversy. This is done by examining whether the currently popular thesis of content externalism (in the philosophy of mind) favors any side of the debate in epistemology. Finally, having identified the question of the compatibility of content externalism with privileged self-knowledge as the controversial assumption in the most plausible argument to link content externalism with the internalism/externalism debate in justification theory, my overall conclusion will be skewed toward perceiving the two issues as being independent of one another.

Part II of the book, introduces the problem of skepticism and the skeptical challenges to our ordinary knowledge-claims. This is done by discussing certain sources of skeptical doubt and evaluating the force of various maneuvers that have been adopted to establish the (Cartesian) skeptical claims. In this connection, I discuss arguments involving the principles of epistemic universalizability, deductive closure, and under-determination (in Chapters 5 and 6 respectively). Although my reactions to these arguments are mixed and qualified, it will be claimed that the skeptic would still be able to undermine much of what we ordinarily claim to know. I also consider the well-known problem of the criterion (in Chapter 4), and, having delineated its structure against the backdrop of some recent attempts to the same effect, go on to argue why it is such a powerful source of skeptical doubt by showing how certain (externalist) attempts fail to resolve it.

Part III is concerned with assessing some well-known responses to the skeptical challenge. These include Davidson's externalist argument from the principle of charity (Chapter 7), arguments from epistemic conservatism (Chapter 8), arguments from inference to the best explanation (Chapter 9), and Kantian transcendental arguments (Chapter 10). My conclusions in this part are generally negative. It is concluded that while one can gain much valuable insight into such key epistemological notions as justification and evidence by examining skeptical scenarios and arguments (as we did in Part I), skepticism does not seem to have any easy solution. In any case, as already argued in Part I, dissolving the problem of skepticism, was never conceived of as an adequacy condition on a proper theory of justification. One does not have to *solve* a theoretical problem in order to gain insight into the nature of the theoretical framework within which it is formulated. Thus, despite skepticism being an intractable problem, we can get by with what we have explained about the nature of epistemic justification.

Part I
Epistemic Justification

In this part of the book, I set out to articulate a particular conception of justification and defend it against competing alternatives. To do so, I begin by identifying two basic elements in an agent's epistemic situation, vis-à-vis the epistemic status of his beliefs, which any theory of justification should accommodate and be accountable to (viz., truth conducivity and the agent's perspective). Commensurate with these dimensions, epistemic justification will be both a function of how things appear from an agent's perspective as well as how things in actual fact are. Having elaborated on these constraints (in Chapter 1), I shall illustrate their significance for the concept of justification through certain examples including the so-called (skeptical) demon scenarios. Next I turn to certain well-known accounts of epistemic justification and show that, one way or another, they either fail to do justice to the constraints outlined earlier or end up accommodating them in an ad hoc manner.

From another angle, theories of epistemic justification are usually described as belonging to either deontological or non-deontological categories of justification with the former construing the concept of justification as involving the fulfillment of epistemic duty. Despite being the dominant view among traditional epistemologists, the deontological conception has been subjected to severe criticisms by a number of epistemologists. In Chapter 2, I shall argue that there is something deeply unsatisfying about the way these different conceptions of justification are usually introduced and contrasted with each other leaving it unclear just what it is that renders a particular conception deontological. Having clarified the pertinent issues, it will then be argued that the deontological conception of justification satisfies the constraints on epistemic justification spelled out earlier. Deontological justification has also been criticized on the ground that it presupposes the implausible doctrine of doxastic voluntarism. I shall argue that this charge is inconclusive.

It is also widely thought that the deontological conception of justification leads to internalism. The internalism/externalism distinction arises out of concerns for a proper explication of the concept of epistemic justification. On one side of the debate there are those epistemologists (internalists) who require that the justifying factors of a belief be cognitively accessible to the agent. Then there are those (externalists) who construe the concept of justification in terms of some relation (e.g., causal/nomological) between the cognizer and the world that might lie entirely outside his conception of the situation. Following my account of what the perspective character of justification involves, I shall challenge the claim that deontological justification leads to internalism, and try to steer a course between the two extremes of internalism and externalism in Chapter 3. An attempt is then made to identify the rationale behind the internalism/externalism controversy. Not being content with the current discussions of this debate, I then try to approach the controversy from a different angle and consider what bearing, if any, the currently popular thesis of content externalism has on this issue in epistemology, and whether, in particular, it favors justification internalism. I set out to present, what I take to be, the strongest argument for the incompatibility of content externalism and justification internalism while highlighting the controversial character of one of its main premises, namely, that content externalism is incompatible with privileged self-knowledge. Accordingly, I close the argument by rejecting the claim that the thesis of content externalism has significant bearing on the internalism/externalism debate in justification theory. This would leave intact our earlier conclusion about both sides of the debate being untenable.

1
Elements of a Theory of Justification

Although it is fair to say that the concept of epistemic justification has occupied the center stage in contemporary epistemological thought, the questions involving its own nature and characteristics are still very much matters of dispute. The situation has further been aggravated by the recent controversy over the internalist/externalist character of justification with both sides of the debate taking their cues from what they consider to be the nature of that concept.

Epistemic justification is usually thought of as that species of justification which is tied to beliefs and judgments. It is that which is needed, among other things, to turn a true belief into knowledge. For to ask whether an agent knows something, we are, in effect, enquiring whether he has sufficient or adequate grounds for his belief. Although attempts at explicating "knowledge" have not, by general consensus, met with success, epistemologists still carry on talking about epistemic justification as an epistemic property that is valuable in its own right. It differs from truth in being defeasible and being a matter of degree. And again, unlike truth, justification has a contextual nature. For whether a particular belief is justified for an agent is a function of that agent's epistemic situation. Thus, what is justified for a person at a certain time may be unjustified for that person at another time. What underlies the difference is usually characterized in terms of the relevant body of evidence that the agent possesses at different times. Traditionally, justified belief has been characterized as a type of belief that is epistemically permissible to hold highlighting its so-called "normative" character as involving what we should or should not believe. On the other hand, it is widely held that epistemic justification is distinct from other species of justification like moral or pragmatic justification in that it is intended to serve the goal of believing truth and avoiding falsity which is precisely why it is regarded as necessary for knowledge. I shall say more about these features of epistemic justification in the course of examining its nature throughout this chapter.

There are, however, two distinct features of justification whose analyses will dominate our discussion, namely, perspective and truth conducivity. Generally speaking, every epistemic situation involving a cognizer forming a belief can be diagnosed along two dimensions: the perspective and the objective. The perspective dimension is characterized in terms of the phenomenology of the cognizer's epistemic situation, in terms of how things appear from his perspective. The objective dimension, on the other hand, is construed in terms of how things actually are independently of the cognizer. Commensurate with the two dimensions, justification will be both a function of how things appear from the cognizer's perspective as well as how things in actual fact are. The latter is what underlies our intuitions regarding the truth-conducive nature of epistemic justification. The perspective character of justification, on the other hand, is usually highlighted by our intuitions regarding the justificational status of beliefs in, say, the so-called "demon scenarios." Consider a possible world that is indistinguishable from the actual world as far as our experiences are concerned, but in which a demon has seen to it that our perceptual beliefs are invariably false. Since the demon world is indistinguishable from the actual world, perceptual beliefs in that world should enjoy as much justification as they do in the actual world despite being, by hypothesis, invariably false.

It is my contention in this chapter that any adequate theory of justification should be able to accommodate these two features of epistemic justification. I shall thus begin by analyzing, in more detail, what these two ingredients of justification actually involve before proceeding to examine how certain well-known accounts of epistemic justification fare in regard to accommodating them.

1.1   The perspective character of epistemic justification

Conferring positive epistemic status on a belief of an agent is, in part, a function of how he has behaved in forming the belief in question in the light of the resources at his disposal and in view of how things have appeared to him then. In short, the justificational status of a belief is to be gauged with regard to how the belief has been formed from the perspective of the agent, in turn, construed in terms of beliefs and other doxastic attitudes that the agent possesses at that time. The positive epistemic status of the judgments made by an agent is, thus, affected by how things appear from his perspective. That is to say, whether a particular belief is justified for a particular person depends on his epistemic situation. The belief that, say, there are nine planets in the solar system may be unjustified for an agent, S, at t_1, and justified for him, or another person, at another time, t_2, because S happens to lack the relevant evidence at t_1 which he later comes to possess at t_2. The epistemic status of a belief is, thus, partly, a function of how complete an agent's epistemic situation is. A cognizer's epistemic situation is incomplete or otherwise defective if all the relevant evidence (for a particular belief) is not available to him.

"Availability" is, however, an epistemic notion suggesting cognitive accessibility. It underscores the fact that to assess a belief, action, or decision from a particular perspective, one has to take into account those facts or reasons that are cognitively accessible to the pertinent agent. After all, how could those reasons be *his* reasons if he lacks cognitive access to them? Accordingly, the perspective constraint on epistemic justification is constitutively linked to the notion of available evidence. Equally relevant to the perspective character of justification is how responsibly an agent behaves vis-à-vis the evidence available to him when forming a belief. For, intuitively speaking, in asking whether an agent's belief is justified we wish to know whether he has done his best, that is, has been epistemically responsible, in taking all the available evidence into account in order to bring about the epistemic goal the belief in question is intended to serve.

The connection between justification and responsibility, however, is best seen in moral contexts. Objectively speaking, an agent's actions may fail to bring about greater good, though they may still be morally justified because he has done his best to see to it that they lead to greater good. In that case, we tend to regard the agent as having behaved responsibly vis-à-vis the obtaining of that aim. The same is true of an agent's doxastic situation where his perspective influences the positive epistemic status of the beliefs he forms in that situation. The perspective character of epistemic justification may be illustrated by two types of scenarios. What characterizes the first type of scenarios is our reluctance to confer positive epistemic status on an agent's beliefs despite the fact that they happen to be invariably true whereas the second type of scenarios seek to reverse the direction; we find ourselves inclined to confer positive epistemic status on an agent's beliefs despite those beliefs being invariably false. What is important to note, however, is that both types of scenarios are intended to make the same point, namely, that the subject's perspective is an important factor in determining the justificational status of his beliefs.

For the first type of scenarios, consider the following example (enunciated by BonJour) where an agent, Norman, is a reliable clairvoyant who spontaneously and forcefully finds himself with beliefs emanating from this source. He accepts these beliefs without bothering to find out if they are true and possesses no available evidence for or against the reliability of such power or of himself possessing it. One day, as a result of exercising such power, Norman comes to believe that the president is in New York. Now, from an objective point of view, Norman is a reliable register of information about his environment in just the same way that a thermometer reliably registers information about its environmental climate. However, thus conceived, an agent's belief is something that involves no contribution on the part of the agent. From his perspective the beliefs are no different from mere hunches or arbitrary convictions. It seems clear that Norman is not justified in accepting the beliefs in question. They are something that happen to him purely as a result of some nomological relation between him and his environment. But why, one may wonder, should the holding of such a relation, entirely outside Norman's ken, render his beliefs epistemically justified. All that follows is that Norman's beliefs are not accidentally true.

> But how is this supposed to justify Norman's belief? From his subjective perspective, it *is* an accident that the belief is true. And the suggestion here is that the rationality or justifiability of Norman's belief should be judged from Norman's own perspective rather than from one which is unavailable to him. (BonJour 1985, p. 44)

The same point about the indispensability of the agent's perspective can be made in the opposite direction by the second type of scenarios (the so-called "demon scenarios") where, as we have seen, the agent's beliefs, though invariably false, seem to be intuitively justified.

It is very important, however, to be clear about the import of the perspective constraint. As noted earlier, what it highlights is the availability of reasons for a belief to the agent holding that belief. In other words, all it requires is that a belief's justification-conferring grounds must include only those that the agent can easily recognize or know (in an attenuated sense of the term) to obtain. The perspective requirement says nothing about the "mode" of such access. It certainly does not confine the evidence pertinent to the justification of a belief to those that are only reflectively accessible. Other modes of awareness (such as a posteriori knowledge) are not ruled out since some of those readily knowable evidential facts, like track records, and so on, might be external rather than internal. For example, a perceptual process's track record is not the sort of property that can be accessed through mere reflection. So for evidence to be available to a subject, it does not have to be available to him through mere reflection. The perspective constraint, at best, requires that the grounds of one's beliefs be accessible to the agent without suggesting any particular mode of awareness or any distinct route to such knowledge.

To illustrate the point, suppose we are lying in our bed listening to the singing of a bird in our balcony. Subsequently, on the basis of what we know, we form the belief that a pigeon is nearby. Our evidence for the belief in question is our association of this kind of noise with the presence of pigeons so that when we hear a similar noise on this occasion we take it as a reliable indicator that a pigeon is nearby. Our knowledge (or awareness) of the evidence in question comes through sense experience. Usually, under normal circumstances, such knowledge is taken for granted and is not made explicit. Nonetheless, we are in possession of such knowledge. It is just that, being plain and obvious, it is hardly worth mentioning and we feel no need to highlight it. It is difficult to see how, without recognizing the noise we hear *as* evidence, it could function as *our* reason for the belief in question.[1]

Having accentuated the perspectival character of epistemic justification and suggesting what it involves, I will close this section by providing an example of a theory of justification that seems to do justice to this constraint. The theory I have in mind is the so-called "deontological" conception of epistemic justification. I shall fully analyze this conception in Chapter 2, but, for now, I only wish to present it as an example of how the perspective element can be satisfactorily incorporated in an account of epistemic justification. The idea behind the deontological justification is that justification is a function of how well an agent has formed his beliefs vis-à-vis the fulfillment or violations of his epistemic obligations and duties. Thus, to say that a belief is deontologically justified is to say that in holding that belief, the agent has flouted no epistemic obligations, and is, thus, subject to no blame or disapproval. The concept of epistemic obligation, however, is, as with its ethical counterpart, ambiguous between objective and subjective obligations. The former are identified from an objective point of view (how things in fact are), while the latter are measured from the agent's perspective, that is, in terms of how things appear to him. Now, since deontological justification primarily involves epistemic responsibility on the part of the agent, deontological justification is a function of what the agent (justifiably) takes his obligations to be. A responsible belief is a belief that in forming it, the agent has, from his point of view (perspective), violated none of the relevant epistemic obligations. Thus, deontological justification very naturally incorporates the perspectival ingredient of epistemic justification.

For the sake of concreteness, suppose we take one's primary epistemic obligation to consist of forming beliefs on the basis of adequate grounds. Thus, following Chisholm, we may say that a person is (deontologically) justified if he has done his best to form beliefs that have adequate bases. The term "trying one's best" is intended to reflect the idea that deontological justification is a function of an agent's perspective on the world and, at the same time, distances it from radically subjective theories. Having behaved in the manner, the agent would be a responsible epistemic agent. Moreover, what this, in turn, implies is that the belief an agent forms is based on adequate evidence that he *recognizes* as obtaining, otherwise he would not be acting in accordance with his obligations, thus, failing to be an epistemically responsible agent. Of course, despite his best efforts, the agent may still fail to form beliefs on the basis of adequate grounds. But that is fine. Indeed, being prone to error is conceptually connected to the idea of epistemic justification having a perspective character, in turn, explaining why a justified belief can be false. We thus get a neat incorporation of the perspective element in the deontological approach to epistemic justification. A fortiori, our intuitions regarding the justificational status of beliefs in problematic scenarios can be easily explained once we invoke the deontological conception. In the Norman example, his beliefs are not justified because they are not responsibly formed as he fails to do his best in meeting his intellectual obligations, while beliefs in the demon scenarios are justified because they are, by hypothesis, responsibly formed. I shall now turn to analyzing the truth conducivity element of epistemic justification.

1.2   Epistemic justification and truth conducivity

It is, I believe, generally agreed that, on any plausible account of epistemic justification, there must be an intimate link between truth and justification (but see Ginet 1975; Pollock 1974). This is, in fact, what is supposed to distinguish epistemic justification from other species of justification such as moral or prudential justification. On a truth-conducive account of epistemic justification, this relation is often spelled out in probabilistic terms: given the satisfaction of the conditions of justification, it is highly probable that the pertinent beliefs are true. So a justified belief is a belief that is more likely to be true.[2] What has however obscured this seemingly innocent notion is the fact that it is often defended by those who uphold different views about the nature of epistemic justification. For example, while the reliability theory of justification is generally thought to be a paradigm case of both a truth-conducive as well as an externalist account of justification, there are internalist theories that explicitly regard their accounts of justification as being truth-conducive for they take truth as being the main aim of cognition.

> *[I]f our standards of epistemic justification are appropriately chosen*, bringing it about that our beliefs are epistemically justified will also tend to bring it about ... that they are true. If epistemic justification were not conducive to truth in this way, if finding epistemically justified beliefs did not substantially increase the likelihood of finding true ones, then epistemic justification would be irrelevant to our main cognitive goal and dubious worth. (BonJour 1985, p. 8)

Still other internalists seem to think that an externalist, truth-conducive conception of justification leaves no room for justified false beliefs.

> According to this traditional conception of "internal" epistemic justification, there is no logical connection between epistemic justification and truth. A belief may be internally justified and yet be false. The externalist feels that an adequate account of epistemic justification should exhibit *some* logical connection between epistemic justification and truth. (Chisholm 1988, p. 286)

I am not going to adjudicate between these versions of internalism vis-à-vis their attitude toward the truth conducivity of epistemic justification, as I shall reject internalism later on when I come to discuss this topic in Chapter 3. My main aim in referring to these views here is simply to point out how the notion of truth conducivity has been variously treated by theorists with diverse epistemic perspectives as well as those sharing the same conception.

As can be seen from the preceding remarks, despite their differences, most theorists share the view that the basic goal of cognition is to believe what is true and to avoid what is false (let us call this the "truth goal"). This raises the question of how one is to conceive of the connection between the truth goal and the purported truth-conducive character of epistemic justification. According to Alston "[t]he claim that justification is essentially truth-conducive is often supported by taking the basic aim of cognition to be the acquisition of true beliefs and the avoidance of false beliefs" (Alston 1996, p. 242). Here is how he expands on the nature of this aim.

> [Epistemic justification] has to do with a specifically *epistemic* dimension of evaluation. ... Epistemic evaluation is undertaken from what we might call the "epistemic point of view." That point of view is defined by the aim of maximizing truth and minimizing falsity in a large body of beliefs. (Alston 1985, p. 83)

But the leap from the truth goal to the thesis that "justification is essentially truth-conducive" is unwarranted without further elaboration of the nature of this goal as there are theorists who avowedly endorse the truth goal while, seemingly, rejecting the truth conducivity of epistemic justification: "However, to say that the goal that helps distinguish epistemic rationality from other kinds of rationality is a truth-directed goal is not to say that truth is a prerequisite of epistemic rationality. In particular, it is not to say that it is impossible for most of what is epistemically rational to be false" (Foley 1987, p. 155). So to see how intimate the connection between the two is we need to have a closer look at the truth goal and the way it should be formulated.

Let us start with Alston's formulation of the truth goal. Epistemic justification, he says, is essentially a matter of serving the aim of maximizing truth and minimizing falsity in a large body of beliefs. It has however been objected that this characterization of the goal of justification leaves no room for justified false beliefs and unjustified true beliefs (Maitzen 1995). For if a belief is true, it is hard to see how it could *fail* to maximize true belief, and if it is false how it could have a *verific* tendency. So all true beliefs will be justified and all false beliefs unjustified. I do not think that this objection is successful, but, in trying to counter it, we would gain a better insight into the nature of the truth goal.

The first thing to do on the way of undermining this objection is to recall the perspective dimension of epistemic justification. As we have already noted, unlike truth, justification is perspectival, that is, it is determined relative to the cognizer's available body of evidence. If a belief is true, then it is true at all times. By contrast, the justification of a belief depends on the epistemic circumstances of the cognizer holding that belief, vis-à-vis, the body of evidence at his disposal. Thus, an agent who is unjustified in holding a belief at a certain time may become justified later on once he comes to possess further relevant evidence. Now, given the goal of justification, we wish to maximize our stock of true beliefs and minimize our stock of false beliefs, but, in view of the perspective character of justification, we are *bound* to do it relative to the body of evidence (E) at our disposal. As it turns out, however, the epistemic situation of a cognizer is often incomplete or defective, that is, it fails to include all the relevant evidence. So E might be equally incomplete or defective. Now relative to E, a belief p may be more likely to be true and so, according to the truth goal, justified, whereas it is in fact false. Or, it may be that, relative to E, p is more likely to be false, and, thus, unjustified, whereas it is, in fact, true. So, given the perspective character of epistemic justification, there would be room for unjustified true beliefs and justified false beliefs on the truth goal.

What is important to note, however, is that the truth goal is not just a function of truth-ratio in a body of belief at a particular time. For then it would be difficult to see how a false belief can be justified, that is, it can be said to serve the truth goal. The fact is that the truth goal is a *historical* concept. It is to be understood in terms of the overall maximization of truth and minimization of falsity in one's belief repertoire *in the long run*. So it is not just the truth-ratio (at a particular time) that determines whether believing p is a good thing from the epistemic point of view but also how the belief is formed or sustained. This is, in other words, to adopt a diachronic, rather than a synchronic, conception of the truth goal. We would then be able to explain how, say, a false belief can be justified in virtue of promoting the goal of maximizing truth in one's belief system. This is how the explanation would proceed. Given the perspective character of justification, our available body of evidence E might indicate that a belief p is more likely to be true, whereas it is in fact false. Relative to E, then, believing p is a good thing from the epistemic point of view because it is adequately grounded and, thus, justified. But we have to treat like cases alike, that is, take well-grounded beliefs in future as justified as well. As a norm, however, most of the well-grounded beliefs turn out to be true. That is why a false belief can be said to be justified in virtue of maximizing true beliefs in the long run. A parallel argument can be used to explain the possibility of unjustified true beliefs. The diachronic conception of the truth goal makes the justification of a belief sensitive to how the belief has been formed in a non-accidental and reliable way. The synchronic truth-ratio version of the truth goal, by contrast, ignores the way a belief has been formed.

In defending the diachronic version of the truth goal, I have appealed to the thesis that like cases have to be treated alike. For example, if we regard a belief as justified (because it is adequately grounded), we have to treat other adequately grounded beliefs as justified as well. This is nothing other than an application of the so-called thesis of epistemic supervenience according to which epistemic properties (e.g., being justified) supervene on non-epistemic properties such as being reliably formed, being adequately grounded, and so on. If we have two beliefs which are adequately grounded and one is justified so is the other. So to say that believing p is a good thing from the epistemic point of view of maximizing true beliefs is just to say that believing p has a *tendency*, in virtue of the adequacy of its grounds, to bring about an overall maximization of true beliefs in our belief repertoire (in the long run). This tendency is ensured by the "fact" that justification is a supervenient concept requiring us to universalize our epistemic judgment about a particular case to other similar cases. That is, when confronted with a case that invites a judgment (of certain kind), we ought to treat that case in the manner that we have treated cases like that in the past (assuming, of course, that we are still sticking to our previous assessments). This highlights the historical nature of the concept of supervenience as its application connects the past and future judgments (involving the ascription of a property) under a single unifying principle. It is, thus, no wonder that, with justification being a supervenient concept, the aim that it is supposed to serve (viz., the truth goal) should exhibit a diachronic nature.

Of course not everybody goes along with taking the truth goal as being our primary epistemic goal or having a diachronic nature. Michael DePaul, for example, has criticized the truth goal on the ground that if we take truth as being our only epistemic goal, then we would not be able to explain how knowledge is better than mere true belief: "But if we are pluralists about epistemic value and take justification to be good apart from any connection it might have to the truth, then we can explain the superior value of knowledge" (DePaul 2001, p. 180). To give an example, he says, it is very reasonable to value a victory obtained by exercising a brilliant strategy more than a victory brought about by luck. But this is because, he says, more than one value is at stake here. In addition to taking victory as a good thing, we also regard excellence and competence as good as well.

Likewise for the case of valuing knowledge over mere true belief. But this value pluralism is plausible only if we focus on a particular time slice of our goals. So long as our aim is to win a battle at a time t, then preferring a well-conducted victory over a haphazard and accidental one requires that we take two values into account, that is, victory and competence. But if our aim is "winning battles in the long run," not just at a particular time *t*, then, to prefer a well-conducted victory over an accidental one, we need not take up value pluralism. We are bound to prefer a well-conducted victory so long as our aim is to win battles in the long run. Likewise, we value knowledge because we want to be a reliable register of facts about the world, thereby, forming true beliefs in the long run rather than just at a particular moment. Once we adopt a diachronic conception of the aim of justification as overall maximization of truth (or "truth in the long run"), we can ensure that knowledge is more valuable than mere true belief without embracing value pluralism.

It might be objected that, given the preceding remarks, our epistemic aim is no longer believing true and avoiding false propositions, but, rather, in having adequately grounded or reliably formed beliefs (Maitzen 1995; David 2001). But even if we regard the goal of justification as forming beliefs by way of reliable mechanisms, that still does not dispose of the truth goal. For any feature of beliefs that is probably correlated with truth, counts toward the original aim of maximizing true and minimizing false beliefs. These factors include, reliable belief formation, being the best explanation of certain phenomenon, and so on. To deny this is, as we said, to understand the aim of maximizing true beliefs in much too crude a sense. By being sensitive to how a belief has been formed, the aim of justification should be understood as having a diachronic nature. I believe we now have sufficient grounds to substantiate the claim made at the beginning of this section: As long as epistemic justification is thought of as serving the truth goal (in a diachronic sense), that is, as long as this goal is built into the notion of justification by definition, then justification will emerge as a truth-conducive concept in just the sense that a justified belief would be more likely to be true.

The truth conducivity of epistemic justification is, however, quite compatible, as we have seen, with the possibility of justified beliefs being false. It is even compatible with justified beliefs turning out to be false on a massive scale (as in demon scenarios). This follows from the perspective dimension of epistemic justification, the fact that it is always determined relative to the agent's available body of evidence. This latter claim requires some elucidation which I shall now proceed to provide. Perhaps the best way of articulating what is meant by this claim is through an example.

Suppose Smith visits a museum and is particularly impressed by certain archaic objects (like vases, bowls, etc.) that he sees in the central room of the museum. These objects are kept inside illuminated window boxes. He is so impressed that he decides to take his son to visit the museum the next day. Unfortunately, the night following Smith's visit, the museum becomes the object of a well-planned robbery where the thieves manage to steal all the antique objects in the central room. Concerned about their reputation, the museum authorities decide to fill the empty window boxes in the central room with exact and convincing holograms of the missing objects till they can recover and return them to the museum. So the next day when Smith is guiding his son through the room (with the help of the museum's brochure) everything seems to him to be exactly like it was yesterday. He forms, once more, varieties of beliefs about the "objects" in the room similar to the types he had formed yesterday (to strengthen the case, let us assume that the original objects have, by now, all been destroyed by the thieves).

Intuitively, Smith's beliefs are all justified despite being invariably false. Moreover, they are justified in just the same sense that they were justified yesterday. Just as yesterday, he can entertain thoughts like, "given this particular visual sensation that I have now, it is more likely that there is a vase with these particular features in front of me." However, despite the fact that Smith's phenomenological perspective is indistinguishable from the one he possessed yesterday, what has changed about him is that his epistemic situation has become defective today. He now fails to possess all the evidence (e.g., evidence about the fraud) that is pertinent to his epistemic situation. But this does not deprive him from having justified beliefs about the "objects" in the room in the very same (truth-conducive) sense that he had yesterday even though these beliefs, as well as the beliefs formed later, are all false. (Demon scenarios are just highly dramatized versions of this example but the intended epistemic morale remains intact.)

So, given the perspective character of justification, one can imagine an agent forming justified but false beliefs on the basis of adequate grounds (because his body of evidence fails to include all the relevant evidence). It is quite conceivable that such an epistemic situation remains always defective. (A real life example would include the case of scientific theories if something like pessimistic induction were true about them. Here we have scientists continuously forming false but justified beliefs because, with their epistemic situation remaining defective, they fail to consider all the evidence relevant to their theories.) In that case, although the agent would be forming beliefs on the basis of, let us assume, available adequate grounds, his justified beliefs would remain invariably false. This would not however undermine the truth-conducive character of justification that his beliefs enjoy. Accordingly, the possibility of mostly false but justified beliefs (in a truth-conducive sense) is a coherent one.

Before concluding this section, it is worth noting that, thus far, we have only been seeking to draw the contours of the notion of epistemic justification rather showing whether or not this concept is instantiated. These are two different projects. Put differently, dissolving the problem of skepticism should not be thought of as an adequacy condition on a proper theory of justification (a theory giving the truth conditions of such locutions as "*S* is justified in believing *p*"). Consider, as an illustration, a concept akin to the concept of justification, that is, the concept of knowledge. Ever since Gettier proposed his counterexamples, a great many attempts were made to patch up this concept. However, none of these attempts were guided by the assumption that a proper account of knowledge should also be able to show that this concept is instantiated. The only adequacy condition on a proper analysis of knowledge that these subsequent endeavors sought to satisfy was that such an analysis should leave no room for knowledge by luck, that is, a theory of knowledge should have the consequence that when its requirements are satisfied the (relevant) belief is not true by accident. Solving the problem of skepticism was never part of the program of presenting an adequate analysis of knowledge.

Compare: The only adequacy condition in Tarski's analysis of truth in formal languages is the satisfaction of convention *T*. It was never expected that such an analysis should also be able to show that, say, arithmetical statements are in fact true. Resolving the problem of realism was never part of Tarski's program in providing a theory of truth for formal languages. To conclude, in providing an analysis of the perspective and truth-conducive features of epistemic justification, one need not be bogged down by one's inability to dissolve the problem of skepticism. Here I concur with Alston, "[H]uman knowledge and justified belief is a subject matter that, like others, we can study without first having to show that it is there to be studied" (Alston 1989, p. 2). In a similar vein, referring to the difficulty of explicating the notion of "relevance" when defending his relevant alternative theory of knowledge, Goldman writes, "I leave open the question of whether there is a 'correct' set of relevant alternatives, and if so, what it is. To this extent, I also leave open the question of whether skeptics or their opponents are 'right' " (Goldman 1992, p. 90).

> This is not the failure of the theory, in my opinion. An adequate account of the term "know" should make the temptations of skepticism comprehensible, which my theory does. ... In any event, I put forward my account of perceptual knowledge not primarily as an antidote to skepticism, but as a more accurate rendering of what the term "know" actually means. (Goldman 1992, pp. 101–2)

Having expounded what the two constraints of perspective and truth conducivity on epistemic justification involve, I shall now proceed to examine certain well-known theories of justification to see how they fare in meeting these requirements.

1.3   Foley: egocentric rationality

I begin by assessing one important theory of justification (put forth by Foley) which claims to incorporate both the truth goal as well as the subject's perspective on his epistemic situation. Foley regards rationality (justification) as a goal-directed notion and defines it in terms of the point of view one adopts (Foley 1987, 1993). This point of view consists of a goal, a perspective and a set of resources. A perspective is essentially a set of beliefs, and what perspective one adopts in making a rationality judgment depends on one's interests as well as the context. Resources consist of information and the data represented in one's beliefs, and they vary in accordance with the theory of justification under question. On a foundationalist account, for example, resources consist of psychological states such as belief, experience, and so on. We can, thus, define rationality along the following lines: It is rational for S to believe q because he has resources R and because from perspective P it seems that, given R, believing q is an effective way of satisfying the goal G. Foley is now able to articulate his conception of epistemic rationality which turns out to be a radically subjective account. He takes, as his goal, the synchronic goal of now having an accurate and comprehensive belief system with the "perspective" construed in egocentric terms, namely, that of individual believers. Thus, it is egocentrically rational for an agent to believe a proposition only if he would think on deep reflection that believing it is conducive to having an accurate and comprehensive belief system. But how deep should a "deep reflection" go? Foley postulates a stopping point: We have to go on till further reflection can no longer affect our judgment. This is where we reach the point of stability, the point when we become invulnerable to self-criticism. At this point reflection would reveal the agent's deepest epistemic standards. So the rationality of a belief depends on how it would be assessed in terms of the agent's deepest epistemic standards.

Thus, Foley construes egocentric rationality as depending subjunctively on deep reflection. But he goes on to add that "you need not have actually engaged in lengthy reflection in order to rationally believe (or rationally withhold on) a proposition. It is enough for your current opinion to conform with what your stable opinion would be"

(Foley 1993, p. 100). He gives an example in which a man and a woman, who are both ideally reflective, come to believe a proposition on exactly the same evidence. However, he not she would come to believe that the evidence in question is inadequate (upon reflection). According to Foley this counterfactual difference affects their epistemic status regardless of whether this difference is reflected in their current beliefs. This difference is enough to make her, rather than him, egocentrically rational to believe that proposition.

It seems quite clear that Foley's account of justification (rationality) does justice to the perspective character of epistemic justification. Indeed, it seems that his account gives it more prominence than it deserves. For, as our analysis of the case involving deontological justification showed, to comply with the perspective constraint on epistemic justification, one's theory of justification need not go so far down the subjective plane that Foley's account demands. Indeed, as I shall explain shortly, Foley's attempt to blend a radically subjective account of epistemic justification with a radically objective account of truth (via the adoption of the truth goal) is the source of some tension in his theory which, in turn, explains why he tends to reject the truth conducivity of justification. To elaborate, let us first focus on the nature of the truth goal that his account of rationality incorporates, and see if it consistently upholds that version of the goal. In this regard, it would be helpful to begin by recalling that a historical account of justification, for example, reliabilism, "has to maintain that the truth goal is the diachronic goal of having true beliefs in the long run" (David 2001, p. 166). The reason being that, by taking the past as well as the future performance of belief-forming processes into account, reliabilism naturally promotes a diachronic understanding of the truth goal. Now, as we have seen, Foley explicitly subscribes to a synchronic reading of the truth goal. However, this seems to be undermined by the "reliabilist" ingredients of his account. Let me explain.

Foley regards rationality (justification) as a goal-directed notion and defines it in terms of the point of view one adopts (consisting of a goal, a perspective, and a set of resources). As we saw, the perspective in question is an egocentric one, namely, that of individual believers. So it is egocentrically rational for you to believe a proposition only if you would think on deep reflection that believing it is conducive to having an accurate and comprehensive belief system. This leads Foley to construe egocentric rationality as depending subjunctively on reflection. However, it is not any old notion of reflection that he has in mind. The reflection should be deep in that the agent has to go on till further reflection can no longer affect his judgment. This is where we reach the point of stability, the point when we become invulnerable to self-criticism. He further requires that during the process of reflection the agent should not be subject to distorting influences such as drowsiness, drunkenness, and so on. According to Foley, under such conditions reflection would be indicative of an agent's deepest epistemic standards. Now by *relativizing* rationality to an agent's point of view, the process of reflection, with the kind of constraints that Foley imposes on it, emerges as functioning like a reliable process (a reliable indicator of an agent's deepest epistemic standards construed, in turn, in terms of the truth goal).

However, these reliabilist ingredients, innocent as they might initially appear, come into conflict with certain suppositions in Foley's account. First, they undermine his claim about the nature of the truth goal. For if, as explained, the reliability of a process is a function of the process's past and future performance, the truth goal cannot be, as he claims, of a synchronic nature. And, in any case, given what was earlier said about the conceptual connection between the truth goal, properly under-stood, and truth conducivity, denying the latter would be tantamount to denying that the truth goal is, after all, the sole goal of cognition. Moreover, the reliabilist elements are also the source of a related tension in his account. This is because once we take the process of reflection to be a reliable indicator of an agent's deepest epistemic standards, then we must concede that one's theory of justification (rationality) is truth-conducive after all. There are, however, certain statements made by Foley that seem to go against this conclusion.

> Epistemic rationality is distinguished from other kinds of rationality by its truth-directed goal. ... However ... [this] is not to say that truth is a prerequisite of epistemic rationality. In particular, it is not to say that it is impossible for what is epistemically rational to be false, and likewise it is not even to say that it is impossible for most of what is epistemically rational to be false. (Foley 1987, p. 155)

Of course, these remarks, viewed one way, are quite compatible with epistemic justification being truth-conducive. For, as we have seen, given the perspective character of justification, the possibility of justified false beliefs, even on a massive scale, can be coherently countenanced.

There are, however, other remarks by Foley that cannot be so easily accommodated. For example, he says that "there is no guarantee that what we on reflection would think to be an effective means to our goal will yield better results than a flip of the coin or some other random method" (Foley 1987, p. 173). But this is going too far for an account of justification that professes to be committed to the truth goal. For what seems to be at issue in Foley's remark is not merely the epistemic worry of whether we can aim at something even when we will not know whether we have attained it. Rather, Foley seems to be making the (metaphysical) claim that, as far as the obtaining of the truth goal is concerned, all methods, random or otherwise, are on a par. But this, if true, says more about the viability of the truth goal than the method used to attain it. For if the adoption of egocentric rationality as a means of obtaining the truth goal is just as good as any "random method," then why take believing truth and avoiding falsehood as our basic cognitive goal? Any other goal would do the job if our theory of epistemic rationality were to exhibit such a random nature as a means of obtaining that goal. Here I concur with David: "[A]s Foley ... emphasizes, when we reflect about egocentric rationality, we realize that there is no particularly good reason for thinking that being egocentrically rational will promote the goal of believing the truth one bit. One cannot help but feel that there is something odd about this situation" (David 1996, p. 952).

1.4   Goldman: process reliabilism

Process reliabilism is basically the view that justification (knowledge) arises from reliable cognitive processes. Dubbed by its most prominent exponent (Alvin Goldman) as a "historical" theory, process reliabilism makes the positive epistemic status of a belief a function of its history and of how it has been formed. In a more recent statement of the theory, Goldman presents it in a framework of rules and says that a belief is justified if it is permitted by a right system of J-rules (Goldman 1986). A system R of J-rules is said to be right if and only if R permits certain (basic) psychological processes whose instantiation would result in a truth-ratio of beliefs that meets some specified high threshold. From this very brief introduction, it clearly emerges that process reliabilism does incorporate the truth conducivity of epistemic justification: "It makes sense to regard someone's justified belief in p as evidence for the *truth* of p if justified belief is belief formed by reliable processes" (Goldman 1986, p. 58).

It is, however, in accounting for the perspective character of epistemic justification, namely, the positive role that the subject's perspective, vis-à-vis his epistemic situation, seems to play in the determination of the justificatory status of his beliefs that the reliability theory runs into serious problems. As mentioned earlier, one way in which the perspective character of justification can be illustrated is through our intuitions regarding the epistemic status of beliefs in the so-called demon scenarios. Consider, once again, a possible world that is indistinguishable from the actual world as far as our experiences are concerned, but in which a demon has seen to it that our perceptual beliefs are invariably false. Since the demon world is indistinguishable from the actual world, perceptual beliefs in that world should enjoy as much justification as they do in the actual world. But these beliefs are, by hypothesis, not reliably formed, and are thus, according to the reliability theory, unjustified.

Goldman has, however, been acutely aware of this problem and has tried to tackle it head on. In fact his numerous attempts to deal with this problem can be seen as marking various stages in the development of the reliability theory. In an early response, referring to his notion of right *J*-rules, Goldman suggests that "rightness" is a rigid designator, but it is rigidified as a function of reliability in normal worlds, not reliability in the actual world. Normal worlds are those consistent with our general beliefs about the actual world. He, thus, has this to say in response to the demon counterexample (or the perspective problem).

> The justificational status of a [D]-world belief does not depend on the reliability of the causing processes in [D]. Rather, it depends on the reliability of the processes *in normal worlds*. ... So it does not matter that the processes in question are highly unreliable in [the demon] world. It only matters whether they are reliable in normal worlds, and that is apparently the case. (Goldman 1986, p. 113)

So what matters about belief-producing processes in the demon world is whether they are reliable in normal worlds which seem to be the case. Thus, beliefs produced in the demon world are justified and the tension turns out to be only apparent. However, Goldman goes on to abandon the normal worlds theory because of the problems that came to be associated with the very notion of "normal worlds." I shall not rehearse these objections here, but point, rather, to a more straightforward problem with the normal worlds approach. It seems that the normal worlds strategy actually amounts to the relativization of epistemic assessments of beliefs, something which defeats the purpose for which it was designed. Beliefs are justified if they are produced by processes that are reliable relative to the normal worlds. But what we were wondering was how to reconcile our intuitions about the justificational status of beliefs *in* the demon world with the fact that they are not reliably produced. It is no good to be told that those beliefs are justified *relative* to (or in) normal worlds. This does not explain our intuitions that are *tied to* the demon world itself rather than to another world. The problem becomes especially acute if the actual world itself turns out to be a demon world.

In any case, as was noted, Goldman abandons the normal worlds account, and instead proposes a modified version of reliabilism by effectively bifurcating the sense of "justification" (Goldman 1988). He proposes a contrasting pair of conceptions of justification, and holds that both are legitimate and defensible. He distinguishes between the "weak" and "strong" senses of justification. On the strong conception, a justified belief is a well-formed belief, while, on the weak conception, a justified belief is that of a blameless, non-culpable belief. However, Goldman proceeds to add the following caveat.

> We must be careful here, however. A well-formed belief, whose method is well-acquired and non-undermined, is also presumably blameless. So the strong notion of justifiedness entails blamelessness. But I want the notions of strong and weak justification to be *opposing* notions. This means that the weak notion of justification that interests me is not precisely that of blamelessness, but the narrower notion of *mere* blamelessness. That is, the weak notion is that of *ill-formed*-but-blameless belief. (Goldman 1988, p. 56)

Goldman further elaborates on the conditions that are sufficient for weakly justified beliefs. A belief is weakly justified iff it is blameless though ill-formed in the sense of being produced by an unreliable cognitive process which the agent does not believe to be unreliable and neither possesses, nor has available to him a reliable way of determining whether the process is unreliable. Given the above apparatus, one can supposedly handle the demon scenario in the following way. Since the beliefs in the demon world are unreliably produced, they are not strongly justified, but, being blameless and non-culpable and satisfying the above conditions, they are weakly justified.

Is Goldman's strategy successful? The first thing to note is that bifurcating justification into strong and weak senses, if not simply an ad hoc maneuver, is at least a significant retreat from the pure reliabilist approach to the justification theory. Moreover, the modified theory is fraught with internal problems. Let us start with Goldman's notion of strong justification. This is, of course, no more than the old reliabilist conception of justification. But Goldman now makes a further claim about it, namely, that "[it] is also presumably blameless," and this is why he wants his weak justification to be an opposing notion. But this claim is confusing. To see why, let us recall the example involving our reliable clairvoyant agent, Norman, who has no evidence for or against the reliability of clairvoyance, or of himself possessing it. Nor does he have any evidence for or against the belief he comes to hold as a result of this power (that the president is in New York). Now although this latter belief satisfies Goldman's strictures on strong justification, it is not an epistemically responsible belief. Goldman's attempts to respond to this objection have never been sufficiently compelling. And the reason is, by now, a familiar one involving the perspective character of epistemic justification. It would not harm to restate it here.

A strongly justified belief is one that is produced by a reliable cognitive process (assuming that Goldman's non-undermining condition is also satisfied). And if reliabilism is to be believed, it is a belief that the agent effortlessly finds himself with, and may have no knowledge about how it has been produced or whether it has been produced in a reliable way. Whereas, the notion of a responsibly formed belief is tied to what the agent *does*, and it is attributable to him only if he can be held accountable for holding the belief on the basis of what seems to him to be adequate grounds. The notion of responsibility is, thus, intimately connected to how things seem from the subject's perspective, a feature that is completely alien to the notion of strong justification thus conceived.

Furthermore, the notion of weak justification seems equally inadequate to perform the task it is intended for. Goldman claims that a weakly justified belief is a blameless one, satisfying the conditions referred to earlier, and that the victims of the demon world are weakly justified in their beliefs. Although this sounds initially plausible, the notion of weak justification is in fact epistemically inept as illustrated through the following modified version of the demon scenario.[3] Consider, once again, a demon world whose inhabitants' perceptual and inferential processes sink them systematically into error while their mental lives are indistinguishable from ours. Imagine two agents A and B in that world. While A is a good reasoner, reasoning in accordance with the canons of inductive inference, B, by contrast, gives in to emotion and wishful thinking, and so on, when engaging in reasoning. By hypothesis, however, A's and B's beliefs are produced by unreliable processes which the agents do not believe to be unreliable and none has available to himself a reliable way of determining whether the exploited processes are reliable (the demon sees to this). Now, in Goldman's opinion, the beliefs of A and B are both weakly justified, but there is no doubt that, intuitively speaking, A is a more responsible and a better epistemic agent than B. The notion of weak justification, thus, fails to capture the perspective, responsibilist ingredient in the concept of justification that Goldman rightly sought to incorporate in his modified version of the reliability theory.[4]

The problem becomes, if anything, more compounded when, in his most recent analysis of the demon scenario, he seemingly abandons the strong/weak framework in favor of the objective/subjective conceptions of justification (Goldman 2001). A belief, he says, is objectively justified if it results from appropriate processes (e.g., reliable processes). This seems to correspond with his earlier strong justification. A belief is, on the other hand, subjectively justified if it is produced by, what the agent regards as, appropriate processes. This does not, however, seem to be equivalent to his weak notion of justification. And indeed he approvingly refers (in a footnote) to Foley's egocentric rationality as "[t]he most systematic development of a subjectivist account of justification" (Goldman 2001, fn. 8). This all looks very confusing not only because Foley's theory is generally thought to be of an internalist nature, but also because, as we have seen, unlike Goldman, Foley avowedly advocates a nonhistorical, synchronic version of the truth goal as the goal of justification (rationality).

The trouble with Goldman's account, I believe, is that while he rightly seeks to present a theory of justification that incorporates both the elements of truth conducivity and the subject's perspective, he also wants the emerging notions of justification to be opposing ones. But there is no need to bifurcate the notion of justification in the way that Goldman intends as both these elements of truth conducivity and how things seem from the subject's perspective might be incorporated in a single conception of justification. As I shall argue in Chapter 2 deontological justification is just such a conception.

In fact Goldman's wavering attitude in handling the intuitions highlighted by the demon scenarios can only be matched by his volatile attitude toward the deontological theory. In *Epistemology and Cognition* he presents his reliability theory within a deontological framework characterizing "justifiedness ... as a deontic notion" (Goldman 1986, p. 25). In "Strong and Weak Justification," while articulating his notion of weak justification in terms of non-culpability, Goldman emphasizes that "justifiedness as freedom from blameworthiness is one of the conceptions discussed by Alston (1985)" (Goldman 1988, fn.3). The conception that Alston articulates in that paper in terms of freedom from blameworthiness is the deontological conception of justification. So it seems that Goldman regards his weak justification as a species of deontological justification. However, in his more recent "Internalism Exposed" when trying to see if the deontological conception of justification entails internalism, he expresses a hostile attitude toward it in the following tangential remark: "Although I do not accept the [deontological] conception of justification, I take it as given for the purposes of the present discussion and explore where it leads" (Goldman 1999, p. 211). I conclude, therefore, that process reliabilism fails to do justice to the multifaceted nature of epistemic justification. Next, I turn to Sosa's virtue-based justification theory that claims to be an improvement on process reliabilism.

1.5   Sosa: virtue perspectivism

Virtue perspectivism is intended to be an improved version of simple or generic reliabilism. The idea being that while, according to generic reliabilism, justified beliefs are the results of reliable processes, virtue perspectivism seeks to restrict the range of allowable processes. This is done by appealing to those intellectual virtues or faculties of the agents, understood as dispositions, which generally issue in true beliefs. More formally, according to virtue perspectivism, an agent S has an intellectual virtue in regard to a field of propositions F, a set of circumstances C, if and only if S, when in C, is very likely to believe correctly with regard to a proposition that falls within F (Sosa 2000, p. 284).

Sosa further introduces a number of important distinctions that turn out to be essential to his epistemic apparatus when dealing with various problems that his theory is designed to solve. One such distinction is that between "aptness" and "justification." An apt belief is one that is produced by a reliable or virtuous faculty in the environment in which it is operating. A justified belief, on the other hand, is construed in terms of the notion of an "epistemic perspective," which is, in turn, cashed out as consisting of meta-beliefs concerning the faculty (responsible for producing the target belief) and its reliability. According to Sosa, it is in virtue of this epistemic perspective that a body of beliefs is rendered justified (rather than merely apt). This seems to suggest that justification is a matter of having reasons for one's beliefs and an internal concept. Commensurate with this distinction, Sosa makes another distinction between animal knowledge (which requires only apt belief) and reflective knowledge (requiring both apt and justified belief).

There is, of course, a lot to be said about Sosa's version of virtue-based epistemology, but it is not my intention here to assess his theory on any grand scale. Rather, I wish to see how his account fares vis-à-vis the satisfaction of the two constraints of perspective and truth conducivity on epistemic justification. This is, by no means, an easy feat to achieve as Sosa tends to change his terminology (and his views) in the course of developing his theory. In any case, I believe, one can grant that virtue perspectivism satisfies the truth conducivity requirement as "aptness" is a truth-conducive concept. But when it is the perspective constraint that is at issue, one has to exercise extreme caution in passing a similar judgment, although, it has to be admitted that, by trying to incorporate the subject's perspective, Sosa's theory quite consciously moves in the desired direction (see the relevant articles in Sosa 1991). Let us then see if this move is successful.

As I just pointed out, Sosa is quite conscious of the indispensability of the role of subject's perspective in determining the justificational status of the beliefs he holds (thus, the name "virtue perspectivism"). He explicitly singles out the two problems of the epistemic status of beliefs in demon scenarios and in BonJour's cases (he calls the latter "the meta-incoherence" problem), and claims that his theory resolves them in a satisfactory way. Let us begin with his treatment of the demon scenarios. Sosa's answer to this problem involves appealing to the distinction between aptness and justification, but, in so doing, he relativizes assessment of the epistemic status of the victim's beliefs in the demon world: "Relative to the demon's [environment] D, the victim's belief may be inapt and even unjustified. ... Even so, relative to our environment ... the beliefs of the demon's victim may still be both apt and valuably justified" (Sosa 1991, p. 290).

It is, however, hard to see how this relativizing move solves the problem posed by the demon scenarios. To begin with, recall that, according to Sosa, aptness has a purely external character, understood in terms of the reliability of the faculty or virtue producing the relevant belief. Thus, aptness turns out to be equivalent to Goldman's "strong justification." And, in fact, Sosa's relativizing maneuver turns out to be very similar to Goldman's early response to the demon world problem in terms of normal worlds. Recall that Goldman claimed that the "rightness" of *J*-rules – in terms of which justification was supposed to be construed – is a rigid designator but that it is rigidified as a function of reliability in normal worlds (worlds consistent with our general beliefs about the actual world). This is just another way of saying that the justificational status of beliefs in the demon world should not be assessed relative to the reliability of cognitive processes in that world but relative to the reliability of the processes in normal worlds. This is effectively what Sosa does except that instead of relativizing aptness to normal worlds, he relativizes it to our actual (normal) world.

Moreover, what renders the problem of demon scenarios intractable is that we seem to have the intuition that the inhabitants of the demon world are justified in their perceptual beliefs in *that* world. It is no accounting of these intuitions to be told that those beliefs are justified (apt) relative to *our* (normal) world. What is at issue is what the epistemic status of those beliefs is in the very environment in which they are produced. As far as *this* question is concerned, it is quite irrelevant to be told what their status is relative to *another* environment. The situation here is rather reminiscent of the controversy associated with David Lewis's proposed solution to the problem of transworld identity which involves determining a person's identity across worlds relative to that of his counterparts in those worlds. According to Lewis, the truth conditions of "Humphrey might have won the election" are given in the following terms; "there is a possible world in which someone else, Humphrey's counterpart, wins the election." But, as Kripke famously remarked, Humphrey could not care less whether someone else would have won the election in another world (Kripke 1980, p. 45). What we wish to know is what happens to Humphrey himself, rather than someone else, under counterfactual circumstances.

Let us now consider, what Sosa calls, "the meta-incoherence problem." This is just the problem posed by BonJour's counterexamples to the purely externalist reliability theories. Consider, once more, the case of our reliable clairvoyant agent, Norman. We observed that, intuitively speaking, he is not justified in his belief that the president is in New York, despite the belief being reliably produced. Sosa concurs. Although Norman's belief is apt, it is not, he says, justified because, by hypothesis, he lacks any perspective that could be relevant to that belief (Sosa 1991, ch.8). This appears to be a plausible explanation of the intuitions involved, but any such impression fades away once we begin to probe deeper into what his conception of justification involves.

As already noted, Sosa distinguishes between aptness and justification. While aptness is of an entirely external character, justification is essentially internal. Sosa is not ideally clear about the relationship between the notions of "justification" and "aptness." But, from what he says in a number of places, it looks as if, for him, these notions are independent of one another (see Foley 1994; Fumerton 1994; BonJour 2000). An apt belief is not automatically justified, and a justified belief need not be apt. This interpretation is further supported by Sosa's claim that while animal knowledge involves only apt belief, reflective knowledge requires both apt and justified belief.

One has *animal knowledge* about one's environment, one's past, and one's own experience if one's judgments and beliefs about these are direct responses to their impact – e.g., through perception or memory. ... One has *reflective knowledge* if one's judgment or belief manifests not only direct response to the fact known but also understanding of its place in a wider whole that includes one's belief and knowledge of it and how these come about. (Sosa 1991, p. 240)

As it is clear from the above passage, the fact that both justification and aptness are required for reflective knowledge shows that neither implies the other. And this is as it should be for Sosa regards "justification [as] amount[ing] to a sort of inner coherence" (Sosa 1991, p. 289). It is a sort of relation that holds between the agent's meta-beliefs and his first-order beliefs: "The justification of a belief B requires that B have a basis in its inference or coherence relations to other beliefs in the believer's mind" (Sosa 1991, p. 289). This sounds very much like a coherence theory of justification, and it is, thus, no wonder that it should be thought of as being independent of a truth-conducive notion like aptness. We are all too familiar with the objections (most notably the possibility of alternative but equally coherent systems) to the claim that the internal coherence of a belief system is evidence of the truth of its members.

However, although the resulting conception of justification violates our truth-conducive stricture on epistemic justification, this may not be much of a worry to Sosa for he still has the truth-conducive notion of aptness. But now a different problem arises for his account. For if justification is, according to Sosa, a matter of possessing reasons for a belief, in turn, understood as consisting of coherence relations between the agent's meta-beliefs and his first-order beliefs, then it is not clear why things should get any worse, vis-à-vis the coherence of the agent's belief system, if the system is stripped of the agent's meta-beliefs. If that is correct, then the internal coherence of the agent's first-order beliefs should be equally sufficient for the justification of those beliefs. This would undermine Sosa's solution to the meta-incoherence problem. For now, although the agent lacks the pertinent meta-beliefs, his set of first-order beliefs, being coherent, would be automatically justified. This means that, *pace* Sosa, Norman's beliefs are justified after all.

Finally, with the severing of the link between justification and truth, Sosa's way of handling the Norman example would actually cease to be a response to the perspective problem that the example is intended to highlight. For, on Sosa's account, the reason why Norman is not justified in his belief is that it is not accompanied by the appropriate meta-belief that connects the target belief to its source and says how it has resulted from that source. But if it is only the lack of a connecting meta-belief that is pertinent to the justification of a certain object-belief, then Sosa's response (to the Norman case) can best be seen as addressing a different problem, namely, the problem of basing relation. To see more clearly the issue I am trying to highlight, consider the following example by Sosa. He considers, as an illustration, the justificational status of the beliefs of an agent who tries to identify shapes on a screen: "[Such an agent] is justified well enough in taking it that, in his circumstances, what looks to have a certain shape does have that shape. He implicitly trusts that *connection*, as is revealed by his inferential 'habits' of moving from experiencing the look to believing the seen object to have the corresponding shape. So the 'belief' involved is a highly implicit belief, manifested chiefly in such a 'habit' " (Sosa 1994a, p. 42).

With this example in mind, it seems to me that what is really getting addressed in Sosa's remarks about justification requiring the relevant meta-beliefs is the problem of basing relation. This is the problem that when holding a belief for a reason, the reason should enter into some specific relation with the belief. It is not enough to merely *have* a reason for the belief. If the belief is to be justified it must also be *based* on the reason in question. Despite the fact that a belief's being based on a reason is a necessary condition of its being justified, it has proved to be notoriously difficult to articulate just what this relation consists in. There are basically two views about the nature of this relation. One view construes it in causal terms while another view (the doxastic view) construes it in terms of holding a meta-belief to the effect that a support relation holds from the reason to the proposition believed. This meta-belief, often called "the connecting belief requirement," is seen, by the proponents of doxastic view to be a necessary condition of a belief being based on the reason. Both views face formidable difficulties but it is not my intention to discuss their merits here (see Korcz 1997). Rather, my suggestion is that when Sosa construes justification as a purely internal coherence relation between the agent's meta-beliefs and his first-order beliefs, he is best seen as addressing the problem of basing relation rather than the perspective problem. I conclude therefore that Sosa's virtue perspectivism, like its precursor "generic reliabilism," fails to account for the perspectival character of epistemic justification.[5] I shall now turn to a totally different approach to the question of justification.

1.6   Alston: abandoning epistemic justification

After producing some of the most illuminating articles on the nature of epistemic justification and what a justification theory should look like, William Alston has recently suggested that we should abandon epistemic justification and try to do epistemology without it (Alston 1993b, forthcoming). The main reason for Alston's U-turn seems to do with the "persistent failure to identify any one objective epistemic status concerning which the various accounts of epistemic justification are differing" (Alston forthcoming, p. 1). He now thinks that there is no such unique common item concerning the nature of which theorists dispute. But if we are to stop looking for the objectively necessary and sufficient conditions for the justification of a belief, how are we supposed to proceed with the epistemic evaluation of beliefs? According to Alston, the best approach is to consider the conditions that are denied or affirmed as constituting the nature of epistemic justification by epistemologists as being *desiderata* for the cognitive enterprise. These desiderata include such conditions as "having adequate grounds for a belief," "truth conductivity," "cognitive access to justifiers," "high level requirements," "coherence," and "satisfying intellectual obligations."

The main task of the epistemology of belief will then be conceived, according to Alston, in terms of evaluating these desiderata and identifying the contexts and interests relative to which a given desideratum tends to become more important than the others. He thinks this approach resolves a number of standoffs involving cases where it is a disputed matter whether the concept of justification applies. Once we deny that "epistemically justified" picks out a unique status, he says, we can see that these cases are marked by exhibiting one epistemically important desideratum and lacking another. For example the standoff concerning whether the victim of the demon scenario is justified in his belief can be avoided if we deny that "epistemic justification" picks out an objective status and just note that the controversy arises because while one party to the dispute attaches more importance to a certain epistemic desideratum, reliability, for epistemic evaluation, the other puts more weight on another desideratum, non-culpability. So, in a nutshell, Alston's idea is that denying that "justification" picks out a uniquely important desideratum would allow us to explore and identify the contexts and concerns, relative to which, certain desiderata become salient to the exclusion of others. So since "there seems to be no single desideratum or set of desiderata that are epistemically crucial in all contexts" (Alston forthcoming, p. 15), all desiderata, mentioned earlier, possess positive epistemic value – though one set may be more important than others.

I do not however think that Alston's desiderata approach presents a radical departure from the current epistemological thought. An initial problem with Alston's new project is that although he claims that his epistemic desiderata all possess epistemic value, he does not appear to take this claim seriously. For when he goes on to discuss their legitimacy and importance, he seems to be denying that some of them are really viable. For example, when referring to the "deontological" desideratum involving the idea that beliefs can be evaluated in terms of whether doxastic standards or norms permit their adoption, he says, "I have [already] expressed the view that this is not a viable desideratum, for it presupposes an effective voluntary control over our prepositional attitudes that we lack" (Alston 1993b, p. 542). As for the "cognitive-access" desideratum, which requires reflective access to justifiers, he asks, "can [reasons for belief] be adequately surveyed just by reflection, so that anything there that supports the target belief one will be sure to spot? That seems unlikely" (Alston 1993b, p. 543).

He thus seems clearly suspicious of those desiderata that, in his view, are of an internalist nature. This suspicion is confirmed when he directly addresses the internalist constraints on justification: "[T]he internalist will have to construe the 'adequacy' or 'sufficiency' of evidence in such a way that the subject can spot this ... just on reflection. And what construal satisfies that requirement? In my view this constitutes one of Achilles' heels of internalism" (Alston 1993b, p. 546). In a later article he softens his position to some extent by giving such desiderata a derivative status (compared to, what he calls, the "primary truth-conducive desiderata"): "For the most part the emphasis on [such] desiderata ... is intimately connected with a conviction that their realization can be expected to carry with it a truth-conducive tendency" (Alston forthcoming, p. 17). Regardless of the validity of these claims, such remarks clearly undermine Alston's main thesis that all of his epistemic desiderata possess positive epistemic value.

Finally, even ignoring the above problems, it remains doubtful whether Alston's program is a "revolutionary one, [and] a bold departure from the well trodden pathways of the discipline" (Alston 1993b, p. 541). He claims that, by giving up on the notion of epistemic justification, his approach allows us to appreciate a "plethora of values in the cognitive enterprise" (Alston 1993b, p. 549). Presumably this means that given the context and concerns relative to which a belief is formed, we can appreciate which epistemic desiderata are salient in that context.

But what does this amount to? Obviously, the satisfaction of the relevant desiderata would have to impart some positive epistemic value on the belief in question as would the realization of other desiderata on other beliefs in different contexts. Let us use the blanket term "positive epistemic status" for the epistemic value in question. Now Alston's idea seems to be that there is no single epistemic desideratum (or a unique set of desiderata) that are necessary and sufficient for the conferment of this positive epistemic status to beliefs in all contexts. Rather in each context, a subset of the realized epistemic desiderata would tend to confer that status on the belief in question.

Now this looks increasingly like a cluster theory of the nature of the property, "having a positive epistemic status." Accordingly, it is not a single set of desiderata that is necessary and sufficient for the application of that concept to an epistemic situation. Rather, there is always a cluster of desiderata associated with the concept of "having a positive epistemic status" and its application in the relevant contexts, just as something is a game because it has enough features from a set of properties usually associated with games. Now what goes for "having a positive epistemic status" goes for "being justified." Thus one may take Alston for his word when he says that it would be futile to look for the nature of the supposedly objective status called "justified," but all this would be consistent with seeing his epistemic desiderata approach as presenting a *cluster* theory of justification (when the search for necessary and sufficient conditions of a belief's justification is no longer pursued). As such, Alston's approach does not mark a "bold departure from the well trodden pathways of the discipline." In Chapter 2, I shall present and defend a conception of justification that satisfactorily accommodates the perspective and truth-conducive ingredients of epistemic justification.

2
The Deontological Conception of Justification

In Chapter 1 we highlighted the two dimensions of perspective and truth conducivity that any adequate theory of epistemic justification should incorporate and be accountable to. We then discussed a number of well-known accounts of the nature of epistemic justification and found that, one way or another, they failed to respect and heed these constraints, thus, only compounding the confusion over the precise nature of epistemic justification. The increasing sophistication (often in an ad hoc manner) of current theories of justification and the ensuing disarray have prompted some theorists to deny its privileged place in epistemology, and redefine the debate in different terms (cf. my discussion of Alston in section 1.6; Plantinga 1993; Haack 1993). In this chapter, I shall try to articulate and defend one theory of justification (the so-called "deontological" conception) that, I claim, is able to accommodate the above concerns. Let us then begin by setting the stage for introducing the deontological conception of epistemic justification.

Judging by our previous discussions, while there are currently a number of different alternative accounts of justification on offer, they can, nonetheless, be divided into the two broad categories of deontological and nondeontological theories. There are, on the one hand, those (deontological) theories that link epistemic justification with epistemically responsible action and there are, on the other hand, those which deny that justification involves the fulfillment of epistemic duty. It is, nonetheless, generally agreed that the most basic and fundamental notion of epistemic justification is the traditional Cartesian-Lockean conception usually construed in terms of the fulfillment of epistemic duty or obligation. Many find the notion of justification as somehow devoid of content when "cut loose from considerations of obligation and blame" (Alston 1985, fn. 21). Generally known as the deontological conception of epistemic justification, it takes justification to be a function of how an agent has formed his beliefs vis-à-vis the fulfillment or violation of his epistemic obligations and duties. Thus, to say that a belief is deontologically justified (J_d) is to say that in holding that belief, the cognizer has flouted no epistemic obligations, and is, thus, subject to no blame or disapproval.

It is important, however, to note that epistemic obligations are sharply distinguished from, say, moral or prudential obligations. This is sometimes done by emphasizing the impartial and disinterested perspective that gives rise to such obligations (Ginet 1975; Feldman 1988), but, more naturally, epistemic obligations are marked as being concerned with ways of achieving, what we have called the "truth goal," namely, the goal of believing the true and not believing the false. Despite its illustrious history, however, the deontological conception of justification has, in recent years, come under attack primarily on the grounds of presupposing the implausible thesis of doxastic voluntarism and for failing to be truth-conducive. In what follows, I shall argue that both these charges are unfounded. I begin however by examining certain attempts at introducing and articulating the deontological conception of justification. A closer look at the debate would reveal that these attempts usually help themselves with question-begging assumptions and unargued premises.

One of the most extensive treatments of this conception of justification is that of William Alston who, in a series of articles, seeks to identify its proper form and assess its feasibility by comparing it to other accounts of epistemic justification (Alston 1985, 1988). While discussions of this topic are often carried out against the background of internalism/ externalism debate, a plausible feature of Alston's treatment is that he tries to steer his discussion away from those controversies. Accordingly, I find it more appropriate to focus on his account of the debate when seeking to contrast deontological and non-deontological conceptions of justification. In what follows, I begin by evaluating Alston's strategy in delineating the deontological conception, and then try to show that the main reasons often adduced in rejecting this conception are inadequate. In the course of the discussion I shall also consider the contributions of other theorists to the debate when appropriate.

2.1 The deontological approach

We may recall that to say of a belief that it is epistemically justified is to appraise it favorably from the epistemic point of view and assign a positive status to it. Epistemic justification is regarded by many theorists as that which is capable of turning a true belief into knowledge (when conjoined with other suitable conditions), and it is indeed this feature that distinguishes it from other species of justification. As we have seen, there are many ways of thinking about this favorable evaluative status. One of the major trends in this area sees epistemic justification as necessarily involving a deontic dimension. It thus analyses the favorable epistemic status in terms of the fulfillment of one's intellectual duties and obligations. To say that a belief is (deontologically) justified (J_d) is to say that, in holding that belief, the cognizer has flouted no epistemic duties, that he has been epistemically responsible and is subject to no blame or disapproval. Distinct modes of these obligations or duties, however, as well as their content, give rise to different varieties of deontological theories of justification. Epistemic obligations can be taken in objective, subjective, and other modes resulting, in turn, in the corresponding modes of justification. We might, thus, say of a cognizer (S) that he is objectively justified in believing that p iff he is not violating any objective obligation in believing that p.

The content of these obligations, on the other hand, could equally be construed in a number of different ways, requiring the formation of beliefs that, say, cohere with the rest of one's belief system that are produced by reliable cognitive processes and so on. Since we have already emphasized that a belief is justified in so far as it serves or promotes the truth goal, we shall take our epistemic duty to consist of forming beliefs on the basis of adequate evidence. This leaves us with the modes of this obligation. Alston discerns four such modes and then seeks to find out which the resulting versions of deontological justification best captures the spirit of that concept (Alston 1985, p. 88).

(X)   S is objectively justified in believing that p iff S has adequate evidence for p.

(XI)   S is subjectively justified in believing that p iff S believes that he has adequate evidence for p.

(XII)   S is cognitively justified in believing that p iff S is justified in believing that he has adequate evidence for p.

(XIII)   S is motivationally justified in believing that p iff S believes that p on the basis of adequate evidence, or, alternatively, on the basis of what he believed, or was justified in believing, was adequate evidence.

Which of these contenders best represents deontological justification? Alston dismisses (XI) on the ground that it makes it too easy to be justified.

The mere belief that one has good reasons for *p* provides no epistemically good excuse for holding *P*. He also rejects the objective version (X) because J_d is, primarily, a concept of freedom from blameworthiness, and this feature is lost in (X). Provided I have not been epistemically negligent in forming my belief on the basis of the evidence available to me, that is, as long as I am justified in supposing that my evidence is adequate, my belief is blameless even if the evidence is, in fact, inadequate. This means that it is the cognitive version (XII) that really brings out what it is to be J_d in holding a belief. As for the motivational mode, it is actually parasitic on other modes. Let us, however, assume that a motivational rider should be put on (XII), although I shall mostly ignore it for the sake of simplicity. Having identified the proper form of deontological justification, Alston then turns to its evaluation.

He initially criticizes the deontological conception on the ground that it presupposes the implausible doctrine of doxastic voluntarism according to which we have direct voluntary control over our beliefs. However he goes on to say that once we stop thinking of epistemic obligations on the model of obligations to do things over which we have voluntary control, the deontic conception can be modified accordingly. But he nevertheless rejects it on the ground that it fails to give us what we expect of epistemic justification, namely, truth conducivity. I shall return to the doxastic voluntarism objection later on in this chapter. For now, I wish to focus on his objection that such an account of justification fails to be truth-conducive.

2.1.1 Deontological justification and truth conducivity

To show that deontological justification is not truth-conducive, Alston tries to contrast it with a decidedly truth-conducive conception of justification which he calls, an "evaluative" sense of epistemic justification (J_e) that no longer involves a deontic dimension, and can, in one natural interpretation, be fleshed out as follows. To say of *S* that he is J_e in believing that *p* is to say that he has adequate grounds for his belief, where the adequacy is measured by whether the grounds are sufficiently indicative of the truth of *p*. Now, as with the deontological conception, there are different modes of thinking about the adequacy of the grounds. They might be thought of as being in fact adequate, believed (or justifiably believed) by the cognizer to be adequate and so on, resulting, in turn, in the corresponding objective, subjective, and cognitive versions of being J_e in holding a belief.

Alston rejects the subjective version for the same reasons that led him to dismiss the subjective version of J_d. Unlike the deontological case, however, he rejects the cognitive version because being J_e in believing that p is, primarily, a question of whether believing that p is a good thing from the epistemic point of view regardless of whether or not the cognizer is subject to blame. It is therefore the objective mode that brings out what it takes to be J_e, and, ignoring further complications, it can be defined as follows:

(DJ$_e$) S is J_e in believing that p iff S's believing that p, as S did, was a good thing from the epistemic point of view, in that S's belief that p was based on adequate grounds.

Alston claims that it is J_e, rather than J_d, that most fully embodies what we expect of epistemic justification because it is only the former that is genuinely truth-conducive.[1] In this section, I shall focus on assessing Alston's reasons for his claim.

In identifying the right form of J_d among its different versions, Alston seems to be guided by the following two principles.

(a) "J_d is, most centrally, a concept of freedom from blameworthiness" (Alston 1985, p. 89).
(b) Any discussion of justification should proceed on the assumption that "there is something wrong with believing in the absence of adequate evidence" (Alston 1985, p. 89).

These principles allow him to adjudicate between different versions of J_d. It is (a) rather than (b), however, that is given the pride of place in the context of identifying the proper form of deontological justification. The objective version of J_d, (X), is rejected on the ground that it fails to do justice to (a), even though it satisfies (b). For precisely the opposite reason, Alston takes the cognitive version, (XII), as exhibiting the central features of deontological justification. So, ignoring the motivational rider for the sake of simplicity, J_d can be defined as follows.

(XII) S is J_d in believing that p iff S is justified in believing that he has adequate evidence for p.

The question that immediately springs to mind in regard to the above definition concerns the sense in which "justified" is used on the RHS of "iff." It cannot, surely, be the cognitive sense of deontological justification, for that would threaten the definition with circularity as well as engendering an infinite regress of beliefs. It cannot also be the objective sense of J_d, for, as we just saw, Alston rejects it for not being a deontologically respectable concept. We thus seem to be *forced* to say that the sense in which "justified" is used on the RHS of "iff" is a non-deontological sense very much in the spirit of Alston's preferred conception, namely, the "evaluative" sense of epistemic justification (J_e). We thus arrive at a more precise formulation of deontological justification.

(DJ_d) S is J_d in believing that p iff S is J_e in believing that he has adequate evidence for p.

There is, initially, something rather puzzling about (DJ_d). For by identifying justification on the RHS of the definition with J_e, we seem to be, in effect, saying that justification is, after all, a *non*-deontological concept. This does not square very well with Alston's (supposedly) non-partisan strategy of *first* introducing deontological and non-deontological conceptions of epistemic justification, and *then* embarking on the task of finding out which one most fully exhibits what we expect of justification. We may, however, ignore this strategical problem and just view (DJ_d) as defining J_d in terms of J_e. Let us now see how this bears on Alston's truth-conducivity objection to deontological justification.

Alston criticizes the deontological conception of epistemic justification for failing to "give us what we expect of epistemic justification."

> The most serious defect is that it does not hook up in the right way with an adequate truth-conducive ground. I may have done what could reasonably be expected of me in the management and cultivation of my doxastic life and still hold a belief on outrageously inadequate grounds. (Alston 1985, p. 95)

He cites "several possible sources of such a discrepancy." These include, what he calls, "cultural isolation" and "deficiency in cognitive powers." The first involves an agent who grows up in an isolated community in which everyone unquestioningly accepts the traditions of the tribe as authoritative. Having had no opportunity to come across circumstances in which this authority is challenged, and being actually unable to expose himself to undermining evidence, the agent can hardly be blamed for holding beliefs that are grounded in the traditions. He is thus J_d in holding those beliefs despite the fact that "it is the tradition of the tribe that p may be a very poor reason for believing that p" (Alston 1985, p. 95). Alston's reasoning here in rejecting the deontological conception is almost the reverse of what he presented when he sought to identify its proper form. There he allowed one of his guiding principles (viz., (a)) to override the other (b), thus, highlighting the role of duty fulfillment in characterizing the deontic conception of epistemic justification. Now in evaluating its credibility as a concept of epistemic justification he allows (b) to take precedence over (a). Another case, highlighted by Alston, involves "cognitive deficiency." Consider a student who, having read parts of Book IV of Locke's Essay, takes Locke's view to be that everything is a matter of opinion. He is "simply incapable of distinguishing" between that view and Locke's view that one's knowledge is restricted to one's own ideas. Since he is doing the best he can, his belief is blamelessly formed and yet it is ill-grounded and therefore not justified (in the truth-conducive sense of J_e).

I have two main problems with Alston's argument regarding the alleged failure of deontological justification being truth-conducive. First of all, it does not seem to me that his examples genuinely illustrate his claim. Second, even granting that such cases are epistemically cogent, what they show, at best, is the possibility of divergence of J_d and J_e. But this stops far short of establishing the claim that deontological justification is not truth-conducive. I shall explain each of these problems in turn. Let us start with the first problem. Consider, once more, the cultural isolation case. Before highlighting my first worry with Alston's argument, it would be instructive, however, to dispose of an early objection to it (put forth by Steup) as it also reveals the argument's lack of focus. It has been claimed by Steup that in the cultural isolation case, the agent who forms his beliefs on the basis of the tribe's traditions is clearly unjustified, but, being a rational agent, he is equally not free from blame. This is because "[b]eing a rational agent involves the capacity to find out, with respect to any belief, whether or not it is being held on good grounds" (Steup 1988, p. 78). Since the agent has failed to find out that his grounds (tradition) are inadequate, he is blameworthy and, thus, not deontologically justified. In reply, Alston accuses Steup of displaying insensitivity to cultural differences.

> He supposes that there are standards recognized that determine what is adequate evidence. … On the contrary, the criteria for this vary significantly from one culture to another. … Hence what can reasonably be expected of a subject with respect to, for instance, critical examination of beliefs and their bases will differ across cultures. … Deontological justification is sensitive to cultural differences. … But truth conducivity does not so depend. Hence they can diverge. (Alston 1988a, p. 146)

I believe, however, that Alston's remarks miss their target and are, in fact, inconsistent with his own characterization of deontological justification. For if, in his view, (DJ_d) is supposed to bring out what it takes to be J_d in holding a belief, then it is no longer relevant whether or not the cognizer is to blame for failing to discover the adequacy of the reasons for p. Assuming that "justification," as it appears on the RHS of the definition of J_d, is an objective, truth-conducive one, what *would* matter is whether the grounds for the agent's (higher order) belief in the adequacy of his reasons for p are *in fact* adequate. Alston's remarks seem to suggest an objective, non-relativist criterion for the adequacy of the cognizer's reasons for p, but a relativist, cultural-sensitive one for the adequacy of the grounds of his (higher order) belief in the adequacy of his reasons for p. This is definitely not in keeping with the definition of J_d.[2] I think the problem with Steup's objection is rather straightforward. It stems from his pre-theoretical appeal to such notions as "rationality," "epistemic responsibility," and their purported connections in setting up his objection. For it is precisely an understanding of such notions and their purported connections that is the focus of Alston's argument. Any unargued appeal to such notions and their alleged interrelations would be a question-begging maneuver at best. The trouble with Alston's examples, I believe, is more of a structural nature where a number of assumptions come into conflict with one another. Let me explain.

Alston's cultural isolation case, for example, is not sufficiently described to allow a thorough understanding of what is going on there. However, we are presumably expected to assume that the traditions of the tribe are a poor guide to truth. And this should not be understood in the mere sense of being an approximation to truth (as in the case of, say, beliefs in Newtonian physics which work pretty well in our daily practices), but in the more substantial sense of having noticeable false implications for our day-to-day judgments. Otherwise, these traditions would be reliable indicators of the truth of the beliefs they give rise to and these beliefs would be justified in a truth-conducive sense. But if they are a poor guide to truth (in the sense described), they must frequently go wrong. (Incidentally, this does not square well with the story. If the agent has never encountered any counterevidence, and cannot "reasonably be expected" to do so, then the same must be true of other members of the community who "unhesitatingly accept the traditions of the tribe as authoritative." But this would be a case where these traditions are more likely to be reliable, contrary to our supposition. This would further support the charge that Alston's case is under-described.)

However, by Alston's lights, trying to see if one has considered all the relevant evidence, or trying to be less subservient to authority, and so on, constitute legitimate epistemic obligations whose violation bars an agent from being deontologically justified (Alston 1993, p. 530). Now, given that the traditions of the tribe are a poor guide to truth, they would infect the fabric of daily judgments (of the members of the community) they give rise to, resulting, in turn, in those judgments frequently go wrong. So there must be quite a few counterexamples around and by ignoring them our agent has formed his beliefs in an irresponsible and culpable manner. Thus, *contra* Alston, the agent is not deontologically justified in his beliefs formed on the basis of the tribe's traditions.

Same is true of the "cognitive deficiency" example where a student is simply incapable of discerning Locke's view that one's knowledge is restricted to one's own ideas. Actually, given Alston's views on the bearing of doxastic voluntarism on the legitimacy of epistemic obligations, this is a rather odd choice for illustrating the claim that deontological justification is not truth-conducive. As we shall see later on in this chapter, Alston believes that lack of voluntary control over one's beliefs makes the corresponding epistemic obligations obsolete. However, by hypothesis, the agent's psychological make up renders him "simply incapable" of appreciating Locke's view or doing things that would enable him to understand it: "There is nothing that he could and should have done such that had he done so, he would have gotten [Locke's view] straight" (Alston 1985, p. 96). Now just as lack of voluntary control over one's beliefs renders, in Alston's view, the relevant epistemic obligations obsolete, the student's cognitive and psychological deficiency would bar his belief-forming activities from being subject to relevant intellectual obligations. Since the agent has no such obligations to violate or to fulfill, the question whether he is deontologically justified in his belief does not arise. Thus, Alston's views on the legitimacy of intellectual obligations render this example unsuitable for the purposes he has in mind.

It might, however, be objected that, Alston's views about obligations notwithstanding, the student's belief is nevertheless blameless since this was the best he could do in his particular circumstances. The belief in question is thus deontologically justified while, being ill-grounded, not truth-conducively so. This claim, the objection continues, can be supported by comparing the student's plight with that of another student who, not suffering from cognitive malfunction, is in a better epistemic situation and, thus, correctly identifies Locke's view. If the latter student's belief is justified (as seems to be the case), the belief of the student suffering from cognitive deficiency must be lacking in positive epistemic status (see Pryor 2001 for an argument along these lines). But this argument is inconclusive. It is true that the latter student is in a superior epistemic situation, but that does not deprive the dysfunctional student's belief from having a positive epistemic status (in a truth-conducive sense) even though it is false. The reason being that a similar situation can arise within an account of justification which is decidedly truth-conducive (as in Alston's J_e according to which a belief is justified if it is based on adequate grounds).

We may recall that, in accordance with the perspective constraint on epistemic justification, the epistemic status of a belief is always measured against the agent's available body of evidence. Consider now an agent, say Watson, investigating a crime scene, and concluding falsely that the butler is the murderer (because he infers his belief from an incomplete but, let us assume, *adequate* body of evidence). Imagine now another agent, Holmes, investigating the same crime and correctly concluding that the gardener is the culprit because he is in possession of all the relevant evidence (some of which Watson has non-culpably ignored). Obviously, Holmes is in a better epistemic situation than Watson, but this does not deprive Watson's belief from possessing a positive epistemic status (in a truth-conducive sense) because the grounds of his belief were assumed to be adequate, and, on the present account, this is sufficient to render it justified. The same is true of the positive epistemic status of the student's belief suffering from cognitive deficiency for although his epistemic situation is clearly defective, the body of evidence at his disposal might still prompt him to form the false belief in question.

One must however grant that, on Alston's preferred approach, the relevance of the adequacy of a belief's grounds to its justificatory status (and therefore the truth-conducive character of justification) is more directly visible. But, as we have seen, a deontological conception of justification can easily incorporate this feature. All one needs to do is to take our main intellectual obligation to consist in forming beliefs on the basis of adequate grounds. Thus, *S* would be deontologically justified in believing *p* if and only if he fulfills his intellectual obligation of forming beliefs on the basis of adequate grounds. (Obviously such an obligation needs to be construed more subjectively. Here we may follow Chisholm and say that a belief is deontologically justified iff the agent has done *his best* in forming his beliefs on the basis of adequate grounds.)

In a recent discussion of this topic, Alston, referring to this way of incorporating the notion of truth in the deontological conception of justification, adds the following cautionary remarks.

> [This would be] a different role from the one it plays in truth-conducive conceptions of justification. In the latter there was a straightforward conceptual connection between justification of the belief and the likelihood of its truth. Here [in the case of J_d] the connection is more indirect. ...[T]ruth comes in by virtue of the fact that a prominent place, among intellectual obligations, is typically given to the obligations to believe what is true and to avoid believing what is false. (Alston 1996, pp. 246–7)

But this does not seem to be an *epistemically* significant difference. Epistemologically speaking, truth comes in directly in the formulation of both conceptions of justification. What is indirect about the connection between truth and justification in the case of deontological justification is only of a *motivational* nature. The difference consists only in the fact that while in the case of the deontological conception we say of "believing on the basis of adequate grounds" that it is a matter of fulfilling an intellectual duty, on a non-deontological conception we regard it as that which best serves the aim of attaining true beliefs and avoiding false beliefs. So the connection between justification and truth in both conceptions is *epistemically* direct though *motivationally* indirect in the case of the deontological conception.

That these motivational differences are not epistemically significant, thus presenting no bar to the truth conducivity of deontological justification, is confirmed (as noted in Chapter 1) by the fact that certain decidedly truth-conducive accounts of justification take their stance to be of a deontological nature. For example, while, on Alston's account, the reliability theory of justification is regarded as a paradigm case of a truth-conducive conception of justification, Goldman presents his version of the theory in a deontological framework: "I will treat justifiedness ... as a deontic notion and examine it in a framework of rules" (Goldman 1986, p. 25).

And in his most recent works, Alston himself seems to acknowledge the truth-conducive character of deontological justification. Classifying what he terms as "epistemic desiderata" for evaluating the cognitive enterprise, he focuses on the desideratum of satisfying intellectual obligations and makes the following comments on its apparent difference with those desiderata that are explicitly truth-conducive.

But that is not the whole story ... [for] virtually all epistemologists, including those who emphasize "internalist" conditions of justification such as [the satisfaction of intellectual obligations] accept likelihood of truth as a prime epistemic desideratum. For the most part the emphasis on [such] desiderata ... is intimately connected with a conviction that their realization can be expected to carry with it a truth-conducive tendency, even though that is not built into the conception of the desideratum. (Alston forthcoming, p. 17)

I conclude therefore that Alston's cases fail to show that the deontological conception of justification is not truth-conducive.

Let me now turn to my second problem with Alston's argument against the truth conducivity of deontological justification. To motivate this problem, I begin by raising the following question: Why does Alston take the trouble of going through such cases as cultural isolation? The simple answer is that he wants to highlight the shortcomings of deontological conception of justification by showing that it can diverge from, what he regards as, truth-conducive justification. Such cases, he says, illustrate "the possibility of a gap between deontological justification and truth-conducive justification" (Alston 1988, p. 147). But if the credibility of J_d really hangs on whether or not it can diverge from J_e, Alston need not have bothered himself with going through such scenarios, or defend their cogency against his critics. For if (DJ_d) is to represent the proper form of deontological justification, the possibility of such a gap is already guaranteed from the very beginning.

To see this let us first note that Alston, along with other contemporary epistemologists, refrains from claiming that justification implies truth (Alston 1985, pp. 98–9). This means that a belief can be objectively justified (i.e., being J_e) and yet be false. Now recall the definition of J_d: S is J_d in believing that p iff S is J_e (objectively justified) in believing that he has adequate evidence for p. Given the stated difference between justification and truth, it follows that S can be J_e in believing that his evidence for p is adequate, thus satisfying the RHS of the definition, and yet the evidence be *in fact* inadequate. This means that S can be J_d in believing that p and yet fail to be J_e in holding the very same belief. The possibility of a gap between deontological justification and truth-conducive justification, thus, simply follows from the failure of epistemic justification to be truth-entailing and the peculiar form of (DJ_d) which involves the justification of the higher order belief in the adequacy of the reasons for the target belief.

If the earlier remarks are correct, it means that Alston has gone astray in tracing the "*sources* of discrepancy" between the competing conceptions of justification to cases involving cultural isolation and deficiency in cognitive powers. These cases merely *illustrate*, if at all, how these conceptions can come apart. What underlies the possibility of such a divergence has, rather, to do with the distinguishing features of epistemic justification and (DJ_d). This also shows that Steup's attempt at denying the possibility of divergence by suggesting a different diagnosis of Alston's cases is misguided. I shall now turn to an attempt by Richard Feldman who also seeks to deny the possibility of such a cleavage by approaching the issue from a very different perspective (Feldman 1988a).

Feldman is not concerned with the nature or viability of the deontological conception. He is rather interested in the commonly drawn distinction between subjective and objective justification. It turns out, however, that his proposed definitions of these species of justification are extensionally equivalent to those that have, thus far, been the main focus of this chapter. That is why he feels compelled to respond to Alston's critique of deontological justification. After a careful examination of a number of proposed definitions of subjective and objective justification, Feldman eventually ends up with the following.

(DJ$_o$) S is objectively epistemically justified (J_o) in believing p iff S has good reasons to believe p.

(DJ$_s$) S is subjectively epistemically justified (J_s) in believing p iff S is objectively justified in believing that he has good reasons to believe p.

He then goes on to claim that subjective epistemic justification and objective epistemic justification are equivalent. He calls this "The Equivalency Thesis" and contrasts it with the case of ethical justification.

[T]here can be actions that are subjectively justified, but are not objectively justified. For similar reasons, actions can be objectively justified without being subjectively justified. In this section I will argue that objective and moderate subjective epistemic justification are not similarly related. (Feldman 1988a, p. 415)

It is obvious that Feldman's objective and subjective epistemic justification are, respectively, what Alston, typically, calls "objective" and "cognitive" justification (ignoring for the moment their underlying motivations). That is why (DJ_o) and (DJ_s) are of the same form as our (DJ_e) and (DJ_d). Now what we said about the possibility of divergence of J_d from J_e and the reasons that underlie it, is equally true of the case of J_s and J_o. S can be objectively justified (J_o) in believing that he has good reasons to believe p and yet those reasons could be in fact inadequate. So, by (DJ_s), S can be subjectively justified (J_s) in believing that p without being objectively so justified. The possibility of divergence is already built into the concepts of J_s and J_o once we also grant, as explicitly does Feldman, that justification is not truth-entailing (Feldman 1988a, p. 410). Feldman does not directly address this issue, but he does consider Alston's contention, derived from his "cultural isolation" case and the like, that J_d and J_o can come apart. To counter this claim, he considers a similar scenario and tries to show why, despite appearances to the contrary, subjective and objective justification will nevertheless coincide.

Suppose a student is told by her otherwise reliable logic teacher that the Gambler's Fallacy (G) is a good rule of inference. According to G if a certain face of a (fair) die does not come up after a long series of tosses, the likelihood of its coming up on the next toss is very high. Let us assume that the student realizes that a certain face has failed to come up in a long series of tosses (call this evidence E). On the basis of E and her justified belief in (G), she forms a belief about the corresponding consequent (W). This latter belief is subjectively justified, but, being based on inadequate reasons, it is not objectively justified.

Feldman disputes this conclusion. He claims that it is the student's total evidence (E^*), rather than E alone, that should be assessed for adequacy. E^* also includes the testimonial evidence (T) she has for rule (G) ("My teacher says that G is true"). Unlike E, E^* is really a good reason to believe W, and, consequently, makes that belief objectively justified. So "if one justifiably believes that E is a good reason for W, then one has a good reason E^*, for W" (Feldman 1988a, p. 416). Feldman concludes by saying that this strategy can be used generally to show why every subjectively justified belief is also objectively justified. It is, however, rather difficult to see how this strategy can lend credibility to the Equivalency Thesis. The problem can be discussed both at the level of evidence and at the level of justification. We can either seek to find out if the agent has adequate reasons for W, or whether the objective justification of that belief can, somehow, be directly derived from her other objectively justified beliefs. Let us start with evidence. Feldman claims that, unlike E, E^* is a good reason for W since it also includes the testimonial evidence (T) that the student has for rule (G). But replacing

E by E^* does not seem to yield support to the Equivalency Thesis. To see the point, let us consider the conditions under which E can be said to function as evidence for W.

One of the main lessons of the paradoxes of confirmation has been that a set of observations confirms, disconfirms, or is irrelevant to a hypothesis (prediction, retrodiction, etc.) only relative to a set of background assumptions (Sober 1988, and our discussion in Chapter 9). Contrary to Hempel's claim that observations can bear on hypotheses in the absence of any empirical background assumptions, confirmation has turned out to be a three-place relationship between hypothesis, observations, and background assumptions with the latter forging an evidential link between the first two, that is, allowing observations to bear on the hypothesis. This means that only in the context of a background theory can E be said to have evidential significance for W. The question whether E counts as adequate evidence for W, thus, reduces to the question whether the background theory (which includes G) is itself adequately grounded. That is why we are inclined to say, with Feldman, that E is not a good reason for W because the background theory is hopelessly inadequate. If it *were* adequate, E would suffice for the objective justification of W. Widening the scope of evidence to include T as well as E does not change the situation, for E^* still has to function against an inadequately grounded theory. It cannot therefore count as a good reason for W.

We might, on the other hand, wish to argue for the objective justification of the agent's belief in W by directly deriving it from her other objectively justified beliefs without bothering about the adequacy of its grounds. Our agent, let us assume, is objectively justified in believing both E and if E then (very probably) W. Do these objectively justified beliefs suffice to show that W is also objectively justified? Feldman thinks so: "Surely she is objectively justified in believing what she knows to follow by *modus ponens* from other things she is objectively justified in believing" (Feldman 1988a, p. 416). But this argument trades on an ambiguity. It can be taken as suggesting that since (1) we are objectively justified in believing E and (2) if we are objectively justified in believing E, then we are objectively justified in believing W, then, by *modus ponens*, (3) we are objectively justified in believing W. But (2) is not available to us. All we are entitled to, on the basis of the above-mentioned assumptions, is (2'): we are objectively justified in believing that if E then W. No application of *modus ponens* to (1) and (2') will give us (3). To get (3) from (1) and (2') we need some version of the closure principle according to which if one is justified in believing that p and that p entails q, then one is justified in believing that q. This requires, however, a thorough analysis of the (controversial) principle of closure especially in view of the fact that the principle's entailment relation has to be given a liberal interpretation to include the probabilistic connection between E and W in the above example (see Chapter 5 for an assessment of Closure).

We have now investigated the possibility of divergence of J_d and J_e from various perspectives, and have concluded that, given a distinctive feature of epistemic justification, the possibility in question is already built into those concepts in view of their explication. But what does this tell us about the viability of J_d as a concept of epistemic justification? Does this phenomenon undermine the credibility of a deontological analysis of justification as is claimed by Alston? Hardly. Neither the phenomenon of divergence of J_d and J_e undermines the feasibility of the deontological conception of justification nor does it show that this species of justification is not truth-conducive. As for the first horn of this claim, we may proceed to justify it in the following manner.

If we can show that the phenomenon that Alston refers to would also arise in a hypothetical language which is very much like English except that the deontological analysis of justification is stipulated to be correct, then the fact that it arises in English cannot discredit the hypothesis that our concept of justification is deontological. Here I am exploiting Kripke's famous test for any alleged counterexample to a proposed analysis (Kripke 1977). To show that the phenomenon of semantic ambiguity in definite descriptions, cited by Donnellan, does not discredit the Russellian analysis of definite descriptions, Kripke considers various forms of, what he calls, "Russell languages" in which definite descriptions are understood along the lines of their Russellian analysis. Having shown that Donnellan's phenomenon would arise in all the Russell languages, he concludes that the fact that it does arise in English does not rule out the possibility that English is a Russell language.

Suppose now, to go back to our own case, we consider a D-language ("D" for deontological) in which justification is analyzed deontologically, that is, justification-conferring sentences are stipulated to have the same truth conditions (or meaning) as those given on a deontological analysis (typified by (DJ_d)). So whenever we say, in the D-language, that S is justified in believing that P, we mean S is objectively justified (J_e) in believing that she has adequate evidence for p (or, alternatively, S is J_e in believing that she is J_e in believing that P). Now, once again, it is obvious, given the fact that a justified belief can be false, that S can be justified (in the D-language) in believing that p without being evaluatively justified (J_e) in holding that belief. So since the phenomenon of divergence would also arise in the D-language, the fact that it arises in English does not show that English is not a D-language, that is, it does not show that our concept of justification is not a deontological one or that it is not a viable concept of justification.

Now for my claim that the phenomenon of divergence does not undermine the truth-conducive character of deontological justification. To see this, recall how J_d was defined: S is J_d in believing that p iff S is J_e in believing that he has adequate grounds for p. (Alternatively; S is J_d in believing that p iff S is J_e in believing that he is J_e in believing that p.) Now since J_d is defined in terms of J_e and the latter is truth-conducive so is J_d. The iteration of J_e (conceived as an operator on "belief") in the definition of J_d does not deprive it of having a truth-conducive character. As noted above, we can happily acknowledge the fact that the two conceptions of J_d and J_e can come apart. But there is no reason why the possibility of such a cleavage should undermine the truth conducivity of deontological justification. Consider, for example, a theorist who propounds an exclusively truth-conducive conception of justification but who also happens to be an internalist. So he would presumably require that in order to attribute a justified belief to a cognizer, he must be aware of (in some strong sense, e.g., having a justified belief in) the adequacy of the grounds of his belief (call this internalist conception of justification "J_i" – with "i" denoting the internalist requirement). So to be justified (J_i) in believing that p, he must be J_e in believing that he is J_e in believing that p. Now, it is obvious that J_i and J_e can come apart (again, given the fact that a justified belief can be false), but this would not show that J_i is not truth-conducive.

It is however true that J_d is not sufficient for truth. But neither is J_e. As was explained in Chapter 1, given the perspective character of epistemic justification, one can imagine an agent forming justified but false beliefs on the basis of adequate grounds (because, say, his body of evidence fails to include all the relevant evidence). The truth conducivity of epistemic justification is, thus, quite compatible with falsity of these beliefs even on a massive scale as it is quite conceivable that an agent's epistemic situation always remains defective. It is now time to turn to the second main objection to deontological justification, namely, that it presupposes the implausible doctrine of doxastic voluntarism.

2.2   The problem of doxastic voluntarism

According to the thesis of doxastic voluntarism, beliefs, like free actions, are under our voluntary control. This claim has, however, struck many philosophers as being, at least, psychologically implausible as no one seems to have the relevant sort of "direct" control over his beliefs that the thesis requires (more on direct/indirect qualifiers later). But, once this is granted, then it seems that there cannot be epistemic obligations; for something can be thought of as being obligatory only if it is something over which we can exercise sufficient control. Thus Alston states: "It is … obvious that it makes no sense to speak of S's being permitted or forbidden to do A if S lacks an effective choice as to whether to do A. Therefore the most fundamental issue raised by [the deontological conception of justification] is as to whether belief is under voluntary control" (Alston 1988, p. 118).[3] In the same vein, Alvin Plantinga has argued that if "accept[ing]…[a proposition is] not up to me … then accepting [that] proposition cannot be a way in which I can fulfill my obligation to the truth, or, indeed, *any* obligation to try to bring about some states of affairs. Suppose I've just fallen off a cliff: Could I be subject to an obligation to try to bring something about, which is such that I can better fulfill it by falling *down* rather than, say, by falling up or remaining suspended in midair? Hardly" (Plantinga 1993, p. 38).

It seems to me however that when the question concerns the legitimacy of deontological conception, the issue of doxastic voluntarism is really a red herring. To show this, I begin by analyzing a well-known defense (stated by Feldman) of the legitimacy of epistemic obligations in the face of the above objection (Feldman 1988b). This is how Feldman reconstructs the argument embedded in the proceeding remarks which he calls "The Voluntarism Argument."

1. Doxastic voluntarism is false.
2. If doxastic voluntarism is false, then no one has epistemic obligations.
∴3. No one has epistemic obligations.

He rightly refrains from challenging the first premise, but thinks that (2) is false, and, thus, rejects the Voluntarism Argument on that basis. His basic point against (2) is that many obligations remain in force even when an agent is unable to fulfill them. To give an example, suppose, in order to buy a house, I am forced to borrow from a bank. Consequently, I am required to pay a certain amount of money to the bank on a monthly basis. However, as a result of a sharp decline in my salary, I find myself unable to fulfill my legal obligations. This does not mean, says Feldman, that I have no longer any such obligations. For another example, consider a student telling his supervisor that, due to a brain lesion, he cannot concentrate for a long period on a subject and consequently cannot do the term paper he has been asked to submit as part of his course requirements. Under these circumstances, it is best, says Feldman, to ask him to do something else. But this "inability plainly does not make it the case that he does not have these academic obligations or course requirements" (Feldman 1988b, p. 242).

Feldman concludes that there can be academic or moral obligations that one cannot fulfill, and thinks that, equally likely, there can be epistemic obligations that one cannot fulfill: "There can be epistemic obligations even if doxastic voluntarism is false" (Feldman 1988b, p. 252). After examining and rejecting various candidates for what our basic epistemic obligation is, Feldman proposes the following alternative candidate.

(F) For any person S and proposition p and time t, S epistemically ought to believe p at t if and only if p is supported by the evidence S has at t.

He then claims that, consonant with his rejection of (2), (F) "is an account of epistemic obligation that does not require the truth of doxastic voluntarism" (Feldman 1988b, p. 254). Why? Because "psychological or other factors may force or preclude one from believing what is supported by one's evidence" (Feldman 1988b, p. 254).

But something seems to be amiss in Feldman's argument for the claim that (F) is the sort of epistemic obligation that does not presuppose doxastic voluntarism. How could the fact that certain factors (psychological or otherwise) may force or preclude one from believing what is supported by one's evidence show that (F), as an epistemic obligation, can remain in force even when the thesis of doxastic voluntarism is assumed to be false? Recall that according to this thesis we have direct voluntary control over our beliefs just as we have direct voluntary control over the movements of our limbs. But to say that we have direct voluntary control over our basic actions is not to say that we can perform such actions under *all* circumstances. If certain relevant factors, such as various muscle failures, intervene, I will not be able to raise my arm. However, the interrupting influence of such factors does not undermine the fact that basic actions are under our voluntary control. So in saying that basic actions are voluntary, what is meant is that, absent the interrupting factors, we have control over, say, the movements of our limbs.

Likewise, what the thesis of doxastic voluntarism says is that, absent the interrupting factors, we can choose our beliefs at will. The thesis does not claim that we can decide what to believe under *any* circumstances. So once we postulate, with Feldman, the presence of interrupting "psychological or other factors," we have effectively destroyed the kind of environment where by we can decide what to believe, just as, by assuming muscle failures, we ruin the kind of circumstances whereby we can raise our arm at will. In other words, the preventive effects of certain relevant factors on performing a basic action by an agent fails to undermine the claim that such actions are voluntary. Likewise, Feldman's reference to the interrupting effects of the relevant factors on the formation of one's doxastic attitudes does not really show that (*F*) presents "an account of epistemic obligation that does not require the truth of doxastic voluntarism." Consequently, his remarks fail to make explicit the connection between the thesis of doxastic voluntarism and the legitimacy of epistemic obligations. What has gone wrong?

To get a clearer picture of what is going on, let us return to Feldman's general strategy in defusing the Voluntarism Argument. We saw that he claimed that his examples, purportedly showing that obligations can remain in force even when an agent is not in a position to fulfill them, actually undermine premise (2) of the argument. But do they? All that those examples show, if anything at all, is that, given an agent's circumstances, there can be obligations that are not fulfillable under those circumstances. But this does nothing to undermine the premise (2), namely, if doxastic voluntarism is false, then no one has epistemic obligations. To see this, recall his example of the student (*S*) with brain lesion. An argument, resembling the Voluntarism Argument, can be constructed to show that our hero does not have the relevant academic obligations (A-obligations, for short) as described in the example.

    I. *S* has a brain lesion.
    II. If one has a brain lesion, then A-obligations are not fulfillable.
    III. If there are A-obligations, then they are fulfillable.
∴IV. *S* does not have A-obligations.

Now what Feldman challenges in the above-mentioned argument is the general premise (III), rather than (II), namely, that if there are academic obligations, then they are fulfillable: "I conclude from these examples that there can be nonmoral and non-prudential obligations that one can't fulfill and ones that one can't avoid fulfilling" (Feldman 1988b, p. 241).

The proceeding observations show that the Voluntarism Argument has actually the following structure.

1*. Doxastic voluntarism is false.
2*. If doxastic voluntarism is false, then epistemic obligations are not fulfillable.
3*. If there are epistemic obligations, then they are fulfillable.
∴4*. No one has epistemic obligations.

Note that, structurally speaking, the falsity of the thesis of doxastic voluntarism here plays a role similar to that played by the proposition that there is a brain lesion in the previous argument regarding the nonexistence of academic obligations. They both act as means to prevent the fulfillment of the relevant obligations. Of course factors other than these might play the preventive role. Nothing in the respective arguments rules this possibility out. Indeed, Feldman himself cites "psychological or other factors" as what might prevent the fulfillment of his favorite epistemic obligation (*F*).

Consonant with our analysis of the argument involving academic obligations, what Feldman is really challenging in the Voluntarism Argument is the general premise (3*). For just after the last sentence in the above quote, he continues: "Thus, I think that it is plausible to hold that there can be epistemic obligations that one can't fulfill and ones that one can't avoid fulfilling" (Feldman 1988b, p. 241). This shows why it is misleading to say, as Feldman does, that in challenging the original version of the Voluntarism Argument, he has shown that "[t]here can be epistemic obligations even if doxastic voluntarism is false." For his challenge only calls into question the general premises of type (III) and (3*), namely, that all obligations are always fulfillable. It does not really address the question of how the thesis of doxastic voluntarism bears on the existence or legitimacy of epistemic obligations. This explains why his later claim about the epistemic obligation (*F*) not presupposing the truth of doxastic voluntarism was so confusing.

This is not, of course, to dispute Feldman's claim that there are epistemic obligations that cannot be fulfilled which, if true, would be sufficient to upset the Voluntarism Argument. Rather, what I am claiming is that his analysis of the Voluntarism Argument fails to provide us with a convincing statement as to how the thesis of doxastic voluntarism bears on the legitimacy of epistemic obligations, and, thus, on the viability of deontological justification. In fact, a wholesale rejection of epistemic obligations, on the ground of the untenability of doxastic voluntarism, is not the policy that all opponents of the deontological conception of justification would want to pursue. Alston, for one, adopts a discriminative stance toward the legitimacy of epistemic obligations. Let us then see if the rationale he adduces for taking such a stance can throw more light on the question of the bearing of doxastic voluntarism on the legitimacy of epistemic obligations.

Here is how Alston propounds his position in a later paper: "It is held that one is justified in believing that *p* only if one fails to violate any intellectual obligations *in believing that p* ... I reject this as a viable suggestion for a condition on justification, since it presupposes that belief is under effective voluntary control. ... However I have no doubt that there are intellectual obligations, e.g., to look for more evidence under certain conditions and to train oneself to be less credulous" (Alston 1993b, p. 530). In a subsequent footnote he further clarifies his position by classifying illegitimate obligations as those "that attach directly to believing and refraining from believing" (Alston 1993b, fn.8). How are we to understand Alston's use of the direct/indirect distinction in this context? To gain a better insight into what he intends by these remarks, we need to know where he stands vis-à-vis the truth of the thesis of doxastic voluntarism.

From what we have seen so far it is obvious that he rejects the thesis (Alston 1988). But this rejection is qualified. He unquestionably denies that we have direct voluntary control over beliefs, though grants a rather weak degree of "long range" control over some of our beliefs. What is important for our purposes, however, is that he thinks we can *indirectly* influence or exert control over beliefs. The situation is rather similar, he says, to our attitude toward certain of our bodily properties. We cannot, for example, control our cholesterol build up in the way we decide the position of our limbs. But we can still control our cholesterol level by, say, reducing our fat intake. The latter is something which is under our effective control. Likewise, "even if propositional attitudes are not under our effective voluntary control, we might still be held responsible for them, provided we could and should have prevented them; provided there is something we could and should have done such that if we had done it we would not have had the attitude in question" (Alston 1988, p. 137). Alston gives some examples involving things that influence our beliefs and over which we have voluntary control. These include getting all the relevant evidence, seeking more evidence, considering the matter more carefully, being more critical of gossip, and so on.

Now the kind of epistemic obligations that Alston finds legitimate, as when he declares that he has "no doubt that there are intellectual obligations," are actually obligations that arise in connection with the above factors on belief formation. This might provide us with some clues to get a better grip on the rationale behind his distinction between legitimate and illegitimate obligations. As a preliminary step toward this goal, let us begin by noting that what the preceding remarks about how one can indirectly influence beliefs suggest is that belief formation is counterfactually dependent on the relevant contributing factors. Or, equivalently, assuming a counterfactual analysis of causation, it is to say that such factors causally influence the ensuing belief. Recalling the cholesterol example, one might accordingly say that had my fat intake been different, I would have had a different cholesterol build up. Thus, although I cannot have direct control over my cholesterol level, I can indirectly influence it. But now, far from undermining the relevant obligations, these observations seem to go some way to ground their legitimacy. For would it not be plausible now to require, as a primary health care, that people are obliged to keep their cholesterol build up below a certain level? Surely, as long as the contributing factors, such as fat intake, are within our control, such obligations make perfect sense. As long as I can bring about an aim, albeit indirectly, then a require- ment or obligation involving the realization of that aim would be quite legitimate.

The same is true of the case of propositional attitudes. The legitimacy of epistemic obligations does not depend on our having direct control over them. What is important is whether our beliefs counterfactually depend on the contributing factors relevant to their formation. As long as we can exercise direct control over those factors, there is no reason why lack of direct control over the ensuing belief should cast doubt on the legitimacy of the relevant obligations involving that belief. This radically undermines Alston's reasons for rejecting certain epistemic obligations as illegitimate as when he argues against Chisholm's version of our basic intellectual obligation according to which every person is required to try his best to bring it about that, for every proposition *h* that he considers, he accepts *h* iff *h* is true: "Chisholm envisages a person thinking of a certain proposition as a candidate for belief, considering what grounds there might be for belief or refraining from belief, and then effectively choosing belief or abstention on the basis of those considerations" (Alston 1985, p. 91). The preceding observations also make it mystifying why Alston thinks that classifying illegitimate obligations as those that "attach directly to believing and refraining from believing" marks a genuine distinction.

Surely if, for instance, the fault with Chisholm's favored epistemic obligation is that it attaches directly to believing, then the kind of obligations that Alston himself deems legitimate can be paraphrased as directly attaching to believing. For example, one might say that one is *obliged to believe* a proposition only if one has gathered enough relevant evidence, has been critical of gossip, and so on. It is thus quite puzzling why Alston thinks that "attaching directly to believing" would mark illegitimate obligations, and how this purported criterion is to be understood. One way to cash it out might be spelled out in terms of the "distance" or proximity of the causal factors to the resulting belief. But, apart from its ambiguity, this proposal fails to be of much help in clarifying the issue as the direct/indirect divide, in the context of Alston's remarks, is to be understood as making an epistemic rather than a metaphysical distinction. In the light of the above considerations, I conclude that, as far as the legitimacy of the deontological conception of justification is concerned, the issue of doxastic voluntarism is actually more of a red herring. In fact, Alston himself goes on to say that deontological justification need only involve *indirect* voluntary control over our beliefs and thus modifies its definition accordingly to arrive at a "deontological concept of epistemic justification that does not require belief to be under direct voluntary control" (Alston 1985, p. 94). I conclude therefore that none of the main charges that are usually leveled against the deontological conception really stick leaving it a viable and coherent account of the nature of epistemic justification.

To conclude, as we emphasized in Chapter 1, epistemic justification is both a function of how things appear from the cognizer's perspective as well as how things in actual fact are. The latter is what underlies our intuitions regarding the truth-conducive nature of epistemic justification, and, as we have shown in this chapter, the deontological conception of justification has the resources to accommodate this characteristic in a satisfying manner. As for the perspective ingredient of epistemic justification, it was argued, in Chapter 1, how the deontological approach most naturally incorporates this feature. It thus seems to me that, with the theory of justification still being a coherent epistemic enterprise, the deontological approach offers the best conception of epistemic justification that is accountable to the two essential features of truth-conducivity and the subject's perspective vis-à-vis his relevant epistemic situation.

3
The Internalism/Externalism Divide

The internalism/externalism distinction arises out of concerns for a proper explication of the concept of epistemic justification. On the one side of the debate there are those epistemologists (internalists) who require the justifying factors of a belief to be cognitively accessible to the agent. Accordingly, something can be regarded as a justifier, that is, confer justification on a belief only if it is reflectively accessible to the subject. Externalism, by contrast, denies that any accessibility relation is required. As long as some sort of (causal/nomological) relation holds between the belief state and the circumstances that make it true, the belief is justified. The division is not, of course, as clear-cut as it appears to be. Different interpretations of the cognitive accessibility requirement would, accordingly, result in different strengths of internalism or externalism. Thus if one thought of the justifying factors (evidence) in a way that required of the cognizer to be actually aware of them, then that would be an example of a strong form of internalism, a version that recognizes as justifiers only those putative grounds that are within the cognizer's perspective on the world. Weaker versions would, however, emerge by loosening the accessibility requirement.

In view of the conclusions reached in the previous chapters in regard to the proper form of a theory of justification, it is imperative that we take a stance on this debate especially because it is widely thought that it is the deontological conception of epistemic justification that leads to internalism. In what follows, I am going to dispute this claim. Indeed, I am going to reject internalism as an unstable position. And, in so far as the other horn of this dilemma is concerned, what we have said about the perspective character of epistemic justification is equally at odds with a purely externalist position. Finally, having identified the rationale behind the controversy, I shall open a new angle on the debate through a detailed analysis of the question whether the currently popular thesis of content externalism (in the philosophy of the mind) favors any side in the epistemological controversy. The conclusion will be skewed toward perceiving the two issues as being independent of one another. Let us then begin by analyzing the standing of the deontological theory vis-à-vis the internalism/externalism debate.

3.1 The internalism/externalism controversy: rejecting both horns of the dilemma

It has been repeatedly claimed that the deontological conception of justification results in the imposition of internalist constraints on epistemic justification. For if justification is to be understood in terms of freedom from blameworthiness, then the factors that form the basis of justified belief must be internal to the subject. We may recall that, according to the deontological conception, as long as an agent is not violating any intellectual duties, as long as she is not being epistemically negligent, then it is permissible for her to form the relevant beliefs. However, goes the argument, if it is freedom from blameworthiness that is supposed to constitute the justification of a belief, then this can only be the case if the agent knows or is aware of what her epistemic obligations are. One cannot be rightfully blamed for failing to take into account obligations that fall entirely outside her ken. This implies, in turn, that the factors that form the bases of justified beliefs (justifiers) must be internal to the agent in the sense of being reflectively accessible to (knowable by) her.

But this conclusion does not follow. All that the argument entails is that the agents must have *some* way of coming to know what the justifiers of their beliefs are. For all that the deontological conception of justification requires is that we comply with our relevant epistemic obligations, and this only requires us to know (in some manner) what they are. Without further assumptions, it does not follow from this fact that the pertinent evidence for a belief should be reflectively accessible to the cognizer. It only requires that the justification-conferring facts be knowable by the agent (without specifying any particular mode of knowledge or access). And, for all that has been said, some of these readily knowable facts may well turn out to be external, but, of course, there is no problem knowing such facts. So it does not follow, from the premises involving the known features of deontological justification, that justifiers must be reflectively accessible to an agent which is what internalism demands. As Goldman observes, "if *all* routes to knowledge of justifiers are allowed, then knowledge by perception must be allowed ... [and] then facts of an external sort could qualify for the status of justifiers" (Goldman 1999, p. 222; see also Conee and Feldman 2001). The argument from the deontological conception of justification to internalism is, I conclude, too quick.

Now, where does this leave us vis-à-vis the externalist camp? Given what was said in Chapter 1 in regard to the perspective character of epistemic justification, our position, I believe, should by now be clear. The perspective constraint requires that a cognizer's evidence be available to him and "availability," being an epistemic notion, suggests that for a belief to be justified its grounds must be cognitively accessible to the agent. Thus, it is not just the de facto reliability of our evidence that renders them the source of justification but also our recognizing them to be so. To repeat an earlier example, when we come to believe that a pigeon is nearby after hearing a distinct continuous noise, it is not just the fact that, as it so happens, the noise is a reliable indicator of the presence of pigeons that renders our belief justified, but also our associating this kind of noise with the presence of pigeons (in virtue of our previous experiences).

This is well in accord with the import of our argument against the claim that deontological justification leads to internalism. For all that the deontological conception requires is that the justifiers of an agent's beliefs be readily knowable by him. This knowledge, as we saw, may well include knowledge of external facts (obtained through perception). So the deontological justification naturally accounts for the influence of the subject's perspective on the justificational status of the beliefs he holds. And this is precisely what distinguishes our stance from externalism and purely externalist theories of justification like the reliability theories. In fact, as noted in Chapter 1, it was the indispensability of the subject's perspective in determining the epistemic status of his beliefs that led Goldman to qualify and amend, *albeit* unsuccessfully, the purely externalist position he once held through the introduction of the notion of "weak" justification.

Rejecting externalism is not, of course, tantamount to embracing internalism, and, in any case, as we saw, this is not something that the deontological conception of justification is committed to. Indeed, I am now going to argue that internalism is an unstable position. There is, however, no point in rehearsing the familiar objections to the internalist position in the literature which mostly find fault with its accessibility constraint on justifiers. Rather, I would like to add a few wrinkles of my own to the debate by posing a general problem for internalism. But before attending to this task, I wish to dispose of a recent statement and defense of the internalist approach which seeks to shift the focus on the accessibility constraint as the defining characteristic of internalism.

Conee and Feldman have recently defended a form of internalism that does not take the accessibility constraint on justifiers as marking internalism (Conee and Feldman 2001). Rather, they defend a version of internalism they call "mentalism" according to which an agent's beliefs are justified only by things that are internal to his mental life. More formally, mentalism is characterized as the following thesis.

(M) The justificatory status of a person's doxastic attitudes strongly supervenes on the person's occurrent and dispositional mental states, events, and conditions.

It follows from (M) that if two individuals are alike mentally, then they are alike justificationally. Conee and Feldman's defense of (M) consists of pairs of examples whose differences, they contend, can best be explained by appealing to (M). Let us look at some of these examples and see if they lend any support to (M).

The first example describes Bob and Ray as sitting in an air-conditioned hotel lobby reading yesterday's newspaper reporting that it will be very warm today. They both come to believe that it is very warm today on the basis of that report. Then Bob goes outside and actually feels the heat. While they both continue to believe that it is very warm today, Bob's belief, at this point, is better justified. According to Conee and Feldman, the change in the justification of Bob's belief can, in accordance with (M), be traced to the change in Bob's mental conditions. Does this example support (M)? I do not think so. For as the example suggests both Bob and Roy are justified in believing that it is very warm today upon reading the report in the newspaper. But that can only be the case if the paper is a reliable source of information. In other words, it is in virtue of the report being a reliable indicator of the truth about the weather that Bob's and Roy's beliefs are justified (i.e., their justification supervenes on the report's reliability). But "being a reliable indicator of truth" is not a mental property or state in the normal sense of the word "mental." Even if one internalizes the reason for their beliefs in order to say that the latter are justified because they are based on their other *belief* that "the newspaper says it is very warm today," the question of the justificatory status of this latter belief will take us back to the problem identified earlier.

The same analysis applies to explaining the enhancement of the justification of Bob's belief after he is exposed to heat. All that the example shows is that the change in the justificatory status of Bob's belief has been accompanied by a change in Bob's mental conditions. But this lends no support to (*M*). On the contrary, Bob's justification for his belief has been enhanced because his newly acquired evidence (the mental state of feeling hot) is a reliable indicator of the actual state of the weather. If such mental states, formed under normal circumstances, were not reliable indicators of facts beyond them, for example, if they were artificially induced, then Bob's justification for his belief would not be enhanced. This shows that, contrary to what (*M*) states, not just *any* mental change is relevant to the change in the justificatory status of one's beliefs. The example does, however, show that one's evidence or grounds can be mental, but this is consistent with externalism. Many externalists are happy to take doxastic and non-doxastic psychological states as grounds for beliefs. Even cognitive processes (many of which can be seen as sequences of mental states such as beliefs) can be taken as grounds – in a broad sense of this term – for the justification of beliefs on a reliabilist account of justification.

Another example, given by Conee and Feldman in support of (*M*), concerns a novice bird watcher and an expert together looking for birds. They both get a good look at a bird in a nearby tree that happens to be a woodpecker. The expert, but not the novice, knows what woodpeckers look like. So he immediately comes to know that the bird is a woodpecker but the novice "is not justified in believing that it is." According to Conee and Feldman, the epistemic difference between the two bird watchers "arises from something that differentiates [them] internally" (Conee and Feldman 2001, p. 237). Again I do not see how this example supports (*M*). For, to begin with, watching the bird does not even generate in the novice the belief that the bird is a woodpecker, and so the question that he does not have any "good reasons to believe that it is a woodpecker and is not justified in believing that it is" does not arise (Conee and Feldman 2001, p. 237). The novice has, in fact, no such beliefs. The belief that *is* produced in the novice is simply the belief that there is a bird of such and such properties in the tree and this belief is justified. The other problem with this example is similar to that identified with the previous example. In the course of describing the example Conee and Feldman say that "[t]he expert has fully reasonable beliefs about what woodpeckers look like" (Conee and Feldman 2001, p. 237). But what do these beliefs owe their reasonability (justification) to? Except to the fact that the birds' appearances are reliable indicators of their being woodpeckers? Again these beliefs are justified in virtue of being based on grounds that are reliable indicators of the relevant facts.

Our diagnoses of the examples mentioned above should make us suspicious of whether (M) really represents a satisfactory account of justification. What it says is that the justificatory status of an agent's beliefs supervenes on his mental states and conditions. But if our analysis of these examples is correct, what (M) should say is that the justification of a belief supervenes on the *adequacy* of its grounds or evidence (which Conee and Feldman identify with mental states). It is, in other words, in virtue of the adequacy of the evidence or grounds of a belief that a belief is justified. This would actually be in accord with the general thesis of supervenience that takes epistemic justification to supervene on such non-epistemic properties as being reliably formed, being adequately grounded, being appropriately caused by experience, indubitability, coherence, and so on. What is important to note is that all these subvening properties are truth-involving. (In the case of "coherence," it is usually taken, as in BonJour's account, as a justifier on the ground that a coherent system of beliefs is likely to be true.) So all these instances of the supervenience thesis remain faithful to the truth goal. But such a connection is absent in (M). For all that (M) says is that justification supervenes on mental states leaving it quite obscure whether there is any link between justification and the truth goal and how the link is supposed to be conceived. Moreover, if (M) is assumed to express what internalism consists in, then it would be unclear how one should classify those internalist accounts of justification (like BonJour's) that regard it as being supervenient on such properties as coherence for this property can hardly be thought of as being of a mental nature.

Finally, Conee and Feldman's discarding of the accessibilist account of internalism notwithstanding, there is surely an acknowledgment of its significance in their mentalist version (M). For, one might wonder, why they choose to settle upon mental states and conditions as those on which the justificatory status of an agent's beliefs supposedly supervene. Is it not because such conditions are thought to be generally accessible to agents on reflection? But, then, once we embrace this as a constraint on properties on which justification supervenes, their account will be in a peck of trouble. For (M) would then seem to have implausible consequences when conjoined with certain widely held views. To see this, consider, for example, a minimalist physicalist view according to which the mental supervenes on the physical. Thus, the mental states of a human agent are thought to supervene on some neural states of his brain. Now given (M), the physicalist thesis and the transitivity of the supervenience relation, we arrive at the following thesis.

(*P*) The justificatory status of a person's beliefs supervenes on the person's neural states.

Now (*P*) – which we may appropriately call "physicalism" just as (*M*) was called "mentalism" – is a strange thesis as it seems to violate the accessibility constraint on the properties on which justification supposedly supervenes. For a person's neural states are as external to him as anything can be, and if we take the justificatory status of beliefs to supervene on such external factors, then the internalist would stand to lose his case against externalism. (Consider a reliabilist theory that takes justification as being supervenient on such external factors as being reliably produced by a cognitive process.)

To make matters worse for (*M*) we may add further plausible assumptions to the physicalist thesis. For example, we may plausibly assume that an agent comes to possess his neural states in virtue of realizing other physical properties on which they supervene until we reach physical properties that lie outside the agent's body. Again assuming (*M*) conjoined with these further supervenience theses and the repeated application of the transitivity of the supervenience relation, we would arrive at the conclusion that the justificatory status of an agent's beliefs supervenes on (or is determined by) the physical properties outside his body which would be an odd claim, given the accessibility constraint on subvening properties. I conclude therefore that Conee and Feldman's mentalist version of internalism does not work as it seems beset by more problems than those that afflict the more widely held accessibilist version of internalism.

I now wish to elaborate on a general problem for internalism before highlighting what I take to be the basic motivation behind this conception of justification. To prepare the ground, however, I begin by examining a recent statement of internalism due to Steup (Steup 1999). In line with the general contours of the debate, he takes internalism to be a view according to which the things that make beliefs justified or unjustified must be recognizable on reflection. So, for example, when a belief is deemed as unjustified because it is grounded in, say, wishful thinking, then you can tell this because you can recognize on reflection that (1) the belief is grounded in wishful thinking and (2) beliefs grounded in wishful thinking are unjustified. Likewise, you can tell that a belief grounded in perceptual experience is justified because you can recognize on reflection that (1) the belief is supported by perceptual experience and (2) the belief thus supported is justified. The reliability of cognitive processes, on the other hand, says Steup, does not qualify as a justifier because "[w]hether your beliefs are produced by reliable cognitive processes is not always recognizable on reflection" (Steup, p. 375). But there is an immediate problem for the internalist in regard to condition (2) earlier: How can we recognize on reflection that beliefs grounded in wishful thinking are unjustified while beliefs supported by sense experience are justified? The obvious reply would be to say that beliefs grounded in wishful thinking are more likely to be false while those grounded in sense experience are more likely to be true. However, to say this is to appeal to the track records of the processes involved and this is just another way of saying whether they are reliable or not. But this contradicts Steup's subsequent (and justified) claim that reliability "is not … recognizable on reflection."

Moreover, Steup (rightly) goes on to reject an internalist account of knowledge on the ground that, among other things, knowledge requires truth and truth is an external relation. However, a rather similar problem seems also to afflict an internalist account of justification though not in so direct a way. To see this, let us recall that epistemic justification was considered to be truth-conducive in the sense that to regard a belief's ground as truth-conducive is just to say that it is a reliable indicator of its truth. Now, just as truth is considered to be an external relation so should being-a-reliable-indicator-of-truth; neither seems to be accessible to an agent just on reflection. And just as the former fact was thought to undermine an internalist account of knowledge, so should the latter fact be considered as anathema to an internalist account of justification.[1]

This point can also be made more generally in terms of the truth goal. We may recall that justification is an evaluative concept whose attachment to a belief makes the belief worth having from the epistemic point of view, in turn, characterized in terms of the truth goal, namely, the goal of believing truth and avoiding falsehood. I have already elaborated on how this goal should be conceived. But, however we choose to describe it, justification is generally thought of as serving the truth goal. Let us call the factors that help to determine the justification of a belief "*J*-factors." Given the goal toward which justification strives, *J*-factors must be thought of as those factors that help realize or promote this goal. That is to say, what distinguishes *J*-factors from other factors is that the former serve or promote the truth goal, that is, maximize truth and minimize falsehood in a large body of beliefs. They are, thus, *constitutively* linked to the truth goal and it is this connection that makes up their identity as *justifying* factors. Now, according to internalism, *J*-factors must be reflectively accessible. Since *J*-factors are also goal-promoters (in the constitutive sense explained earlier), then the serving of the truth goal must be something that is also reflectively accessible to agents. But surely "maximizing truth and minimizing falsity in a large body of beliefs" is not a property whose realization can be introspectively accessible to a cognizer. This puts an internalist who embraces the truth goal in an embarrassing situation as one would want to know what entitles him to take justification as being constitutively linked to a goal whose realization is beyond his ken. Or, to put the same point differently, one wonders what difference the truth goal could possibly make to an internalist conception of justification when its realization is, by definition, beyond the (reflective) reach of an agent whose belief is supposedly justified because it has successfully served that goal. I conclude, therefore, that internalism, while wedded to the truth goal, is not a stable position.

3.1.1   The internalist/externalist distinction: its rationale

This takes us now to the question of what the driving force behind internalism is. What is it really that separates internalists from externalists? A number of rationales for internalism have been proposed. Some have pointed to the deontic ingredients of justification as what underlies internalism. However, as we have seen, this is not a viable claim. Others have suggested that the motivation behind internalism can be traced to the origin of the concept of justification, namely, the interpersonal practice of criticizing one another's beliefs seeking to specify the grounds on which they are based (Alston 1989, p. 236). This is, according to Alston, what explains the internalist accessibility constraint on justifiers. Such suggestions, however, are more of a genetic, rather than epistemic, disposition.

For my part, I tend to see the main rationale behind the internalists' position as stemming from their attitude toward the threat of skepticism. This follows from the internalists' insistence that "*J*-factor[s] must be ... cognitively accessible to us in such a way that *we can always tell* whether what we believe is justified or not" (Steup 1999, p. 373). To see the point, it is, I believe, instructive to consider the issue against the backdrop of the much older debate between realists and idealists. Ordinarily, we tend to conceive of truth as a relation to an independently existing world. Our commonsense conception of reality construes it as being wholly independent of our beliefs and thoughts, thus, leaving a gap between those beliefs and the world. As these beliefs seem to transcend what is given to us in experience, however firmly we hold them and however coherently they stick to one another, there always remains the possibility of a mismatch between them and what they are supposed to represent. This makes it impossible to tell for sure whether our beliefs are true or false, or so the skeptic claims.

The problem would disappear, however, once one construes statements about the world in terms of the contents of our experience. It is precisely at this juncture that an idealist (phenomenalist) response presents itself as a viable alternative. If what lies at the root of our predicament is the gap between what appears to us in experience and a reality to which we have no independent access, then the easiest way to close the gap is to identify physical objects with the contents of our experiences, or, equivalently, reduce object statements to those about our experiences. Why bother about a reality that is forever beyond our reach? All that can be of (epistemic) significance is that to which we would have immediate cognitive access. Barry Stroud finds this reaction "very natural and immediately appealing."

> If an imperceptible "reality," as it is called on this picture, is forever inaccessible to us, what concern can it be of ours? How can something we can have no contact with, something from which we are permanently sealed off, even make sense to us at all? Our sensory experiences, past, present, and future, will then be thought to be all we are or should be concerned with, and the idea of a "reality" lying beyond them necessarily out of our reach will seem like nothing more than a philosopher's invention. (Stroud 1984, p. 34)

The gap between the contents of our beliefs and the world can be equally construed in terms of justification rather than truth. The idea being that however carefully we may have gone about forming our beliefs in the light of available experience or evidence, our impression of the epistemic status of those beliefs may be totally unlike what they in fact are. Despite our best efforts, we may still fail to identify the epistemic status of our beliefs as their grounds may turn out to be radically different from what we take them to be. For example, despite all the evidence to the contrary, our beliefs may have been formed or grounded in an entirely unreliable way due to the influence of a demon or super-scientist intent on deceiving us. This would deprive us of the ability to determine or to tell, at any time, whether our beliefs are justified or unjustified. The only way to block this possibility, and, thus, be able to tell, at any time, whether our beliefs are justified would be to confine their grounds to those whose presence is detectable by the subject on reflection.

Seeing the situation in this light, makes the internalism/externalism controversy look more like an epistemization of the older debate between idealists (phenomenalists) and realists, as it is now evidence and justifying grounds, rather than physical objects and facts, that become the appropriate objects of cognition and awareness. Just as the phenomenalists were willing to confer the status of an object on something only in so far as it was perceivable, the internalists are led to admit something as a justifying ground (justifier) in so far as it is reflectively accessible to the cognizer. Just as, on the idealist picture, the inaccessible, external reality drops out as irrelevant, on the internalist account of justification the external and inaccessible grounds become epistemically obsolete. There is, thus, no more to justification, for an internalist, than what falls within the cognizer's ken, just as, for the idealist, reality is confined to that which appears to an agent.

This way, the internalists can escape the specter of skepticism (at the level of justified beliefs). For now they "can always tell whether what [they] believe is justified or not" as the justifiers of a belief at any time are those that they can, on reflection, determine whether they obtain or not. By contrast, the externalists' attitude toward skepticism seems completely ineffective and wide of the mark, or so the internalists claim. All that an externalist can say in the face of such a challenge is that *as long as* our beliefs possess a certain external property (e.g., being produced by reliable processes), then they are justified. But, the internalist retorts, this conditional claim does nothing to thwart the challenge of skepticism or even to try to take it seriously. Indeed one of the chief complaints of internalists against an externalist conception of justification has been that it fails to appreciate or do justice to the skeptical challenge. At any rate, I take the preceding remarks to constitute the main driving force behind the internalist account of justification.

Thus far, we have tried to steer a course between the two extremes of internalism and externalism by acknowledging the indispensability of the subject's perspective, in accordance with the perspective character of epistemic justification, on the justifiers of his beliefs for the epistemic status of those beliefs. This perspective, we saw, required no particular mode of knowledge that is essentially reflective in an internalist sense. Nor did our position accorded with the externalist stance in taking the holding of a causal/nomological relation between a belief state and its truth maker as being sufficient to confer justification on that belief. Nonetheless, it may be premature to write off either internalism or externalism completely. Indeed, some theorists have claimed that a certain thesis (in the philosophy of mind) that is currently thought to have attained more or less the status of an orthodoxy, namely, the thesis of content externalism clearly supports the externalist position in justification theory. The rest of this chapter will be devoted to examining this claim.

3.2   Externalism in semantics and epistemology

According to externalist theories of content, the contents of an individual's thoughts do not supervene on her intrinsic properties. Rather, facts about the social and physical environments enter into the individuation of her mental contents. This means that two individuals could be indiscernible as far as their intrinsic physical properties are concerned, and yet differ in respect of the contents of certain of their thoughts. The externalist thesis is motivated by the well-known Twin Earth thought experiments propounded by Putnam and Burge (Putnam 1975; Burge 1979). Consider two individuals, Oscar and Toscar, who are molecular duplicates. Oscar lives on Earth while Toscar lives on Twin Earth, a planet which is an exact duplicate of Earth except for the fact that the liquid that the Twin Earthians call "water," which fills their lakes and falls from the sky, and is superficially indistinguishable from water is not H_2O but has a different chemical composition, XYZ. Now, the widespread intuition is that when both Oscar and Toscar utter the words "Water is wet" they express different thoughts for "water" in their mouths refers to different entities. While Oscar is expressing the thought that water is wet, Toscar expresses the thought that twater – translating his word "water" into Oscar's language – is wet. This difference, according to the externalist, reflects the difference in their environments.

Internalism in justification theory, as we have seen, is thought of as the view that imposes an accessibility constraint on justifiers, that is, those facts that determine the justificatory status of beliefs. However, following the lead of those whose views are under consideration here, and also because this is a widely accepted version of internalism, I take the access in question to involve, at least, justified belief. Now the question that arises in this context is whether content externalism favors any side of the internalism/externalism divide in justification theory. A number of theorists seem to think that content externalism rules out justification internalism (call this the "incompatibility thesis") and instead supports the externalist position. The incompatibility thesis has been addressed in different ways by the likes of Boghossian and BonJour, both of whom try to defend it – although the thrust of their papers is actually directed at different goals. In what follows, I shall discuss each of these views in turn before proposing an argument of my own for the incompatibility thesis, though, as I shall explain, the argument hinges on a controversial premise. Let us begin, however, with Boghossian's pioneering attempt to bring content externalism to bear on the internalism/externalism divide in justification theory.

Boghossian's main objective (in the article in which he raises the issue) is to show that content externalism undermines the thesis of privileged self-knowledge (Boghossian 1989). However, an argument for the incompatibility thesis, along the following lines, can be easily constructed out of the claims he advances. Let us call this the "non-inferentiality argument."

(P) If justification internalism is true then self-knowledge is non-inferential.
(Q) If self-knowledge is non-inferential then content externalism is false.
∴(C) If justification internalism is true then content externalism is false.

By the non-inferentiality argument, content externalism undermines the internalist conception of justification. The argument is valid, so everything depends on whether the premises are true. Boghossian backs up both premises with arguments which we shall subsequently discuss. Let us start with the argument for (P).

Consider two first-order empirical beliefs p and q such that belief p is based on belief q. Boghossian then spells out the following conditions as those that have to be satisfied if I am to be justified (in an internalist sense) in believing that p.

(1) I believe that p.
(2) I believe that q.
(3) The proposition that q justifies the proposition that p.
(4) I know that I believe that q.
(5) I know that a belief that q justifies a belief that p.
(6) I believe that p as a result of the knowledge expressed in (4) and (5).

(4) and (5) constitute Boghossian's favored brand of justification internalism requiring the cognizer to know (justifiably believe) that not only the ground of his belief p (namely, the belief q) obtains, but also know (justifiably believe) that the ground is adequate. In connection with the earlier conditions he makes the following observation.

Now, there is, of course, a *standard* problem in holding that all knowledge of empirical propositions is inferential, that all beliefs can be justified only by reference to other beliefs. This is a problem of the regress
of justification: If the belief that *p* is to count as justified, then the
belief that *q* on which its justification depends must itself be justified.
But if *all* beliefs can be justified only by reference to other beliefs, then
the belief *q* must itself be justified by reference to other beliefs. And
this threatens to lapse into a vicious regress. (Boghossian 1989, p. 10)

By the "standard" problem, Boghossian is referring to the problem
of the structure of knowledge (justified belief). The problem involves the
distinction between inferentially and non-inferentially justified beliefs.
To say that a belief *p* is inferentially justified is to say that it is justified
by being inferred from other justified beliefs, say, *q* and *r*. But the same
question arises for these latter beliefs. Where do they get their justification from? If they, too, are inferentially justified, their justification
must derive from still further justified beliefs and we are off on a vicious
regress. However, Boghossian goes on to add that "there is a *special*
problem sustaining a thoroughly inferential conception of *self-knowledge*,
one that is independent of the *standard* problem of the regress of justification" (Boghossian 1989, p. 9). To show this he waives the standard
problem by not requiring that if a belief, *p*, is to be justified, then it must
rest on another belief, *q*, that is itself justified, for this would give rise
to the regress problem. Rather, he sets his target to be the justification
of "the belief *p* ... *relative* to the belief that *q*, in accordance with standard internalist requirements" (Boghossian 1989, p. 9). This way, we
need not assume that the belief *q* is itself justified, thus, neutralizing the
regress-generating assumption that "[a]ll justification is inferential."

Now, since our concern here is with knowledge of our own beliefs
(self-knowledge[2]), let us take the belief *p* to be a shorthand for the
second-order belief that I believe that, say, *r*. Assuming that this second-
order belief rests on another belief, say, the belief *s*, we wish to know
what are the conditions that have to be satisfied if I am to be justified (in
an internalist sense) in believing that I believe that *r*. Boghossian spells
out the conditions as thus:

(1′) I believe that I believe that *r*.
(2′) I believe that *s*.
(3′) The proposition that *s* justifies the proposition that I believe that *r*.
(4′) I know that I believe that *s*.

(5′) I know that a belief that *s* justifies the belief that I believe that *r*.
(6′) I believe that I believe that *r* as a result of knowledge expressed in (4′) and (5′).

Now, Boghossian claims that there is a special problem with the satisfaction of the above conditions that is independent of the standard problem of the regress of justification. It concerns (4′).

> In order to know that I believe that *r*, I must antecedently know that I believe that s. But how was knowledge [justification] of *this* belief required? *On the assumption that all self-knowledge is inferential*, it could have been acquired only by inference from yet other known [justified] beliefs. And we are now off on a vicious regress. (Boghossian 1989, p. 10; emphasis added)

To bring the regress to an end, he suggests we should invoke the view that all self-knowledge is non-inferential. We, thus, get the first premise (P) in the argument for the incompatibility thesis: If justification internalism is true then self-knowledge is non-inferential. Before assessing Boghossian's argument, it would be instructive to examine a recent critique of the argument (due to Chase) for its failure, as I shall try to show, helps to highlight the substantive issues that Boghossian's argument raises. This would, in turn, set the stage for a better understanding of where Boghossian's argument for (P) goes wrong.

According to Chase although the earlier argument is supposed to establish (P), all it shows is that, given internalism, it is not the case that *all* self-knowledge is inferential (Chase 2001). The point is obvious enough. If a chain of justified beliefs is to come to an end, then the chain naturally includes both inferential and non-inferential beliefs. Thus, to bring the regress generated by (4′) to an end, we are only entitled to the conclusion that *some* self-knowledge is non-inferential. To reinforce this conclusion Chase adds the following remarks. Suppose we follow Chisholm and adopt a foundationalist account of the structure of our justified beliefs where justification is construed internalistically. Then the basic or self-presenting beliefs that play the role of foundations in our belief structure are not inferentially justified. If this is the case, then Boghossian's argument for (P) would fail to go through, says Chase, because the regress automatically ends once we reach the foundational beliefs. These beliefs, he says, will not include "all cases of self-knowledge ... [They] might only include beliefs about sense-data (or sensory-information), experiences of pain and so on" (Chase 2001, p. 232).

But there seems to be some confusion here. As his examples show, Chase's foundational and self-presenting beliefs seem to consist only of first-order beliefs whereas Boghossian is concerned with second-order beliefs when he concludes that not all self-knowledge is inferential. Moreover, Boghossian's way of bringing the regress (generated by (4′)) to an end is precisely to adopt a foundationalist strategy where some justified second-order beliefs are assumed to be non-inferential. And, to be fair to Boghossian, he does not really conclude from his regress argument that all self-knowledge is non-inferential. What he says is, rather, this: "[I]t emerges very clearly that not *all* knowledge of one's beliefs can be inferential. On pain of a vicious regress, it must be possible to know the content of *some* mental states non-inferentially" (Boghossian 1989, p. 10). It is, however, true, as Chase observes, that Boghossian often opts for the position that *all* self-knowledge is non-inferential. I shall later explain why Boghossian wavers between the two positions. In any case, I do not think that Chase really puts his finger on where Boghossian's argument goes wrong. The trouble with Boghossian's argument, I think, runs deeper than a mere disagreement over the scope of non-inferential character of self-knowledge. Rather, it seems to me that his argument fails to show either that all or some self-knowledge is non-inferential. Let me explain.

Recall that to separate what he calls the "special problem" sustaining a thoroughly inferential conception of self-knowledge from the standard problem of the regress of justification, Boghossian chooses to "waive the standard problem" by requiring only that "the belief p be justified *relative* to the belief that q." To repeat, the standard problem of the regress of justification arises when we assume that every justified belief could be justified only by inferring it from some other justified belief, or, more simply put, by assuming that all justification is inferential. However, once we choose to focus on the justification of, say, belief p relative to the belief q, we no longer need to suppose that the belief q itself is justified, and, thus, the threat of the (standard) problem of the regress of justification would not arise. In so doing we are, in effect, neutralizing the assumption that "all justification (of first-order beliefs) is inferential."

Now where the subject matter of our concern is knowledge of one's own beliefs, the belief p, as noted, will stand for the belief that I believe, say, r, and this second-order belief is supposedly based on, say, the belief s. Accordingly, adopting Boghossian's strategy in this case means that we should require only that the belief that I believe that r be justified *relative* to the belief that s, thus neutralizing the assumption that "all justification of second-order beliefs, that is, all self-knowledge is inferential." But if waiving the standard regress problem is what Boghossian is asking us to do in order to highlight the "special problem" sustaining a thoroughly inferential conception of self-knowledge, then he can no longer appeal to the assumption that "all self-knowledge is inferential" to allow (4') to generate a vicious regress. Given the relativization requirement, which effectively neutralizes this assumption, he can no longer say of the (second-order) knowledge (justified belief) expressed by (4') that *"on the assumption that all self-knowledge is inferential*, it could have been acquired only by inference from yet other known [justified] beliefs. And now we are off on a vicious regress." Boghossian's argument for (P) is thus blocked.

So I conclude that Boghossian's failure to establish (P) is not because his argument entitles him only to the conclusion that only some self-knowledge is non-inferential, but because his argument for (P) does not even get off the ground once it is decided to waive the standard problem of the regress of justification by relativizing the justification of one belief to another. The preceding remarks can also explain why Boghossian wavers between the two positions expressed by propositions "All self-knowledge is non-inferential" and "Some self-knowledge is non-inferential." The latter is an obvious offshoot of his foundationalist solution to the chain of regress of justification. For on a foundationalist solution to the chain of inferentially justified beliefs – which generates a vicious regress – and in order to avoid circularity, one has to assume that in tracing back this chain we arrive at one or more non-inferentially justified (second-order) beliefs that terminate the regress. Thus, in bringing the regress to an end in the above manner, one has to acknowledge, naturally enough, that the chain includes both instances of inferential and non-inferential self-knowledge as its members. On the other hand, when reflecting on the differences between the ways in which one comes to know one's own thoughts and the thought of others, he is propelled to the former position.

Another reason for Boghossian's wavering attitude might be the fact that he uses "indirectly" and "inferentially" interchangeably as the following quote clearly demonstrates: "In the case of others, I have no choice but to *infer* what they think from observation about what they do or say. In my own case, by contrast, inference is neither required nor relevant. ... I know what I think *directly*" (Boghossian 1989, p. 7). But these two notions are not identical. Not every instance of an indirect knowledge (justification) is inferential. When construing self-knowledge as a species of direct knowledge, epistemologists do not generally have in mind a lack of spatial or causal link between the knower and the known. The term is rather used in an epistemic sense meaning that direct knowledge (justification) is a species of knowledge that is not based on another piece of knowledge (justification). On the other hand, some indirect perceptual beliefs that we acquire are not obtained through inference from some other set of beliefs. We are usually unaware of such inferences and may not even be able to reconstruct such inferences because it is often difficult to form beliefs about how things appear to us in perception (Alston 1971).

The preceding diagnosis of Boghossian's argument also shows that, on his way of setting up the problem, it is actually the regress-of-justification problem (now involving second-order beliefs) that is doing all the work and not the internalist conception of justification.[3] In fact, given certain assumptions, we may derive the conclusion that "some self-knowledge is non-inferential" by applying the standard regress argument to justified second-order beliefs without presupposing either an internalist or externalist conception of justification. If the justification of all first-order or second-order beliefs is assumed to be inferential, then we have two main options at our disposal in order to deal with the generated regress. We can either adopt a foundationalist stance by ruling that some first-order or second-order beliefs are non-inferentially justified, or we can opt for a circle and then switch from local to holistic coherentism. Either way, this means that it is our ways of handling the regress problem, rather than anything to do with internalist/externalist conceptions of justification, that is brought to bear on the question of whether or not justification (of first-order or second-order beliefs) is inferential.

Chase has claimed that, despite Boghossian's failure to establish (P), one can still present the following qualified version of Boghossian's argument for the incompatibility thesis. Recall that, according to Chase, given justification internalism, Boghossian's argument for (P), at most, gives us the conclusion that some self-knowledge is non-inferential. This provides the basis for a qualified version of the incompatibility argument.

(P′) If justification internalism is true then some self-knowledge is non-inferential.

(Q′) If some self-knowledge is non-inferential then content externalism is false.

∴(Q′) If justification internalism is true then content externalism is false.

Chase's reaction to this argument consists of denying (Q'), because content externalism does not entail that *all* self-knowledge is inferential. The latter is true if all instances of self-knowledge involve wide content concepts. But, says Chase, "Twin Earth cases only show that some, rather than all, concepts are wide. ... [So] [b]eing committed to the claim that some instances of self-knowledge involve only narrow content concepts is not being committed to much" (Chase 2001, p. 236). Chase concludes that Boghossian has failed to show that justification internalism is incompatible with content externalism.

There are, however, a number of problems with Chase's treatment of the qualified version of Boghossian's incompatibility argument. To begin with, in order to be able to construct this version of the argument, he needs to show that the class of the instances of non-inferential self-knowledge whose existence he takes to follow from Boghossian's argument for (P') coincides with the class of the instances of non-inferential self-knowledge that, he says, only involve narrow content concepts. However, even granting that Boghossian's regress argument establishes, at least, (P'), there is no indication that instances of non-inferential self-knowledge whose existence is supposedly acknowledged by the argument all involve narrow content concepts. Moreover, *pace* Chase's claim, Boghossian himself is quite aware that Twin Earth cases only show that some concepts are wide:

> The commitment to relationism is evident, of course, in *wide* or *anti-individualistic* conception of thought content. According to such views, *many* of a person's thought contents are necessarily dependent on relations that the person bears to the physical or, in some cases, social environment. The view is supported by a series of now-famous thought experiments. (Boghossian 1989, pp. 11–12)

I take the preceding remarks as showing that Chase fails to address the substantial issues that Boghossian's argument from non-inferentiality of self-knowledge raises.

My own assessment of the incompatibility argument is, by now, quite clear. It fails because Boghossian's argument for (P) is seriously flawed. It neither delivers (P) nor (P'). Nevertheless, I think, there are certain intuitions that one can preserve from Boghossian's failed attempt in order to erect a new argument for the incompatibility thesis. The argument that I am going to submit will principally draw on the recent controversy concerning the possible bearing of content externalism on the alleged privileged character of self-knowledge. By way of setting the stage for presenting the argument, it will be helpful to consider briefly some terse remarks that BonJour has made in this connection which focuses on the accessibility of content. Here is all he says in defense of the incompatibility thesis.

> The adoption of an externalist account of mental content would seem to support an externalist account of justification in the following way: if part or all of the content of a belief is inaccessible to the believer, then both the justifying status of other beliefs in relation to that content and the status of that content as justifying further beliefs will be similarly inaccessible, thus contradicting the internalist requirements for justification. (BonJour 1992, p. 136)

BonJour's compressed remarks are made in the context of clarifying the internalist/externalist divide in justification theory, and they clearly need clarification. I think a charitable understanding of BonJour's remarks can be obtained if they are seen in the light of the recent controversy over the possible bearing of content externalism on the thesis of privileged self-knowledge. What BonJour seems to be saying is that if the content of a belief A is not accessible to a cognizer, then it cannot play the role of a justifier for another belief B. For if the cognizer is to be justified (in an internalist sense) in believing B, she must know (by reflection alone) whether the ground of that belief obtains. Now if, as content externalism seems to imply, knowing the content of a belief requires empirical investigation, then this means that the justifying factors of the cognizer's beliefs are not internally (i.e., reflectively) available to her. This means that content externalism and justification internalism are incompatible.

We are now in a position to present our argument from privileged access for the incompatibility thesis. It should be noted that I am using "knowledge," as in "self-knowledge," not in the sense of merely having a true belief in the contents of our thoughts. I use it, rather, as, at least, having a *justified* belief in those contents. The argument consists of the following steps.

(E) Justification internalism presupposes self-knowledge.
(F) Self-knowledge is epistemically privileged.
(G) Content externalism is incompatible with privileged self-knowledge.
∴(C) Justification internalism is incompatible with content externalism.

Each of the above steps needs to be obviously substantiated. The argument for (E) is rather straightforward. I have already characterized justification internalism by the accessibility constraint on the justifiers of one's beliefs. It requires of them to be reflectively knowable to the agent. Accordingly, the justifiers of a cognizer's belief p at time t are those facts that she is capable of knowing (in some internal sense), at that time, whether they hold. Thus, if justifiers are themselves beliefs knowing whether they hold and bear the appropriate epistemic relation to the target belief would, ipso facto, require knowing their contents. So justification internalism presupposes self-knowledge. This is especially clear in the case of the strong form of justification internalism that Boghossian, claiming to be following BonJour, seems to advocate. Suppose belief p depends on belief q, then "[a]ccording to internalism, if I am to be justified in believing that p, I must believe that p as a result of both of my recognition [knowledge] that I believe that q, and that a belief that q justifies a belief that p" (Boghossian 1989, p. 9). Thus, justification internalism requires the cognizer to know (or, at least, justifiably believe) the contents of her beliefs' justifiers.[4]

Now for the truth of (F). Since (F) is widely assumed to be obvious, I do not think that it really needs an argument. At least, this is how it is thought of by almost all those who have addressed the question of the compatibility of content externalism and privileged self-knowledge in print. In the case of the knowledge of empirical facts or the thoughts of others, we have to embark on empirical investigation of our environment and the behavior of people. But in the case of knowledge of the contents of our own thoughts – beliefs, desires, and so on – this is obtained independently of any empirical investigation. So the idea is that we have a privileged access to the contents of our thoughts. The idea is not that such a knowledge is incorrigible. Rather, the claim is that "we are able to know, without the benefit of empirical investigation, what our thoughts are in our own case" (Boghossian 1997, p. 271). So the general consensus is that privileged self-knowledge (access) has a broadly a priori character. Here is a typical statement of privileged self-knowledge, which in conformity with our understanding of knowledge, is couched in terms of justification.

(PS) It is conceptually necessary that if we are able to exercise our actual normal capacity to have beliefs about our occurrent thoughts, then if we are able to occurrently think that p, we are able to know that we are thinking that p without our knowledge being justificatorily based on empirical investigation of our environment. (McLaughlin and Tye 1998a, p. 286)

I take it that the preceding remarks establish both the premises (E) and (F) of our incompatibility argument. The argument is also valid, so everything hangs on the premise (G). Is it true?

There are currently two lines of thought to show that content externalism undermines the traditional doctrine according to which we enjoy a privileged access to our intentional states. The first line of argument, due to McKinsey, seeks to show that the combined theses of content externalism and privileged self-knowledge provide a non-empirical route to knowledge of empirical facts which is clearly absurd (McKinsey 1991). The second line of argument (mainly due to Boghossian) is what is generally known as the "slow switching argument" (Boghossian 1989). It claims to show that if externalism is true, then one could discover the contents of one's thoughts only after investigating the physical and/or social environment in which one exists. For example, if we wish to know whether we are thinking about water or twater, we should investigate our environment to see if it contains H_2O or XYZ. This means that we do not have the kind of immediate and direct access to the contents of our thoughts that the thesis of privileged access claims we have. It might be protested, however, that in order for us to know something our evidence need not rule out *all* the alternatives to what is known but only those that are *relevant*, and, under ordinary circumstances, the twater hypothesis is not a relevant alternative. So the fact that we do not seem to be able to rule out the twater hypothesis does not undermine our claim to know that we are thinking about water.

Following Burge's lead, however, Boghossian has suggested that it is easy to describe scenarios in which the twater hypothesis is a relevant alternative. Suppose, unbeknownst to Oscar, he is switched back and forth between Earth and Twin Earth, remaining on each planet long enough to acquire the concepts appropriate to the respective environments. Suppose, having returned from Twin Earth, Oscar is now on earth expressing the thought that water is wet. Does he know that he is thinking about water? Well, given his circumstances, one can attribute such knowledge to him if he is able to rule out the relevant hypothesis that he is thinking about twater. But this would require Oscar to investigate his environment first in order to find what he thinks, which is precisely what the thesis of privileged access denies. Externalism is thus incompatible with self-knowledge.

Obviously an assessment of both lines of argument is too large a task to undertake in this chapter. Fortunately, both arguments have received a good deal of critical attention in the literature, and it would be fair to conclude that neither succeeds in establishing its intended conclusion, and that, in consequence, content externalism remains neutral as far as lending its weight to any particular side in the internalism/externalism debate in justification theory is concerned.[5] This leaves our earlier conclusions in rejecting both horns of the dilemma unaffected and intact.

Part II
The Skeptical Challenge

We have already touched on the problem of skepticism and discussed certain skeptical scenarios in order to draw the contours of the concept of epistemic justification, though, as emphasized, it is no adequacy condition on a proper theory of justification that it shows that we have such epistemic attainments as justification or knowledge. It looks as if one could conceive of a skeptical scenario for almost every knowledge/justification-claim one makes. Skepticism is one of the oldest problems in philosophy, and it is fair to say that, despite numerous efforts to resolve it in the philosophical tradition, it has proved to be a resilient one. Just when a certain attempt at defeating skepticism seems to have had some measure of success, it reemerges in a different guise or at a different level. The enduring appeal and resilience of the problem of skepticism has prompted some theorists to regard it as actually being rooted in the human condition: "[W]hen we first encounter the skeptical reasoning ... we find it immediately gripping. It appeals to something deep in our nature and seems to raise a real problem about the human condition" (Stroud 1984, p. 39). Skeptical theses are usually targeted at the epistemic status of beliefs, and their strength is negatively correlated with the strength of the epistemic achievements they seek to deny. Thus a strong form of skepticism may deny that our beliefs are even justified while milder versions may seek only to show that we lack knowledge or certainty. Here, for the most part, I shall couch the problem in terms of the concept of justification.

Skepticism has many sources. In this part of the book, I choose to focus only on certain sources of skepticism that have been more prominent in the recent tradition of the epistemological thought, though I shall try to approach them from a fresh angle. One notable argument for skepticism has come to be known as the problem of the criterion.

Although with ancient roots, Descartes famously addresses a certain instance of it in his work (now known as the problem of the Cartesian Circle). The problem of the criterion received, however, its most explicit formulation in the works of Chisholm. It will be subjected to scrutiny in Chapter 4 where I shall seek to highlight its skeptical import.

The possibility of error has been regarded as another source of skeptical doubt since ancient times. The idea is that we have made mistakes in the past (even when things have seemed to be otherwise), so it is quite possible that our current beliefs are equally prone to error. However, while the problem that the possibility of error raises is mostly couched in terms of the fallibility of our cognitive faculties, I shall try to consider it (in Chapter 5) in one of its modern guises, involving the so-called "universalizability thesis," and see if it can deliver the goods as well as the more traditional versions of the thesis. The motivating idea behind the modern approach is the same as that of the traditional one except that the modern approach gives it a new twist through the use of the epistemological analogues of universalizability principles in ethics. The idea is that if we find ourselves in circumstances that are epistemically indistinguishable from situations in which we made mistaken judgments in the past, our beliefs in those circumstances would equally fail to attain the epistemic status of knowledge or justifiedness.

Another source of skepticism has been the possibility of alternative hypotheses equally accounting for our sensory experiences. The demon scenarios that have frequently featured in our discussions so far are precisely situations that exploit this kind of possibility. There are currently two distinct ways of arguing from alternative possibilities to skeptical conclusions. One draws on a principle known as the principle of closure which will be examined in Chapter 5. The other line of argument appeals to the so-called "underdetermination" principles which shall be the topic of our discussion in Chapter 6. To anticipate, my reaction to these skeptical arguments will be mixed. While some of them seem to seriously undermine our justification/knowledge-claims, I shall argue that others fail to make a strong case for skepticism.

4
The Problem of the Criterion

One important source of skepticism that deserves to be mentioned is the one that is given expression to by the so-called "problem of the criterion." The idea behind the problem is that any attempt at attaining epistemically justified beliefs incurs the charge of circularity or vicious regress. To be more precise, what the problem of the criterion highlights is the difficulty arising from trying to determine the extent of knowledge (justified belief) as well as formulating the criteria of such epistemic values. Although with ancient roots, the problem of the criterion found its most explicit formulation in the works of Roderick Chisholm. But despite Chisholm's efforts and subsequent discussions, there is as yet no general consensus over the exact structure of the problem. It has been thought to be concerned with phenomena as diverse as truth, knowledge, epistemic principles, and so on, with each version requiring its own special treatment.

In this chapter, I shall try to identify the canonical form of the problem of the criterion by proposing certain constraints (namely, mutual dependence and generality constraints) on what a proper formulation of the problem should satisfy. The legitimacy of these constraints is defended through a critical diagnosis of a recent revisionist attempt to depict the problem as being actually concerned with alethic concepts. This would, in turn, explain why the problem of the criterion is such a potent source of skeptical doubt. To substantiate this claim, I then embark on a detailed analysis of a widely influential account of (and solution to) the problem of the criterion, and reject it on the ground that it fails to satisfy the generality constraint.

4.1 The problem explained

The problem of the criterion arises when we attempt to provide an answer to the following questions: (1) What do we know? And (2) What are the criteria of knowing? What makes the situation problematic is that any answer to any one of these questions seems to presuppose an answer to the other. Thus, to determine the extent of our knowledge, we seem to need the criteria of knowing whereas to specify the latter, we need to be able to identify instances of knowledge. This is how Chisholm poses the problem (Chisholm 1973, 1977, 1989).

> We may distinguish two very general questions. ... "What is the *extent* of our knowledge?" and ... "What are the *criteria* of knowing?" If we know the answer to either one of these questions, then, perhaps, we may devise a procedure that will enable us to answer the other. ... But if we do not have the answer to the first question, then, it would seem, we have no way of answering the second. And if we do not have the answer to the second, then, it would seem, we have no way of answering the first. (Chisholm 1989, p. 6)

The first thing to note about this presentation is that the problem of the criterion actually concerns the boundaries of our epistemic achievements and their standards. It can be equally posed in terms of the notion of justification rather than knowledge. We may wish to determine the extent of our justified belief and its criteria. However, responding to either of these questions does not seem to be possible without responding to the other, and this is what gives rise to the problem of the criterion. But this way of presenting the problem in terms of a set of questions suffers from, what may be called, "procedural ambiguity": What is exactly the content of the claim that any response to such questions as "What do we know?" or "What is the extent of our knowledge?" presupposes an understanding of the standards of knowing? Is the problem one that we cannot *identify what we know* without already possessing the criteria of knowing (and vice versa), or is it simply that we cannot *know* a proposition without already having in possession the criteria of knowing (and vice versa)?

These questions are, as we shall explain later, quite different, and any decision regarding our choice of the proper form of the questions involved will obviously affect the structure of the problem of the criterion and its possible resolutions. My main aim in this chapter is to identify the proper structure of the problem, in the light of proceeding observations, and defend it against competing formulations, although we shall also be looking at some of the suggested solutions to the problem during the process. This will, in turn, help highlight its skeptical potentials. To achieve this goal, I shall start by imposing certain plausible constraints that a statement of the problem of the criterion should satisfy if it is going to do justice to its real import.

4.1.1   Constraints on formulating the problem of the criterion

Although Chisholm's remarks may be far from ideal in revealing the exact structure of the problem of the criterion, it seems evident that what it is really concerned with is the seemingly mutual dependence of attempts to draw the contours of our epistemic concepts (such as knowledge and justification) and the extent of our epistemic achievements. It seems quite plausible, initially at least, to think that in uncovering the nature of epistemic properties and concepts, we are bound to consider their realized instances in our intellectual endeavors. Without reflecting on some real life cases, it would seem impossible to be able to get a grip on the concepts or properties whose instantiations they are. To use a different example, to identify whether a certain activity is a game we need to know what constitutes a game, whereas to attain the latter information we seem to need to look at some real life cases of these activities. Thus, going back to the epistemic case, our problem is that identifying the instances of the relevant epistemic concepts seems to require prior familiarity with their content (and vice versa). There is therefore some sort of seemingly mutual dependence between these Herculean tasks. So our first constraint on a proper formulation of the problem of the criterion is that it should recognize a mutual dependence between the tasks involved. Let us refer to it as the "mutual dependence" constraint.

The other constraint involves the obvious fact that the premises that are supposed to give rise to the problem should enjoy prima facie plausibility. What is important, however, is that they should not owe their plausibility to any particular epistemic theory. In other words, they should be pre-theoretically plausible. So, the second constraint, which may be called the "generality" constraint, is intended to highlight the thought that the problem of the criterion is supposed to arise for all theories and conceptions of knowledge or justifications (and epistemic values, in general). Indeed, this is what makes the problem a formidable challenge to epistemological theorizing in general. So what the generality constraint amounts to is that the premises that lead to the problem of the criterion should be prima facie plausible and their plausibility should be independent of any particular theory of epistemic goodness. In order to provide further support for the enforcement of these constraints, I shall now proceed to consider a recent revisionist attempt (due to Andrew Cling) that seeks to redescribe, in new terms, the tasks that constitute the problem of the criterion (Cling 1994, 1997). He offers some arguments that, if successful, would undermine the legitimacy of the above constraints. However, as I shall explain shortly, these arguments fail.

Cling correctly notes that an ambiguity is involved in Chisholm's presentation of the problem of the criterion, but he entirely dislocates it in the process of changing its focus by redescribing its import as being concerned with alethic values such as truth. In so doing, he explicitly violates the mutual dependence constraint. So let us see if his arguments can sustain such a move. He claims that on one reading—the lower-order reading—Chisholm's questions "are the same as 'which statements are true?' and 'how can we tell which statements are true?' respectively. Sometimes when we ask what is known on a particular subject we want a list of true statements about that subject. 'What do we know about the murderer' Doright may ask, seeking a list of true statements about the criminal he seeks" (Cling 1994, p. 263). So his suggestion is that Chisholm's question "what do we know?" is equivalent to "which statements are true?" The same goes for the other question, "how do we know?" which would be couched in terms of a question about identifying true statements. But this is not correct. When we ask what we know about the murderer, the full answer may be given by the list <we know p, we know q, ...>, but this would be a different list from the list of truths <p, q, ...>. The impression that these are the same lists arises from the fact that knowledge implies truth. That the corresponding questions are not the same can be clearly seen if we reformulate Chisholm's questions in terms of justification – which, as we noted, still gives us the problem of the criterion. Now, on this construal, surely, the questions "Which beliefs are justified?" and "Which beliefs are true?" are different questions (even, on a lower-order reading). Justified beliefs can be false.

Cling goes on to suggest a higher-order reading of Chisholm's questions and claims that, on this reading, a response to "how do we determine whether we know?" would be a proposed "criterion of truth for statements about knowledge" (Cling 1994, p. 264). But this is puzzling, not least because the lower-order question "do we know p?" would prompt the same response (on Cling's account). Moreover, the mentioned question quite unambiguously concerns the criteria of knowledge, and it is explicit enough not to lend itself to different readings. So why does Cling insist on having the answer to the question formulated in terms of a criterion of truth for knowledge statements rather than a criterion of knowing per se? After all, to have a criterion for deciding whether S knows that p is to have a criterion for deciding whether "S knows that p" is true. On the other hand, one way one might go about deciding whether a statement is true is by deciding whether our evidence sufficiently supports it (i.e., whether we are *justified* in believing it). So what can explain Cling's insistence in posing the questions in terms of truth?

The reason seems to be that Cling seeks to identify "the most fundamental" form of the problem of the criterion, and he somehow thinks that since truth is a more general category than knowledge, the problem should be couched in terms of truth and its criteria. In this vein, he claims, without offering any argument, that "the questions which lead to Chisholm's ... version of the problem of the criterion are special cases of 'which statements are true?' and 'how we can tell which statements are true?'." I think Cling's failure in demonstrating that the problem of the criterion should be construed in terms of alethic rather than epistemic values is due to violating the constraints on a proper formulation of the problem of the criterion as I shall explain below. After some sampling, Cling comes up with, what he calls, "the problem of the criterion master argument" (Cling 1994, p. 270).

(1) Good beliefs depend upon an independently good criterion of truth. (premise)
(2) A good criterion of truth depends upon independently good beliefs. (premise)
(1a) We can have no independently good beliefs. (from (1))
(2a) We can have no independently good criterion of truth. (from (2))
(3a) We can have no good beliefs. (from (1) and (2a))
(3b) We can have no good criterion of truth. (from (2) and (1a))

In this argument "good" is a placeholder for terms expressing such epistemic values as knowledge and justification. The first premise says that in order to have any good belief we must first know an independently good criterion of truth, and the second premise states that knowing any good criterion of truth presupposes some good beliefs. The other steps in the argument say that, given the premises, we could neither have any good beliefs nor any good criterion of truth.

The "master argument" fails, however, to satisfy the two adequacy constraints on the construction of the problem of the criterion that, in turn, explains why its premises are far from being prima facie plausible.

(For the sake of concreteness, let us take "good" to designate "justified.") In regard to (1), Cling says "[s]hort of lucky guessing, it seems that the only way to have good [justified] beliefs is to employ a criterion of truth whose own goodness is somehow settled independently of the beliefs it warrants to be true" (Cling 1994, p. 270). But why? What can explain the purported mutual dependence between a justified belief and an adequate theory of truth? Could not one's belief be justified without one's employing a criterion of truth? To deny this would be to make the implausible claim that in ascribing, say, justified perceptual beliefs to ordinary cognizers, we are, *ipso facto*, ascribing to them knowledge of a criterion of truth, especially a criterion whose validity they have "settled independently of the beliefs it warrants to be true."

The second premise is even more implausible. In its defense Cling has this to say, "short of lucky guessing, in order to have a good criterion of truth we must select from among alleged criteria of truth on the basis of independently good [justified] beliefs" (Cling 1994, p. 270). But why? Why should the identification of a criterion of truth depend on having independently recognized *justified* beliefs? Is Cling assuming that "truth" is an inherently epistemic notion? Of course, on a truth-conducive account of justification, a justified belief is one that is more likely to be true (given the available evidence). But what is most naturally hooked up with this idea is a criterion of justification rather than truth that, contrary to Cling's intentions, would take us back to the original formulation of the problem of the criterion. It is only on some highly exotic theories of justification and truth that the second premise might look remotely plausible. The failure of Cling's arguments to justify a radical rethinking of the import of the problem of the criterion would, I think, give us sufficient incentive to employ our constraints in order to pin down its true structure. To achieve this goal, let us, once again, return to Chisholm's original remarks and see what can be extracted from them.

4.2   Two versions of the problem of the criterion

The problem, we may recall, can be said to be constituted by the following statement.

(*) We can answer the question "What are our justified beliefs?" only if we already know the criteria of justification (and vice versa).

As noted earlier, however, this statement is ambiguous. Suppose the set of our justified beliefs is not empty and that we have justified beliefs.

Then one way (*) can be understood as saying is that whether one is justified in holding a belief depends on already knowing the criteria of justification. This is a lower-level reading of that statement. There is, however, another, higher-level, reading where what is at issue is whether we can identify (or know) which beliefs are justified without already knowing the criteria of justification.

While on the lower-level reading it is the state of *being justified* that is at issue, on the higher-level reading we wish to find out if we can *determine* or *show* which beliefs are *justified* without already knowing the criteria of justification. Commensurate with these two readings, we get two different versions of the problem of the criterion constituted respectively by the following pairs of propositions.

Lower-level problem of the criterion version	(1) We can be justified in holding a belief only if we already know the criteria of justification.
(LPC)	(2) We can know the criteria of justification only if we are justified in holding some beliefs.
Higher-level problem of the criterion version	(1) We can determine (know/be justified in believing) which beliefs are justified only if we already know the criteria of justification.
(HPC)	(2) We can know the criteria of justification only if we can determine which beliefs are justified.

Since they involve different levels of epistemic achievements, these two versions of the problem of the criterion need to be treated differently. It is certainly not clear that solutions offered for one version are capable of resolving the other. What is important to note at this point, however, is that epistemologists have often had different versions of the problem of the criterion in mind when talking about it. Cling's "master argument" is clearly a lower-level version of the problem of the criterion. One of its typical premises says that a justified (good) belief depends upon an independently good criterion of truth. This reading of his argument is further confirmed by his description of the skeptic's claim that " 'prior' to having a good criterion of truth we simply could not *have* any good beliefs" (Cling 1994, p. 269).[1] (LPC) is also what Van Cleve seems to have in mind as he explicitly describes the problem of the criterion in terms of the following pair propositions (Van Cleve 1979, fn. 1).

(1) I can know some epistemic principle only if I first know some other propositions from which to derive them.

(2) I can know those other propositions only if first know some epistemic principle.[2]

Chisholm, on the other hand, clearly advocates a higher-level version of the problem of the criterion. Referring to the circle created by the questions "What is the extent of our knowledge?" and "What are the criteria of knowing?" he says there are two ways of escaping the circle.

> (1) We may try to *find out* what we *know* or what we *are justified* in believing without making use of any criterion of knowledge or of justified belief. Or (2) we may try to formulate a criterion of knowledge without *appeal* to any *instances* of knowledge or of justified belief. ... [As for the first way, what we try to do is to] *identify instances of knowing* without applying any *criteria* of knowing or of justification. (Chisholm 1989, pp. 6–7; emphasis added)

These and other relevant passages in his work clearly indicate a higher-level reading of the problem of the criterion.[3] In the remaining part of this section, I shall argue that it is (HPC) that truly represents the structure of the problem of the criterion.

It seems clear that (HPC) satisfies our constraints on a genuine description of the problem of the criterion. It naturally satisfies the mutual dependence constraint. Moreover, the generality constraint is also satisfied. To see this, consider the premise (1) in (HPC). A criterion of justification most naturally takes the following form: If $\Phi(B)$, then the belief B is justified. It says, in other words, that it is by virtue of possessing Φ, that a belief is justified. Since knowing a criterion of justification is tantamount to knowing the justification-conferring property Φ, what the premise (1), in (HPC), actually says is that forming the set of justified beliefs requires knowing the property (Φ) in virtue of which the members of the set are justified. That is to say, knowing Φ would enable us to identify which beliefs are justified (by knowing whether they possess Φ). This can be thought of as an application of the so-called axiom of comprehension according to which for every property we can form a set whose members possess that property. As such, premise (1) sounds pretty innocent and uncontroversial. Moreover, its plausibility is independent of any specific theory of justification as the nature of Φ was deliberately left unspecified. It is equally independent of the conception of justification (internalist/externalist) that might be associated with the theories of justification. Whatever the nature of Φ, it seems that our knowledge of Φ is necessary if we are to determine the extent of our justified belief, and this, as noted earlier, is what makes the problem of the criterion a serious challenge in epistemology, something that any theory of justification (knowledge) should confront.[4]

What about (LPC)? Although, being an outgrowth of Chisholm's remarks about the origin of the problem of the criterion, (LPC) initially satisfies the epistemic-dependence constraint, I do not think that it truly represents the structure of the problem as it fails in regard to the generality constraint. This becomes evident when we ask why the premises of (LPC) should be thought of as being (pre-theoretically) plausible. To begin with, unlike the intuitively plausible premise (2) in (HPC), it is not clear why the second premise in (LPC) is true. If being justified in holding a belief, which is what the premise (2) in (LPC) is concerned with, were tantamount to knowing that one is so justified, then the premise in question would be plausible. But, as things stand, it requires substantiation. The first premise in (LPC) is also questionable. There is no longer an obvious mechanism (like the axiom of comprehension) at work here. Why should our being justified in holding a belief depend on our knowing the criteria of justification? It seems to me that the most natural way of sustaining the plausibility of such claims, namely, the premise (1) in (LPC), is by invoking a certain conception of justification, in this case, an internalist one. This is how this can be done.

The premise in question claims that a necessary condition for being justified in holding a belief is to know a criterion of justification. Such a criterion, as we have seen, is usually cashed out in terms of a property in virtue of which a belief is justified. Since knowing such a criterion is tantamount to knowing the relevant property, what the premise (1) in (LPC) says is that knowing the justification-conferring property is necessary if our beliefs are to be justified. But, again, how can one *explain* the alleged dependence of the justification of one's belief on the possession of the general knowledge that a certain property (say, coherence) is justification-conferring? How could one bring this knowledge to bear on the epistemic status of one's belief? An internalist conception of justification, I suggest, is the most natural way of establishing this link. If it is required of a cognizer that he should be capable of recognizing (on reflection) whether the justification-conferring property (specified by the criterion) obtains in the case of his beliefs, if the beliefs are to be justified, then we have moved some way toward explaining how the first premise of (LPC) can be made plausible.

So the main premise of (LPC) depends for its plausibility on a specific conception of justification and this contravenes the generality constraint. (LPC) represents the problem of a criterion as a "lesser" of a problem that it might have been by getting it hooked up with a particular conception of justification. It would, thus, undermine its reputation as an enduring source of epistemological skepticism as was pointed out earlier. For, once construed as (LPC), the problem would fail to arise for *any* theory of justification, since all one needs to do to resolve it is to deny its premises by invoking a competing account of justification. This is, in fact, what has happened in the case of (LPC) as one influential solution to the problem (due to Van Cleve) has sought to deny its main premise on the basis of a competing account of justification. To support these claims, I shall now set out to examine Van Cleve's solution and its underlying assumptions.

4.2.1   The failure of Van Cleve's (externalist) response

Van Cleve does not directly deal with the problem of the criterion. His target is the problem of the Cartesian Circle, but, he says, he intends his solution to be equally applicable to the problem of the criterion since in "its generalized form, the Cartesian Circle is none other than the problem of the criterion" (Van Cleve 1979, p. 55). We therefore need to begin with a brief statement of the problem of the Cartesian Circle. This problem arises because Descartes seems to commit himself to each of the following propositions.

(I) I can know that whatever I perceive clearly and distinctly is true only if I first know that God exists and is not a deceiver.
(II) I can know that God exists and is not a deceiver only if first I know that whatever I perceive clearly and distinctly is true.

Van Cleve's (particularist) resolution of the Cartesian Circle amounts to the denial of (II), and prominent in his solution is Descartes's rule of clearness and distinctness (A) which he summarizes as follows.

(A) For all P, if I clearly and distinctly perceive that P, then I am certain of that P.

The crux of Van Cleve's way of breaking out of the circle consists of claiming that "(A) is not a principle I have to *apply* in order to gain knowledge; I need only *fall under* it" (Van Cleve 1979, p. 70). To be certain of a proposition one need not know that one clearly and distinctly perceives it, it suffices only that one does clearly and distinctly perceive it. Falling under (A), says Van Cleve, does not even require that "I have the concept of clear and distinct perceptions" (Van Cleve 1979, p. 67).

> (A) says that perceiving something clearly and distinctly is *sufficient* to render me certain of it. It follows that nothing else is *necessary*, unless it is also necessary for the occurrence of clear and distinct perception in the first place. But neither knowledge of (A) nor knowledge of the fact that I am clearly and distinctly perceiving something is necessary for such perception to occur. (Van Cleve 1979, pp. 69–70)

Thus, in virtue of satisfying (A), we acquire a set of certainties such as that God exists, and so on. From this we become certain that God is not a deceiver, and from here we go on to derive (A) itself, namely, that whatever I perceive clearly and distinctly is true.

Cling, however, has claimed that Van Cleve's solution is unsuccessful. He attacks one of the premises in Van Cleve's argument, namely, the one which states that neither my knowledge of (A) nor my knowing that I am clearly and distinctly perceiving that P is necessary for my clearly and distinctly perceiving that P. He thinks this claim is unwarranted as Van Cleve provides no support for it: "Only an account of the nature of clear and distinct perception which entails that clear and distinct perception does not require knowledge of (A) could support [the mentioned premise]. Without such an account, Van Cleve's defense of Descartes is seriously incomplete" (Cling 1997, p. 130). But there are two ways of looking at the mentioned premise in Van Cleve's argument: We can either regard it as a general strategy to show that neither knowledge of an epistemic principle (If ..., then P is justified for S) nor of its antecedent is necessary for the obtaining of its antecedent, or simply concentrate on a particular epistemic principle (in this case (A)) and reject the corresponding argument. As an attack on the general strategy, Cling's criticism fails. He says nothing as to why it is defective. Rather, his remarks draw their seeming plausibility only by focusing on a particular epistemic principle (namely, (A)) whose antecedent is concerned with our clearly and distinctly perceiving a proposition. All that Cling's remarks show is that, as things stand, Van Cleve needs to say more in order to make good his claim about (A), for we have not been told much about what a clear and distinct perception of a proposition consists in. But it is unfair to take this as a criticism of Van Cleve's general strategy as it is actually targeted at the particular epistemic principle it involves.

In fact Van Cleve goes on to represent his argument in a way that no longer hinges on Descartes's rule of clearness and distinctness. His target is the general (anti-foundationalist) claim that epistemic principles must themselves be known (justified) if knowledge (justified belief) is to arise in accordance with them.

> An epistemic principle has the form "if ... then P is justified for S." In other words, it says that the obtaining of whatever condition is specified in its antecedent is *sufficient* for P's being justified for S. Now it is a logical truth that if X is sufficient for Y, then there is no other condition Z that is *necessary* for Y, unless Z is also necessary for X. But knowledge of an epistemic principle is not necessary for the obtaining of its antecedent. Therefore, knowledge of an epistemic principle is not necessary for knowledge to arise in accordance with it. (Van Cleve 1979, p. 77)

Here, Van Cleve's target is no longer the dubious Cartesian principle (A) but *genuine* epistemic principles in general. What he claims is that knowledge of a genuine epistemic principle is not necessary for the obtaining of its antecedent. And this claim seems plausible enough for epistemic principles that are currently in vogue, and which take properties such as coherence, reliability, and so on as being sufficient for the obtaining of justification. Surely, the obtaining of coherence does not depend on our knowledge of the relevant epistemic principle connecting coherence with justification. Neither does the obtaining of reliably formed beliefs presuppose that we know the epistemic principle connecting reliability with justification. In the case of such principles, unlike Descartes's rule of clearness and distinctness, we are faced with a set of relatively well-defined properties that are claimed to be sufficient for the obtaining of justification. So citing these examples gives us enough grounds to support Van Cleve's claim.

It is, however, quite clear that Van Cleve's argument is cogent only if an externalist perspective is assumed, one in which a belief can be justified simply by virtue of possessing a justification-conferring property regarding which the cognizer may have no reason to think that it is obtained in the case of the belief in question. Extending Van Cleve's strategy to cover his preferred version of the problem of the criterion, (LPC), his "solution" would amount to denying the premise (1) in the argument. But this can only be sustained if an externalist account of justification is invoked where "the obtaining of whatever condition is specified in [the] antecedent [of the relevant epistemic principle] is sufficient for [a proposition] being justified for S."[5] This would clearly dispose of the first premise of (LPC) lending support to our earlier claim that (LPC) does not genuinely represent the structure of the problem of the criterion. For the fact that (LPC) can be shown to be invalid by invoking a particular conception of justification shows that it actually violates the generality constraint on the formulation of the problem of the criterion.

To conclude, we started with various ways in which the problem of the criterion has been framed, and sought to identify its canonical form by proposing certain constraints that a proper formulation of the problem should satisfy. The legitimacy of these constraints was then defended by considering and rejecting a revisionist attempt to change the focus of the problem. These resources were exploited to show why a widely influential account of the problem of the criterion fails to reflect its real import. In the light of preceding remarks, it is fair to conclude that the problem of the criterion is still one of the most formidable problems that any serious anti-skeptical epistemological theory must face head on and be able to formulate a response to it.

5
Universalizability and Closure

5.1 The epistemic universalizability thesis

Suppose I claim that it will rain today basing my belief on such body of evidence as the gathering clouds, the increasingly windy weather, and so on. Do I *know* this? It seems so. However, the skeptic is quick to remind us of relevantly similar circumstances in which I had formed a similar belief based on similar grounds but my claim had turned out to be false. Thus, he would demand that unless I can show that my current situation is not a knowledge-precluding one, I will not be able to claim to know that it will rain today. This argument admittedly requires some filling up as we need to have a more precise account of the mechanism through which knowledge-precluding situations, namely, possibilities that have to be ruled out if a claim is to count as knowledge, can be specified.

Some epistemologists (most notably Adler) have sought to introduce a set of closely related principles that, they claim, would inject more precision into the mechanism of specifying the alternatives that must be countenanced when making knowledge-claims, and which, while stopping short of endorsing radical skepticism, have enough power to generate skeptical conclusions (Adler 1981, 1990). Adler calls these "universalizability principles" which are analogous in their form and underlying basis to universalizability principles in ethics. In this chapter, I shall try to show that although the universalizability thesis possesses skeptical potentials, it is only because of certain epistemically significant assumptions embedded in Adler's version of the thesis that it can generate skeptical conclusions. Stripped of these assumptions, we get a more modest version of the principle that is epistemically innocuous functioning, at best, as a means of enforcing certain constraints on the concept of justification.

The term "universalizability" was introduced in ethics by Richard Hare who suggested that moral judgments can be characterized by the two defining features of prescriptivity and universalizability. The latter was intended to highlight the point that an agent who makes a moral judgment is committed, on pain of being inconsistent, to making the same judgment of any relevantly similar action. That is to say, by judging an action as morally good the agent commits himself to holding that any relevantly similar action is morally good. Inspired by the idea behind ethical universalizability, Adler attempts to advance a similar thesis for epistemological contexts. As a first shot he suggests the following universalizability principle (involving knowledge) in order to set the stage for the introduction of a more precise one.

(KUP) If A and B are in *epistemically indistinguishable circumstances* (EIC) and A *does* not know that *p*, then B *cannot* know that *p*.

By being in EIC the cognizers are presumed to be in qualitatively identical epistemic situations, agreeing in "all epistemically relevant factors, including evidence, background information, reasoning abilities, and ... in what they are trying to know" (Adler 1981, p. 144). As Adler points out that (KUP) is false as stated, for A's failure to know could be due to the failure of the truth condition, whereas the interesting cases are those in which knowledge is defeated "because of ... failures in the epistemic, or third condition of knowledge" (Adler 1981, p. 145). This requires a shift away from "knowledge" to "justification," thus, the second universalizability principle.

(FUP) If A and B are in EIC and A's *justification* that *p* was defeated by *d*, then B is not justified in believing that *p* (unless he can rule out the relevant *d*-like defeaters).

These principles allow for a number of variations involving their key terms leading to a much greater range of alternatives than is recognized on the common-sense view. We can, for instance, vary the degree of accessibility of defeaters by gradually widening their epistemic distance from the cognizers themselves, making them subsequently accessible to their respective epistemic communities only, and, eventually, placing them out of their epistemic reach. We can also expand the range of statements that are affected by previous failed justifications to include their correlates in EIC. And, perhaps more significantly, we can go beyond actualized defeaters, and also consider, as relevant, those that are merely *plausible*, that is, those whose occurrence is very likely and not just a mere logical possibility (like our being deceived by a demon).

The skeptical import of these principles, and their variations along the above dimensions, is now clear. For with respect to any familiar, well-entrenched belief (p), it is plausible to think that someone whose justification was subsequently defeated has actually been in EIC to us. Here Adler reminds us of the familiar cases where people have made mistakes, taking, for example, facades for entire houses, holograms for real objects, and such like, and also the familiar (falsified) theories in the history of science. We can proliferate such cases by adding to the actual defeaters the plausible ones. Given these assumptions, the cognizers are, by (FUP)[1], denied having justified belief (knowledge) about similar objects under similar circumstances unless they can rule out the relevant defeaters. They are, in other words, required to offer better justification than their epistemic counterparts whose beliefs have subsequently turned out to be not adequately grounded: "Our minimal principles require only that the agent improve his epistemic circumstances sufficiently to undermine the realistic possibility that his justification will be defeated" (Adler 1981, p. 147).

5.1.1   Two versions of the universalizability thesis

To get a better grip on Adler's skeptical argument and the nature of epistemic universalizability principles, it would help to start by considering the following question: how could these supposedly innocuous and structural principles have such significant epistemic import? To appreciate this question, let us remind ourselves of the status of universalizability principles in ethics which seem to have been the main inspiration behind the introduction of their epistemic counterparts. According to Hare the thesis of (moral) universalizability is a logical thesis by which he means that it is a thesis about the *meanings* of words: "I have been maintaining that the meaning of the word 'ought' and other moral words is such that a person who uses them commits himself to a universal rule" (Hare 1963, p. 30). Thus, someone who judges that an action is morally all right but refuses to pass the same judgment on a similar action and in identical circumstances is guilty of logical inconsistency, and cannot be said to know what "morally all right" means. The universalizability thesis has, therefore, a semantic character embodying a semantic feature of moral words. Likewise, one can regard the thesis of epistemic universalizability as requiring the passing of the same (epistemic) judgments on similar beliefs held under similar circumstances, designating a semantic determinant of the concept of justification.

Given this background, it is rather mystifying how these semantically motivated, structural principles can generate skeptical conclusions.

The problem is rather analogous to what was once a controversial question about the alleged essentialist import of the so-called causal (or direct) theory of reference. Some philosophers had, for example, claimed that one could derive such metaphysically necessary statements as "Water is H_2O" from the causal theory of natural kind terms alone. What seemed puzzling was how a (supposedly) pure semantic theory about natural kind words and proper names could usher in nontrivial essentialist conclusions about natural kinds and individuals. The subsequent unpacking of the claim revealed, however, that it actually helps itself to a number of assumptions one of which is by no means modally neutral and the other has an empirical character. It was not therefore true that the essentialist import of the conclusion derives from the semantic theory of reference alone (see Salmon 1982).

The same, I believe, can be said about the claim that one can derive substantial epistemic conclusions from (semantically motivated) universalizability principles, for its unpacking would disclose certain hidden and significant epistemic assumptions that help the derivation. To show this let me begin by rehearsing an objection that was leveled against Adler's (FUP) by Anthony Brueckner (Brueckner 1984). In formulating the thesis of epistemic universalizability in terms of justification, Adler explicitly states that he is following the Gettier literature when, as in (FUP), he speaks of justification being defeated. That is to say, if e justifies p, then the justification is defeated "if there is some truth d such that $[e]$&d fail to justify $[p]$" (Adler 1981, p. 143). But, as Brueckner points out, the mere existence of a defeater in the context of attributing knowledge to a cognizer (in the sense of the Gettier literature) is consistent with his being justified in the belief in question. This is because in the Gettier literature it is assumed that the justification-condition for knowing is independent of a fourth (defeasibilty) condition (if there is one). So Adler must be assuming that a defeater of whose existence the cognizer is unaware undermines his justification.

In his most recent work on the topic, Adler tries to restructure his earlier argument, an attempt that reveals a different version of the epistemic universalizability principle. He starts by asserting that "knowledge entails certainty or the absence of any reasonable doubt" (Adler 1990a, p. 83). This idea forms the basis of his first premise (M): X is justified in believing that P only if there is no possibility of serious defeaters to that justification. The second premise is a universalizability principle (N): If some agent is justified (for knowledge) in believing P, then anyone in EIC is justified in believing that P (where P is a place holder for statements that are the correlates of P in EIC). From (M) and (N) it follows that (C): If someone is justified in believing P, then no serious defeater to P is possible for anyone in EIC to that agent. But, given varieties of actual and plausible circumstance in which the consequent of (C) fails to be satisfied, it would follow that the agent is not justified in believing P.

As can be seen, the earlier universalizability principle (FUP)—which is, with some modifications, equivalent to (C)—is now broken up into an epistemically significant assumption (M) which is, presumably, intended to take care of Brueckner's objection, and reveal the mechanism whereby justification is undermined; and a more abstract version of the universalizability thesis (N) (which I shall rename as (MUP) for reasons that will become clear shortly).

(MUP)   If A and B are in EIC and A is justified in believing P, then B is
        justified in believing that P.

In unfolding the mechanism of defeat, (M) not only says that justification can be undermined by the existence of known defeaters, but it also requires that the agent's "justification must take account of potential sources of error, even if the knowledge of these sources only surfaces much later than the time for which justification is being assessed" (Adler 1990a, p. 84). The unpacking of (FUP) into (M) and (MUP) shows why (when conjoined with (empirical) assumptions about the relevant records of the cognizers in EIC) it results in skeptical conclusions. Just as the argument from "reference" to "essence" was revealed to incorporate hidden essentialist and empirical assumptions, the argument from epistemic universalizability to skepticism seems to have helped itself with an epistemically significant assumption as well as some empirical ones.

The relation between (MUP) and (FUP) can be usefully compared to that between, what Alston calls, a "minimalist" correspondence theory of truth and a "full-blooded" one (Alston 1996, ch. 1). The minimalist theory can be obtained from generalizing over an analogue of Tarski's convention T: (p) The proposition that p is true iff it is a fact that p. This "correspondence" theory is minimalist because it says nothing about the relation between a proposition and the fact by virtue of which it is made true. It treats propositions as unanalyzed units. A full-blooded theory, on the other hand, takes off from this point, and includes an account of the internal structure of propositions and facts, left unanalyzed in the minimalist version, in order to highlight what correspondence consists in.

Such an account is intended to reveal the mechanism of correspondence as consisting, for example, of some sort of structural isomorphism between propositions and facts (as in the correspondence theories of Russell and Wittgenstein).

An analogous relation holds between the minimalist version of the universalizability principle (MUP) and the full-blooded one (FUP). The latter incorporates, and exploits, the mechanism whereby justification is undermined. The minimalist version (MUP), by contrast, is silent on the nature of such mechanisms, requiring only that we extend our judgments about particular epistemic situations to those that are relevantly similar to ensure consistency in doxastic behavior. In the next section I shall examine what Adler has to say in defense of his universalizability principles, especially the full-blooded version (FUP). This will be followed by an analysis of the minimalist version (MUP).

5.1.2 The epistemic import of universalizability principles

In support of (FUP) Adler merely gives some examples which, he hopes, are plausible enough to motivate the principle and provide a rationale for its application. Consider, as an example, what he calls "the hologram case." In stage one an agent (A) claims to know that there is a vase in the room on the ground that he sees a vase-like object before him. What he sees, however, is a convincing hologram. Nonetheless, his claim is true because there actually is a vase in the room. In stage two, another person (B) is standing in the room and looking at the place where the hologram once stood. This time, however, a genuine vase has replaced the hologram. It is plausible to say that, despite the truth of his belief, B cannot know (be justified) that there is a vase before him unless he can rule out the relevant alternative that he is seeing a hologram, and this coincides with the verdict of (FUP). Adler also claims that his principles can explain some of the (independently) plausible cases discussed in the literature. He cites Harman's example of "undermining evidence one does not possess" which is intended to highlight the social character of knowledge (justification) and Goldman's barn example. It seems to me, however, that his diagnosis of the Goldman example, and his subsequent attempt to draw support from it for his universalizability principles, are flawed. It would be instructive to go through the case as it would reveal the real import of such principles.

Goldman considers a case where an agent (A) is pointing at what looks like a barn in an area where there are lots of similar-looking fake barns around. Goldman (plausibly) claims that A does not know that he is looking at a barn despite the fact that what he sees is a real barn. Adler claims that his (FUP) can explain A's failure to have knowledge under such circumstances. This is because "he could easily be in EIC, where his justification would be defeated (i.e., he could be looking at one of the other objects)" (Adler 1981, p. 149). But this is an improper application of (FUP). For, in the actual case, where A is looking at a real barn and there are fake barns around, he is, by Adler's own assumptions, unjustified in believing that he is looking at a barn. This is because although there are no (rebutting) defeaters in that case, there is an undercutting one. ("There are lots of fake barns around.") This satisfies Adler's own definition of a defeater as it is a truth whose conjunction with the proposition describing the (perceptual) evidence fails to justify A's belief that he is looking at a barn. There is, thus, no need to consider the scenario where A, being in EIC, is looking at a fake barn in order to bring his epistemic status, via (FUP), to bear upon his status in the actual case where he is looking at a real barn. What *would* have occasioned an application of, and thus lent support to, the universalizability principles was if Goldman had claimed that even when A is looking at a real barn and there are no fake barns around, he still does not know. For to explain this, one could then exploit the principle to bring the epistemic status of A's belief in the case where he is looking at a barn and there are fake barns around to bear on his belief in the other case where there are no such barns (this would, incidentally, be similar to the hologram case where although the agent is looking at a real vase, he lacks, says Adler, knowledge and justification).[2]

The preceding remarks (in terms of examples) are all that Adler has to offer in defense of (FUP), and while some of his observations lend intuitive support to the principle, they cannot substantiate it in its entirety. This is primarily because (FUP) incorporates, as we saw, substantive epistemic assumptions regarding the mechanism of defeat of one's justification, something whose involvement demands a more compelling defense of (FUP) than the mere citation of some plausible examples. To gain a better understanding of the dialectic of the situation so far, it would be helpful to try to find out what may lie behind the introduction of (FUP). It is widely believed that the enforcement of certain plausible constraints on the ascription of knowledge would leave the door open for skepticism to creep in. It seems to me that the most plausible candidate for the role of the constraint in question involves an idea that, following Nagel, has been called "epistemic luck." The term was introduced into literature following Williams's discussion of moral luck (Nagel 1976; Williams 1976). The idea is that while a significant portion of what one does depends on factors beyond his control, yet we continue to pass moral judgments on him. But, as both Williams and Nagel concur, there is something about our conception of morality that resists the idea that moral merit or blame should be subject to luck. And it is this very feature that seems to invite moral skepticism. Nagel extends this to epistemology, and claims that although many of our beliefs turn out to depend on factors outside our control, our concept of knowledge also displays a similar kind of resistance to luck. But by being committed to discounting luck, our conception of knowledge inevitably invites skepticism.

Adler acknowledges such a feature of knowledge for, it looks as if, it is precisely to safeguard against epistemic luck that he introduces the universalizability principles: "More generally, the justification [of the principles] stems from the requirement that knowledge not be *accidental*" (Adler 1981, p. 145). So universalizability principles are actually intended to function as built-in safeguards against epistemic luck. I think this is a fair analysis of the legitimacy of certain species of universalizability principles and their skeptical potentials. What is unwarranted, however, is Adler's extension of this moral (in the case of knowledge) to the case of epistemic justification. It is here that, as we have seen, his universalizability principle (FUP) runs into trouble.

The conclusions reached, thus far, vis-à-vis the universalizability principles in epistemology parallels rather neatly the situation involving their ethical counterparts. For although at a certain level of abstraction ethical universalizability (extending one's moral judgment about a particular action to those that are *morally relevant*) is intuitively obvious, there is, nonetheless, as Mackie observes, plenty of room for discussion in regard to how the thesis should be interpreted (Mackie 1983, ch. 4). Mackie cites three different kinds (or stages) of universalization which involve different interpretations of what is to count as a "morally relevant factor." The first stage only rules numerical differences as being morally irrelevant, while the second stage denies the moral relevance of generic differences as well. The third stage requires, in addition, giving equal weight to different tastes and rival desires. As we move away from the minimalist, or, from what Nagel calls, "bare" version of ethical universalizability through these stages, the underlying requirements (and assumptions) become increasingly more substantive and controversial and, as Mackie shows, more difficult to satisfy (Nagel 1990, p. 102). It is, however, only when we are prepared to accept those substantial assumptions and requirements, and embrace a full-blooded version of the thesis that we may hope, as Hare does, to derive such significant ethical conclusions as (some form of) utilitarianism from the universal-izability thesis.

Something very similar is true of the universalizability thesis in epistemology. For, as we have seen, it is only in conjunction with certain substantial epistemic assumptions that an application of epistemic universalizability (as embodied in its full-blooded version (FUP)) can lead to skeptical conclusions. When stripped of these assumptions, we get the minimalist version (MUP). That (MUP) is epistemically innocu-ous follows from the fact that, when applying the universalizability thesis, the real work is done by the accompanying epistemic assumption (*M*) rather than (MUP). If our aim is to generate skeptical doubt in regard to a justification/knowledge-claim, all we need to do is to bring (*M*) to bear directly on that claim. For what (*M*) effectively says is that an agent's belief is justified if there is no possibility of serious defeaters to that justification. However, since one can always conceive of the possibility of such defeaters, in one form or another, there is not much chance for the agent's belief to maintain its positive epistemic status. There is, thus, no need to involve (MUP) to generate the desired skepti-cal doubt. (*M*) alone can be relied on to do the job for us. Of course, everything hangs on whether (*M*) is a plausible assumption, but this is something that is not addressed in Adler's remarks.

As for the status of (MUP), it strikes one as a plausible enough princi-ple (which is perhaps why it lacks enough anti-skeptical firepower). What it says is that if two agents are in epistemically indistinguishable circumstances and one is justified so is the other. One can in fact view it as a semantic determinant of the content of the concept of epistemic justification. This is actually the case with its ethical counterpart. For although the minimalist version of ethical universalizability is generally thought to be uncontroversial, attempts have been made to justify it by linking it to the meaning of moral terms. Any violation of the principle, it is claimed, simply indicates that agents have failed to fully grasp what those terms mean (Hare 1963).[3] Hare, for example, has tried to substantiate the universalizability requirement by showing how it enters into the semantic content of moral terms by virtue of what he calls the "prescriptive" and "descriptive" meanings of such terms (Hare 1963).

Indeed, (MUP) can be seen as an instance of the general principle that like cases ought to be treated alike which is actually what underlies the thesis of epistemic supervenience (again modeled on the case of moral supervenience). Thus, let us remind ourselves of the case of moral supervenience by looking at the following much quoted passage by Hare.

> Suppose that we say "St. Francis was a good man." It is logically impossible to say this and to maintain at the same time that there might have been another man placed exactly in the same circumstances as St. Francis, and who behaved in exactly the same way, but who differed from St. Francis in this respect only, that he was not a good man. (Hare 1952, p. 145)

The idea is that if moral supervenience is denied, then we ought to admit that two objects could differ in respect of the property of goodness, but be indiscernible as far as their natural properties are concerned. And this is absurd. Similar absurdity follows if epistemic supervenience is denied. For it implies that two beliefs may share their non-epistemic properties, but while one is justified, the other is not. This is precisely what gets denied in (MUP). For if an agent A is justified in holding a certain belief, it would presumably be in virtue of his belief having certain non-epistemic properties such as being reliably produced, being part of a coherent system of belief, and so on. Now, if there is another agent B whose epistemic situation is qualitatively indistinguishable from A, he, too, would be equally justified in his belief. This is the import of (MUP) according to which by making an epistemic judgment one is committed, on pain of being inconsistent, to making a similar judgment in relevantly similar situations.

To conclude, we distinguished between the minimalist and full-blooded versions of epistemic universalizability, tracing their difference to whether they incorporate assumptions about the underlying mechanisms of defeat (of justification). It was argued that those universalizability principles (like (FUP)) that seem to have skeptical potentials are epistemically suspect while those principles (like (MUP)) that are epistemically plausible lack enough bite to generate skeptical claims. It thus looks as though the universalizability gloss on the possibility of error as a source of skepticism fails to render it anymore effective. The more traditional versions of the story still seem to be more compelling. In the rest of this chapter, I turn to another purported source of skepticism that exploits the possibility of alternative hypotheses of our sensory experiences.

5.2   The principle of closure

As noted earlier, one source of skeptical doubt that has been widely discussed in philosophical debates over the legitimacy of skepticism is one that involves the possibility of alternative hypotheses to explain our sensory experiences. The idea is that for any knowledge-claim made in a particular context, one can conceive of alternative "skeptical" hypotheses that are equally compatible with our evidence, thus, undermining the epistemic status of the claim in question. One version of this skeptical argument that has acquired a canonical status is the one that takes alternative hypothesis to involve an evil demon (or a super-scientist) seeing to it that we receive appropriate sensory input that we normally take to come from an independently existing world. Let P be some arbitrary proposition about the external world, and let SK be a skeptical hypothesis incompatible with P, such as "I am a brain in a vat with sense experience qualitatively indistinguishable from my actual experience." Then the argument, known as the "Cartesian skeptical argument" (C) (though its historical credentials are dubious), proceeds along the following lines.

(1C) If I know that P, then I know that ~SK.
(2C) I do not know that ~SK.
∴(3C) I do not know that P.

This way the skeptic is able to undermine much of what we ordinarily claim to know. As the argument is unquestionably valid everything hangs on whether its premises are true. A number of attempts have been made to rebut the categorical premise (2C). I shall deal with some of the representative ones in Part III of this book. In this chapter, however, I shall focus on the conditional premise (1C) and the principle that underwrites it, namely, the principle of deductive closure. A compelling discussion of this principle will obviously require a book-length treatment, so, in what follows, I shall confine myself to presenting my own perspective on this question against the backdrop of certain well-known accounts.

Knowledge-claims are often made against the background of a set of competing alternatives so that to know a proposition (p) to be true is to know that the alternatives to p fail to hold. While there is broad agreement about the spirit of this claim, there is much controversy over the range of possibilities that have to be ruled out if knowledge claims are to be sustained. Concerned about the skeptical consequences of such a feature of knowledge, defenders of commonsense have made a number of (unsuccessful) attempts to delimit the range of alternatives in order to leave room for knowledge. In any case, what is being targeted here by the skeptic is the idea that knowledge can be expanded by means of inference with the principle that underlies it known as the principle of deductive closure. This is the principle according to which knowledge (justification) is closed under known entailment. That is to say if one knows (is justified in believing) that p and that p entails q then one knows (is justified in believing) that q. Suppose, for example, you claim to be justified in believing that you are reading this book. You are presumably also justified in believing that if you are reading this book then you are not a demon's victim (or a brain in a vat). But, says the skeptic, you are not justified in believing that you are not a demon's victim and, thus, by *modus tollens*, you are not justified in believing that you are reading this book. Much of our justification/knowledge-claims will, thereby, be undermined.

The issues surrounding the principle of closure are not, however, straightforward at all. Because of the perspective character of the concept of justification, there is a great deal of ambiguity regarding the context where the principle is applied. This contextual ambiguity, as will be shown, gives rise to different instances of the principle each requiring a distinct treatment.[4] The failure to distinguish this variety has led to serious misunderstandings regarding both the nature and function of the principle of closure. Another point that will be stressed concerns the similarities in the behavior of the concepts of justification and confirmation as they both seem to give rise to similar puzzles.[5] Indeed, as I shall explain, the solution to certain paradoxes of confirmation can be exploited to clarify and sharpen our understanding of the principle of closure. Furthermore, it will be argued that the failure of the principle of closure in certain contexts would not deter the skeptic from undermining our knowledge-claims because of the involvement of, what I shall call, the "infectious character of epistemic contexts," namely, the ability of such contexts to affect the epistemic status of the propositions they involve when the status of some of these propositions undergoes some change. I begin, however, with Dretske's pioneering discussion of the principle of closure.

5.2.1 Dretske on closure

Discussing this question in an early article, Dretske posed the problem in terms of penetratability of certain operators (Dretske 1970). Some of these operators such as "it is true that" and "it is necessary that" penetrate to every necessary consequence of the propositions upon which they operate; if it is true that p and p entails q then it is true that q. At the other end of the spectrum lies the class of *non-penetrating* operators such as "it is a mistake that" or "it is accidental that." They fail to penetrate to some of the most elementary logical consequences of a proposition. It may have been a mistake that Bill and Susan married each other but not a mistake that Bill married. Dretske also identifies a class of *semi-penetrating* operators which falls between these two extremes. These include epistemic operators such as "knows that," "has reason to believe that," and so on. One of the examples that Dretske gives is the following.

Suppose you take your son to the zoo where you see several striped animals. When asked about the identity of the animals you tell him that they are zebras. You know this because you know what zebras look like and the animals are kept in a cage marked "zebras." Being a zebra, however, implies that the animal is not a disguised mule. According to the principle of closure by knowing these facts you also know that the animals are not disguised mules. Dretske denies that such a consequence follows and, thus, rejects the closure principle. He argues that your adequate evidence for "That is a zebra" ceases to be adequate for "That is not a mule with stripes painted on it." That evidence has been effectively neutralized. It no longer supports the claim that these are not mules disguised to look like zebras. The evidence did not involve checking with the zoo authorities or examining the animals closely enough.

Dretske also offers an explanation for the failure of the principle of closure. Knowing that this animal is a zebra, he claims, does not necessarily involve knowing that it is not a disguised mule. This is because knowing that x is A always involves knowing it within a framework of *relevant alternatives* B, C, D. So that, by changing the set of contrasts one also changes what a person is said to know. Epistemic operators, thus, penetrate only to those contrast consequences which belong to the set of relevant alternatives. This explains why we can claim to know that this animal is a zebra without knowing that it is not a disguised mule. The possibility of the animal being a disguised mule is not relevant in the (ordinary) context of the example and, thus, need not be ruled out in order for us to know.

Dretske's views on the principle of closure and his espousal of the relevant alternatives account has spawned a large secondary literature devoted to the discussion of these topics. One early and influential response to Dretske was enunciated by Gail Stine which sought to defend and improve on the relevant alternatives account while sticking to the principle of closure (Stine 1976). On the relevant alternatives theory to say that S knows that p is to presuppose that $\sim p$ is a relevant alternative. On Stine's account, however, this is viewed as a pragmatic rather than a semantic presupposition thus having the Gricean property of cancellability (Grice 1961). It is therefore possible for "S knows that p" to be true while "$\sim p$ is a relevant alternative" is false. So although it may sound misleading to claim to know that the animal is not a disguised mule but this does not mean that the claim is false. One can cancel, says Stine, the implication that one has investigated the questions raised by the consequence.

Stine's defense of the relevant alternatives account is not, however, desirably consistent as she seems to be pulled away in opposite directions by conflicting intuitions. After finding fault with Dretske's account of the notion of "relevance," she sides with Goldman to say that "an alternative is relevant only if there is some reason to think that it is true" (Stine 1976, p. 252). She then goes on to add that "it seems safe to say [Descartes] was wrong if he thought that there was some reason to think that there *was* an evil genius. ... [T]he whole trust of the relevant alternative position, as I conceive it, is that such an hypothesis is not relevant" (Stine 1976, p. 253). But she contradicts herself in a proceeding paragraph where she seems to think that the demon hypothesis is sometimes relevant: "[B]y *some* extreme standard, there is some reason to think that there is an evil genius, after all" (Stine 1976, p. 254). Her conflicting views on the subject in turn lead her to make a manifestly curious remark to the effect that while she does not need evidence in order to know that the animal in the cage (which looks like a zebra) is not a painted mule, "I would say that I do not have evidence that it is a zebra, either."

> The point is that one does know what one takes for granted in normal circumstances. I do know that it is not a mule painted to look like a zebra. I do not need evidence for such a proposition. The evidence picture of knowledge has been carried too far. I would say that I do not have evidence that it is a zebra, either. (Stine 1976, p. 258)

This picture of knowledge and the preceding claims are rather confusing. And this has more to do with the account of knowledge (justification) that Stine subscribes to rather than the inherent difficulty of identifying the nature of relevance.

Indeed the latter question has been recognized to be a difficult task on all hands. Perhaps the most promising attempt at resolving the problem was one that sought to cash out on the notion of relevance in terms of the notion of objective probability. But, as many theorists soon recognized, the latter notion, in turn, required identifying a reference class relative to which one has to determine the relevant probabilities. However, as it turns out, it has proven to be extremely difficult to provide a satisfactory explication of the notion of a reference class (Sosa 1988). A recent stab at the problem, by John Greco, has sought to remedy the situation by making use of the possible worlds apparatus (Greco 2000). A possibility is relevant, he says, if it is true in some close possible world, irrelevant if not. There are, however, some rather obvious problems with this proposal. To begin with, for the relevant alternatives theory to be an effective tool against skepticism, what the theory requires is an (epistemic) criterion enabling us to rule out certain skeptical alternatives as being irrelevant to the knowledge-claims we make under normal circumstances. This is what the "objective probability" approach tried but failed to achieve. Greco's proposal, by contrast, is a purely semantic one seeking to delineate the content of the notion of "relevance" in terms of the notion of "close" possible worlds. As such it is not of much help to the relevant alternatives theory in combating skepticism. Moreover, even as a semantic proposal, it merely shifts the problem of analyzing the content of "relevant possibility" to that of delineating the content or semantics of "close possible worlds." (Compare: Popper's account of the notion of verisimilitude was a semantic proposal trying to justify the claim that the notion of closeness to truth is a coherent one, although this was proved to be otherwise. It was not intended to lay down a criterion telling us which of the competing scientific theories is closer to truth.) Fortunately, however, it is possible to assess the validity of the principle of closure regardless of whether there is a satisfactory analysis of the nature of relevance. So in the remainder of this chapter I turn to other assessments of the principle of closure preparing the ground for expounding my own.[6]

To give one more example, Peter Klein has argued that the hostility toward the principle of closure is the result of confusing it with a different but false epistemic principle according to which justification is transitive, that is, if the evidence e justifies p for S and p entails q, then e justifies q for S (Klein 1981). But, Klein claims, justification is not transitive and the principle of closure does not depend on that, for the justification of q is already secured via p itself. If e justifies p for S, then p, on its own, would provide adequate justification for anything that is entailed by it. So in the zebra example, if I am justified in believing that the animal is a zebra, I would, a fortiori, be justified in believing anything entailed by this including the consequence that the animal is not a disguised mule.

As the preceding remarks show there are conflicting intuitions regarding the principle of deductive closure. On the one hand there is Dretske's claim that certain consequences of a proposition raise possibilities that affect the epistemic status of the evidence, thus undermining our claims to know those consequences. On the other hand there is the intuition expressed by others in their claim that entailments are justification (knowledge)-preserving, though each has a different style of explaining away the contrary intuition. The whole issue has, however, been obscured by the fact that the parties involved seem to have all failed to take note of different contexts in which the principle of closure may apply. They only consider the application of the principle across contexts, that is, where the initial context is allowed to change as a result of taking new information into account. There is, however, another instance of the principle of closure when it is considered relative to a fixed context where no additional information besides the evidence is admitted. Once the context is so fixed then, relative to this context, the principle of closure may hold. This seems to be what Lehrer has in mind in the following remarks: "The closure principle is intended to concern what one knows at a single time, however, and then it seems correct. The principle says that if one knows that p and that if p then q all at once, then one knows that q as well" (Lehrer 1990, p. 183).

5.2.2 Closure and context

How are we to account for these conflicting intuitions? Is there a uniform account that could explain them all? To begin with, it should be noted that we shall only be concerned with the application of the principle of closure in justification contexts. Any conclusion we reach will, of course, be true of the application of the principle to those conceptions of knowledge that include a justification clause. So our intended principle of closure states that if the evidence e justifies S in believing that p and that p entails q, then e justifies S in believing that q. As noted earlier, an important point on the way of providing a uniform account of the application of the principle of closure is to remind ourselves of the perspective character of epistemic justification. Justification, we may recall, is a matter of degree with the degree of justification of one's belief being dependent on the position of the cognizer within the epistemic web of evidence and on the amount and strength of that evidence. In short, justification, unlike truth, has a perspective dimension, that is, it is measured relative to the subject's evidence. Accordingly, it is always possible that the cognizer's belief loses its positive epistemic status as further evidence may show his initial evidence was misleading. To see the point consider a case in which, although the subject's evidence in itself provides an adequate basis for his belief that p, that would not have been the case had he been in possession of further relevant evidence. The adequacy of the initial evidence is undermined by the larger context in which it would be considered.

Evidence, however, may provide ground for a belief only against the background of one's other beliefs so that by changing the background beliefs the evidence may cease to support the belief in question. Not only does the context of the background beliefs affect the adequacy of the evidence but it also determines which evidence is to be regarded as misleading in the sense of inclining us to form a false belief. That is to say, whether evidence is misleading can only be determined relative to the set of one's background beliefs. We might come to form a belief as a result of some evidence but the obtaining of new evidence might oblige us to revise our judgment and make new adjustments. In the light of this new evidence the initial evidence might be judged as misleading. This process may be iterated indefinitely. What this shows is that both the adequacy and epistemic relevance of the evidence is measured relative to the doxastic situation of the cognizer.

Let us illustrate these points by considering an extended version of Dretske's zebra story. (1) Smith takes his son to the zoo. They come across a cage marked "zebras" in which there are a number of black and white striped animals. When asked by his son about the identity of the animals he tells him that they are zebras. (2) One of the zoo keepers, Jones, who is a friend of Smith and from whom he has not heard for some time tells him that the manager is using cleverly disguised mules to cover up the zoo's lack of zebras. (3) Jones's doctor who is around at that time tells Smith that Jones is currently undergoing treatment for mental disorder which manifests itself in the form of a disposition to spread false rumors. (4) An acquaintance of both Smith and Jones informs Smith that the doctor is actually Jones's nephew who has been trying to deprive him of some inheritance on the ground of mental illness. (5) And so on.

Let us go through the story step by step to see how the change in the context of the story affects the epistemic status of the evidence. At stage (1) of the story, the evidence supports, but fails to prove beyond any doubt, the claim that the animals are zebras. So Smith is (defeasibly) justified in believing that they are zebras. At stage (2) the evidence undermines, but does not conclusively rule out, the claim that the animals are zebras. The evidence of stage (1) is now regarded to have been misleading. At stage (3) the evidence justifies, but fails to prove beyond any doubt, the claim that the animals are zebras. The evidence of stage (2) is now regarded to have been misleading. At stage (4) the evidence undermines, but does not conclusively rule out, the claim that the animals are zebras. The evidence of stage (3) is now regarded to have been misleading and so on.

This example illustrates that both the adequacy and epistemic relevance of evidence are measured against the context of the background beliefs of the cognizer. What was justification-conferring evidence in one context may cease to be adequate in another context and indeed may be regarded as misleading. This, as we have seen, can only be determined from the perspective of a more comprehensive evidential context. A cognizer's evidential situation, as noted in earlier chapters, is often defective in that it fails to include *all* the relevant evidence. Note that it is irrelevant whether the cognizer persists in placing credence in his belief. That does not change the justificatory status of his belief or of the evidence. Suppose at stage (2) of the story Jones falsely (but honestly) tells Smith of the cover up by the zoo's manager and suppose Smith is persuaded that all the appearances are fake but nevertheless persists, on the basis of visual evidence, in believing that the animals are zebras. In such a case he is not permitted to hold this belief because this permission is undermined by his cognitive state at that time. It is sufficient for undermining that a cognizer believes that certain conditions obtain which, if they did obtain, would imply that the target beliefs are no longer justified (see Goldman 1986, p. 53). I shall now consider the consequences of the preceding remarks for the principle of deductive closure and the problem of skepticism respectively.

It is obvious from our example that what underlies the shift in the epistemic status of the evidence at each stage in the story is the fact that we are assuming that one may be justified in believing something even though one's evidence fails to be conclusive. At no stage in our story did the evidence *conclusively* establish or rule out that the animals are zebras. In each case the possibility of defeat by further evidence was left open. At each stage the change in the belief context introduced possibilities which affected the epistemic status of the earlier evidence. If this is correct then the failure of the principle of closure in such circumstances is no more than a triviality. For if one and the same proposition can change its epistemic status as the context undergoes change, it would be no wonder if its consequences turned out to have different status in those contexts.

Going back to our story, at stage (1) the evidence based on visual appearances justifies the proposition "These animals are zebras." At stage (2) however, the same piece of evidence fails to justify the very same proposition and also its consequence "These animals are not disguised mules." In general if evidence *e* can provide adequate justification for a proposition in one context but fails to do so for that very proposition in another context, then it may, a fortiori, fail to provide justification for the consequences of that proposition. Indeed since p entails p, and p, justified for S in one context, may fail to be justified for him in another context we already have a counterexample to the principle of deductive closure. This also explains why Klein's defense of closure is unsuccessful. He claims that when evidence e justifies p and p entails q, we already have a perfectly sufficient reason for q, namely p itself. But if the above remarks are correct and we are considering the principle of closure across contexts then, as we have seen, as the context undergoes change we may no longer be justified in believing p and, consequently, the belief in p would fail to justify the belief in q.

So as long as we are evaluating the principle of closure across contexts (i.e., we allow the context to change) its failure is a trivial consequence of the perspective character of the concept of epistemic justification. This is not, of course, to claim that any change in the context of a belief will necessarily upset the transmission of justification to its consequences. There may, indeed, be situations where the change in the context is of such a nature as to leave the transmission undisturbed. This is most evident in cases where p is taken to be its own consequence. Here, as elsewhere, the change in the context need not necessarily involve information which has an undermining character. The subject's justification for p may actually be increased as the result of the added information. But as I am concerned with the possibility of the *failure* of the principle of closure, the sort of situations that are considered are those that involve cases where the change has an undermining character, that is, it neutralizes the evidence for p and its consequences.

But this is not the end of the matter for the principle of closure. Its (possible) failure across contexts does not imply that it also fails relative to a single context. We have as yet to evaluate the principle in a setting where the context is fixed and no additional information besides the evidence is admitted. Recall Lehrer's remark that the principle of closure "is intended to concern what one knows at a single time." Before turning to this problem, however, let us consider the implications of the failure of the principle of closure (across contexts) for the skeptical arguments which exploit it.

5.3   The infectious character of epistemic contexts

The skeptic, we may recall, argues that if you know (are justified in believing) that you are, for example, reading this paper then you know (are justified in believing) what it entails, for example, that you are not a brain in a vat. But since you do not know that you are not a brain in a vat then, by *modus tollens*, you do not know that you are reading this paper. Now if the principle of closure is false the skeptic's move is automatically blocked. It seems to me, however, that so long as we are allowing the context to change, the failure of the principle of closure cannot stop the skeptic from undermining much of what we ordinarily regard ourselves as knowing. To clarify this point the following remarks are in order.

We saw that our argument against the principle of closure exploited the perspective character of epistemic justification. It was argued that if we are evaluating the principle of closure across contexts, then we need to take into account the possibilities that these contexts introduce; and we saw that the epistemic status of evidence might undergo radical change once these possibilities are taken into account. It is true that by rejecting the principle of closure the skeptic can no longer appeal to *modus tollens* to deny that, for example, you know you are reading this book despite the fact that you do not know you are not a brain in a vat. But he can still deny that you are reading this book *via* the new context which is introduced as a result of taking the skeptical possibilities into account. This is possible because epistemic contexts are, as I call them, "infectious," in the sense that they affect the epistemic status of the propositions involved with them.

Consider, once again, the story of Smith and the zebras. At stage (1) of the story he is justified in believing that the animals are zebras. At stage (2) the initial context changes as a result of the new information (about the fraud) that Jones adds to it. In the resulting context Jones is not justified in believing that the animals are not disguised mules but he is equally unjustified in believing that the animals are zebras. So when the context decides the epistemic status of some consequences of p, the verdict may change the status of p itself. When additional information is injected into the context, the epistemic status of all the propositions is affected. A belief once justified in a context may lose its status when new information is added to that context. This also explains why Klein's attempt to use the principle of closure to undermine skepticism is unsuccessful. He thinks that the principle of closure can actually be exploited to defeat skepticism. For if you are justified in believing that you are reading this book (p), then, by *modus ponens*, you are justified in believing that you are not a brain in a vat (q). But if what we have said is correct the infectious character of epistemic contexts undermines the subject's justification in believing p. The mere entertaining of skeptical possibilities is enough to create a setting where the evidence is neutralized both for p and q. As indicated earlier, another context which shares the same property with epistemic contexts is the context of the confirmation of theories. It is well known that adding new information to the background knowledge affects the degree of confirmation of the theories involved. I shall say more on this point shortly.

Being infectious is not, however, the same thing as being semi-penetrating. First of all, "being infectious" is a predicate of a context, whereas it is an operator which is semi-penetrating. Operators introduce and operate *in* contexts. They are not identical with contexts. Second, the direction of penetration is always from propositions to their necessary consequences whereas an infectious context may affect propositions in both, and indeed in all, directions. Moreover, it is not the case that all semi-penetrating operators introduce infectious contexts. There are semi-penetrating operators whose contexts are not infectious. It is, I believe, failure to take note of this point that has led philosophers like Dretske to claim that epistemic operators "share the same logic with such operators as 'explains why'." He exploits this claim to undermine the principle of closure. Let us consider the example which he gives in support of his claim.

Suppose we want to explain why Brenda did not order any dessert. To do this, Dretske claims, we have to take into account the range of relevant alternatives. He admits that he does not have a theory about what a relevant alternative is, but the case, he hopes, is intuitive enough. When we explain why Brenda did not order any dessert by saying that she was full, we explain why she did not order any dessert as opposed to ordering some dessert and eating it. If we consider a different set of alternatives, for example, Brenda ordering some dessert and throwing it at the waiter, and so on, the above explanation fails to be an explanation of why Brenda did not order any dessert even though the fact that Brenda did not order some dessert entails the fact that Brenda did not order some dessert and throw it at the waiter. Dretske concludes that to say we do not know the animals in the zoo are zebras because we do not know that they are not disguised mules is "as much a mistake as arguing that we have not explained why Brenda did not order any dessert (within the original, normal, setting) because we did not explain why she did not order some dessert and throw it at the waiter" (Dretske 1970, p. 1023).

But there is a difference. Introducing the competing possibility of Brenda ordering some dessert and throwing it at the waiter does not invalidate the original explanation of why Brenda did not order some dessert because explanatory contexts are not infectious. When we explain why Brenda did not order some dessert by saying that she was full, our contrast class consists of Brenda ordering some dessert and eating it. This explanation, of course, fails when a new contrast class consisting of Brenda ordering some dessert and throwing it at the waiter, and other such, is introduced. But that does not diminish its effectiveness when it is considered against the earlier contrast class. This is because explanatory contexts can be, as it were, partitioned into different sets of alternatives with each partition being completely autonomous. The failure of a certain explanation in one partition does not imply its failure in another partition. But this is not the case with epistemic contexts. Introducing a novel alternative may neutralize a certain bit of evidence, thus, affecting the epistemic status of the proposition whose consequence it is. In the zebra example, the visual evidence justified "This is a zebra" but failed to support "This is not a disguised mule" when the possibility of fraud was raised. The raising of this possibility, however, also affected its ability to justify "This is a zebra." In other words, the failure of the evidence to support one possibility infected its ability to support another. This is because in epistemic contexts we are concerned with the cognitive state of the cognizer and cognitive states cannot be divided into autonomous partitions. They are of such a nature that a slight change in their belief repertoire may affect the epistemic status of all the propositions involved. They are, in other words, infectious. Dretske's conclusions regarding the analogy with explanatory contexts are, thus, unwarranted.

Let us return to the question of the validity of the principle of closure itself. We have already argued that the principle may fail to hold when it is applied across contexts. We saw that in the context in which the possibility of fraud was raised not only the evidence was effectively neutralized for the proposition that the animals are not disguised mules but it also ceased to support the proposition that the animals are zebras. Nothing, however, has so far been said about the principle of closure when it is considered relative to a single context, that is, when no additional information other than the evidence is taken into account, or as Lehrer put it, when the principle is intended to concern what one knows at a single time. So, the question we need to address is whether the principle is correct when the context is fixed. Does, for example, the evidence for "These animals are zebras" lend any support to "These animals are not disguised mules" when that evidence is the only piece of information that is admitted? There seems to be an intuition in favor of a positive reply. How are we to account for these conflicting intuitions? To answer these questions we need a comprehensive theory which *explains* those intuitions. To do this, I shall propose an analogy with one of the paradoxes of confirmation known also as the paradox of the ravens. We have already noticed the concepts of justification and confirmation resemble each other to some degree. The analogy can be taken still further by the following observations.

The ravens paradox, in its simple form, has the following structure. Observations of black ravens confirm the proposition "All ravens are black" while observations of black pens, white swans, and others, are neutral to it. But the proposition "All non-black things are non-ravens" is equivalent to (and, a fortiori, entails) "All ravens are black" and since a white swan confirms the former it should also confirm the latter which seems paradoxical. To resolve the paradox a number of solutions have been proposed. The difference between these solutions can be traced to the amount of background information that is taken into account. Here I rely on Mackie's account of the paradox (Mackie 1963; see also Swinburne 1973). I believe a theory along the lines Mackie proposes to account for the conflicting intuitions in the case of the ravens paradox can also be exploited to account for the conflicting intuitions in the case of the principle of closure.

One early solution to the paradox was proposed by Hempel (1965). Consider the proposition (p) "All sodium salts burn yellow." Suppose we hold a piece of ice into a colorless flame and it does not turn the flame yellow. This confirms the proposition (q) "Whatever does not burn yellow contains no sodium salt" and because the two propositions are equivalent it also confirms p which is paradoxical. But, Hempel argues, the paradox is only apparent. For if we take an object whose chemical structure we do not know and hold it into a flame and it fails to burn yellow and subsequent investigation proves that it contains no sodium salt, then this observation would confirm p. The difference between the two cases is only that in the first one we already knew that the substance is ice and ice contains no sodium salt whereas in the second case we did not know this. So, Hempel concludes, the seemingly paradoxical nature of the first case is only due to our allowing the additional information that the object is ice.

So as long as we ignore any additional information we can solve the paradox in the way Hempel suggests. In a setting where no reference is made to additional knowledge we can say the observation of a non-black non-raven confirms "All non-black things are non-ravens" and its equivalent (and, a fortiori, its consequence) "All ravens are black." But, as Mackie points out, given some additional information, for example about the relative size of the classes of ravens and black things, we can solve the paradox in another way. We can still affirm that the observation of white swans confirm "All ravens are black" but argue that its degree of confirmation is much less than that provided by the observation of black ravens. The admission of more information, as Mackie shows, might further reduce the degree of confirmation provided by the observation of black pens and white swans. So if we completely ignore the background knowledge we can follow Hempel and say that the observation of black pens and white swans confirms "All ravens are black."

I think we are faced with more or less the same situation in the case of the principle of closure. Here we are concerned to know whether the same piece of evidence (visual appearances) which justifies p (These animals are zebras) equally justifies q (These are not disguised mules) when p entails q. Imitating Mackie's account of the paradox, we may now explain the apparent plausibility of this principle when it is considered relative to a context where no information besides the evidence is admitted and its apparent implausibility when the context is allowed to change (in an undermining way).[7] The principle of closure seems to hold at a single time (or in a fixed context) because *no* reference is made to the background information. Just as the observation of a non-black non-raven confirmed "All ravens are black" in a context where the evidence was the only information available, similarly the evidence (based on visual appearances) which justified "These animals are zebras" equally confers justification on "These animals are not disguised mules" in a context where no additional information besides the evidence is taken into account.

So, as long as the principle of closure is considered relative to a context where no additional information besides the evidence is admitted and we ignore all the possibilities and concerns, then it holds. That is to say the evidence also provides adequate ground for asserting that "These animals are not disguised mules." But once we take into account additional information and background knowledge, the evidence might cease to provide justification for "These animals are not disguised mules" just as the consideration of background knowledge led to a sharp reduction of the degree of confirmation of the observation of black pens, and so on, for "All ravens are black." The principle of closure, thus, fails to hold when the context is allowed to change as a result of taking skeptical possibilities into account.[8] Nevertheless, as noted earlier, although the principle of closure may fail in these circumstances, the skeptic can still undermine knowledge/justification-claims because the newly created context not only tends to upset the justificational status of the skeptical consequences of the target belief but, being infectious, it would also affect the positive epistemic status of the target belief itself.

6
Skepticism and Underdetermination

As noted earlier, the possibility of alternative hypotheses equally accounting for our sensory experiences is widely viewed as a source of skeptical doubt. In Chapter 5 we discussed one way of utilizing this insight drawing on the principle of closure to set up a (Cartesian) skeptical argument. In this chapter, I shall deal with another way of constructing such arguments that helps itself with, not the principle of closure but, the so-called underdetermination principles (Yalcin 1992; Brueckner 1994). To explain, I begin by distinguishing between knowledge and justification analogs of the principle of underdetermination. While acknowledging the plausibility of a restricted version of the knowledge version, it shall be argued that this has nothing to do with facts involving underdetermination.

My central thesis, however, is that the (fundamental) justification version of the underdetermination principle is implausible. To support this claim, I shall critically evaluate a number of direct and indirect arguments that have been adduced to show that typical underdetermination principles provide a basis for skeptical reasoning. Having shown that none of these arguments holds water, I shall seek to explain away the intuitive appeal of the underdetermination principle by suggesting that its plausibility actually derives from confusing it with a superficially similar but entirely distinct principle which is plausible but which concerns the epistemic status of the comparative, rather than the individual, content of the competing beliefs.

6.1 Skeptical arguments from underdetermination

Typical Cartesian skeptical arguments, as we saw, take their departure from Descartes's skeptical hypothesis according to which instead of the world one normally supposes to exist, we can imagine a world consisting only of one person, his beliefs and an evil genius (or a mad scientist) causing him to have just those beliefs that he would have were there to be a world consisting of the familiar objects. The fact that these two situations are phenomenologically indistinguishable, Descartes concludes, undermines much of what we ordinarily claim to know. Such arguments, as noted before, usually exploit the principle of closure according to which knowledge is closed under known entailment.

(CK) For all S, ϕ, ψ, if S knows that ϕ and S knows that ϕ entails ψ, then S knows that ψ.

To remind ourselves of the structure of such arguments, let P be some arbitrary proposition about the external world and SK denote a skeptical hypothesis incompatible with P such as "I am a brain in a vat with sense experience qualitatively indistinguishable from my actual experience." The Cartesian argument from closure (C) may then be presented as having the following structure.

(1C) If I know that P, then I know that ~SK. [from (CK)]
(2C) I do not know that ~SK.
∴ (3C) I do not know that P.

Anthony Brueckner has, however, noted that the sort of theses that are normally invoked in support of the premise (2C) have the consequence of depriving the skeptic to utilize the principle of closure to support the premise (1C) (Brueckner 1994). Such theses usually involve certain constraints on the concept of knowledge such as the following "tracking" condition (T) that appears in Nozick's account of what it is for a subject to know a proposition (P) (Nozick 1981).

(T) If P were false, then S would not believe that P.

While (T) lends support to (2C), it undermines, says Brueckner, the principle of closure by allowing a cognizer to know a proposition while failing to know an entailed consequence of that proposition (such as that specified in (1C)).

To rectify the situation, Brueckner, among others, draws attention to the fact that the cognizer's typical evidence under such circumstances seems to fail to discriminate between the hypotheses P and ~SK.[1] To support (2C), the skeptic may thus appeal, he says, to the following "underdetermination principle" (UJ) (Brueckner 1994).

(UJ) For all S, ϕ, ψ, if S's evidence for believing that ϕ does not favor ϕ over some incompatible hypothesis ψ, then S's evidence does not justify ϕ.

Since (UJ) concerns justification, we might as well consider a justification analog of (CK).

(CJ) For all S, ϕ, ψ, if S's evidence justifies ϕ, and ϕ entails ψ, then S's evidence justifies ψ.[2]

Armed with (UJ), the skeptic can now argue that since one's sensory evidence fails to favor SK over ~SK, one is not justified in believing ~SK.[3] This, in conjunction with an appropriate instance of (CJ), easily leads to the skeptical conclusion that one is not justified in believing P, and, assuming that justification is necessary for knowledge, does not know that P. Given the latter assumption, it would also be helpful to have the knowledge version of the underdetermination thesis.

(UK) For all S, ϕ, ψ, if S's evidence for believing that ϕ does not favor ϕ over some incompatible hypothesis ψ, then S does not know that ϕ.

However, as Brueckner notes the skeptical reasoning can be further simplified by applying (UJ) directly to the question whether one knows the proposition P itself and dispensing altogether with the principle of closure. This gives us another version of the Cartesian argument (from underdetermination) (U).

(1U) If my evidence is for believing that P does not favor P over SK, then my evidence does not justify P. [from (UJ)]
(2U) My evidence does not favor P over SK. [premise]
(3U) My evidence does not justify P. [from 1U, 2U]
∴(4U) I do not know that P. [from 3U]

There has been much debate over the relative merits of the arguments from closure (C) and underdetermination (U). The fate of the debate depends obviously on the plausibility of the principles that underlie them. While some epistemologists have claimed that (CJ) and (UJ) are identical, others have gone only as far as admitting that (CJ) entails (UJ). Both groups however are united in acknowledging the force of (U) as a plausible skeptical argument. This is what I am going to challenge in this chapter. To this end, I shall begin by making some general observations about the credibility (or its lack thereof) of the underdetermination principles in epistemology and science in general. This will be followed by examining some of the direct and indirect arguments that have been proposed in support of (UJ).

6.1.1 Underdetermination principles and epistemic stalemate

Much reasoning in epistemology, as elsewhere in philosophy, proceeds by exploiting our initial intuitions regarding the subject matters under investigation. These intuitions may, of course, turn out to be unwarranted, thus, the "initial" prefix. They may, accordingly, be revised while we are sailing through the troubled waters of epistemology. However, we have no alternative but to stay afloat on what is at our disposal. The examples are well publicized. Perhaps the most well known of these cases involve the ongoing attempts to analyze the concepts of knowledge and justification. The process generally consists of testing our intuitions about the intension of such concepts against our intuitions about their extensions through a series of thought experiments. To give an example, consider the analysis of "knowledge" in terms of true belief being caused by the relevant facts. To assess this analysis the following two-stage scenario, with which we are already quite familiar, was proposed (Goldman 1976). At stage (1), we have our agent, Smith, driving in the countryside pointing to a barn in an area where there are lots of barns next to one another. At stage (2) Smith is again pointing to a real barn but in area where there are, unbeknown to him, a number of indistinguishable fake barns. While at stage (1) we are strongly inclined to say that Smith knows that he is seeing a barn, we are not so inclined to attribute knowledge to him at stage (2) despite his true belief being caused by a real barn. The reason being that at stage (2) the belief in question could have easily been false as he might have pointed in a direction of an indistinguishable fake barn. However, we are equally inclined to say that in both cases Smith is justified in believing that he is seeing a barn. Falsity is no bar to a belief being justified. This reflects the fact that conditions for ascribing knowledge and justification may well diverge.

In any case, as far as the analysis of knowledge is concerned, it seems that resistance to luck functions as an adequacy condition on any acceptable account of knowledge which is precisely what underlies our differential attitude in ascribing knowledge to the agent at different stages of the barn example. But these intuitions and the processes utilizing them will be undermined if we allow (UK) or (UJ) to govern our epistemic theorizing. In other words, the activation of these principles results in epistemic stalemate. This is because for any belief, ϕ, we can always concoct a competing skeptical alternative, SK, such that, consonant with the underdetermination principles, it would neutralize the evidence for both ϕ and that alternative. Thus, an unbridled version of the underdetermination principle, as is the case with both (UK) and (UJ), entails that no beliefs could be known or justified. This means that, with these principles in force, we can no longer claim to have knowledge in, say, the stage (1) of the example given above and other Gettier cases. Likewise, neither Nozick nor Dretske would be able to proceed to show that the principle of closure can be false for that would require showing that we can know a certain proposition without knowing its consequences. The situation is much worse in the case of (UJ), since any claim to having a justified belief can be thwarted by allowing our reasoning to be regulated by (UJ). This is, again, because, for any proposition we can construct various alternatives where our evidence fails to discriminate between them, thereby, rendering it epistemically impotent. This is very implausible because, unlike cases in which we wish to refrain from ascribing knowledge to agents, we are strongly inclined to attribute justified beliefs to them under those circumstances (such as in the barn example mentioned above and other Gettier cases).

Setting aside the problem of epistemic stalemate, many respectable theses in epistemology would be rendered mysterious, to say the least, if (UJ) is allowed to be operative. One such thesis is the now familiar claim that justification is supervenient on non-epistemic properties (such as "coherence," "being reliably produced," etc.). The core idea of epistemic supervenience, as we have seen, is that no two believers, with similarly functioning cognitive faculties, can differ in the epistemic status of their beliefs without a difference in the degree of support for those beliefs. Suppose that evidence e is strong enough to justify an appropriate belief ϕ. The thesis can then best be expressed in terms of the strong version of the notion of supervenience.

(SUP) Justification supervenes on evidence $=_{df}$ Necessarily, if any belief has the property of justification (j), then there is a property e (evidential support) such that the belief has e, and necessarily every belief that has e has j.

On a possible world construal of the "necessity" operator, the following worlds are accordingly conceivable. First, there is a possible world, w_1, where a belief, ϕ, is justified because it possesses e (recall our assumption that e is strong enough to justify the relevant beliefs). There is also another possible world, w_2, where another incompatible belief ψ has e and, thus, has j, and finally there is a possible world w_3 where two beliefs ϕ and ψ have both e and j. But w_3 is an impossible world if we are to go along with what (UJ) says.

(UJ) says that if two incompatible beliefs are equally supported by evidence e, they are unjustified (i.e., lack the property j). If we accept what (UJ) says we are confronted with the following mystery: In w_1 and w_2, where beliefs ϕ and ψ are considered independently of one another, each one is justified, but in w_3 where they are considered together none of them is justified. How can this be possible? Why should considering ϕ and ψ alongside one another lead to the neutralization of the evidential force of e? It seems that the only way out, without denying (SUP), is to deny that beliefs in w_1 and w_2 are actually justified. But this would be quite implausible as it would require explaining away our strong intuitions to make justification claims in w_1 and w_2 for, after all, we assumed e to be strong enough to justify the appropriate belief.

Thus, both (UK) and (UJ) immediately entail that the concepts of knowledge and justification are uninstantiatable. Accordingly, epistemology fails to get off the ground once these principles are admitted to regulate our reasoning. In this respect, the status of the principle of underdetermination stands in sharp contrast to that of the principle of closure (CJ) which, as noted before, *is* an initially plausible claim in one form or another. It is not just in epistemology that the application of the underdetermination principles looks dubious. It has been claimed that the phenomenon of underdetermination also plays an important role in scientific reasoning. However not all versions of the underdetermination principle are thought to be of much consequence in scientific thought. For example, the so-called thesis of "methodological" underdetermination according to which theories are underdetermined by available data is generally thought to be innocuous. On the other hand, the strong version of the principle which states that all theories are underdetermined by all actual and possible evidence seems to be epistemically significant not least because of its consequences for a realist view of science. According to this thesis (which closely resembles (UJ)) for any scientific theory there is an empirically equivalent alternative.

However, despite drawing much attention in the literature on the scientific reasoning, many deny that there is a shred of evidence in favor of the underdetermination thesis or that it is even intelligible. Laudan and Leplin, for example, have argued that not only is there no guarantee of the possibility of empirically equivalent alternatives to a given theory, but also the very notion of empirical equivalence is problematic (Laudan and Leplin 1991). First, they reject the idea that there are indefinitely many equivalent alternatives to any theory on the ground of variability of the range of observables and the instability of auxiliary assumptions that either result in the expansion or contraction of the empirical consequence class of the theories. Moreover, they argue that being an empirical consequence of a theory is neither necessary nor sufficient for being evidentially relevant to the theory in question. It is not necessary because a theory may be evidentially supported by results that are not its empirical consequences. For example, instances of a theory may evidentially support one another despite not being the consequences of each other. Observed black ravens lend evidential support to the hypothesis that the next raven we come across is black despite their not being the consequences of one another. The converse point holds as well. Examples can be constructed to show that not all true empirical consequences of a theory would necessarily lend it evidential support. So being an empirical consequence of a hypothesis is not necessarily evidentially pertinent to that hypothesis. These points, if true, seriously undermine the view that underdetermination generally obtains in scientific thought.

Before concluding this section, it is instructive to note an asymmetry between the knowledge and justification versions of the underdetermination principle, namely, (UK) and (UJ). For it seems that a restricted version of (UK) enjoys some intuitive appeal, though, as I shall argue, this has a source different from facts involving underdetermination. We may recall that according to (UK) if our evidence does not favor a hypothesis over its rivals then we do not know either of those hypotheses. As noted earlier, however, this unbridled version of the principle is problematic. But suppose we restrict the range of the rivals of the target hypothesis to those that are relevant to the context in question. Understood thus, (UK) comes very close to what the so-called "relevant alternatives" theory claims about the conditions under which one can ascribe knowledge to agents. In fact the latter theory is embedded in a discriminative account of knowledge (much in the same way that (UK) suggests). The idea of the discrimination approach is that, according to one sense of "know," knowing something involves discriminating or distinguishing it from its relevant alternatives. There have, however, been distinct conceptions of what counts as a relevant alternative. According to Goldman, for example, the alternatives in question are counterfactual alternatives. The idea is that "a true belief fails to be knowledge if there are any relevant alternative situations in which the proposition P would be false, but the process used would cause [the agent] to believe P anyway" (Goldman 1986, p. 46). If this happens to be the case, the utilized process is said to have failed to discriminate the truth of P from those alternatives and the subject is consequently said to have failed to know P.

Thus, in the barn example (stage (2)) Smith's true belief that the object he is pointing at is a barn fails to be knowledge because if he were instead looking at a fake barn he would form the same belief anyway. This is precisely the verdict that our restricted version of (UK) would issue in the context in question. But this has nothing to do with the fact that alternative hypotheses are underdetermined. For, if that were the case, the agent would equally fail to be justified in holding the same belief at the two stages of the story (in accordance with (UJ)), whereas, as noted before, the justificational status of that belief is widely acknowledged. Rather, what seems to underlie the plausibility of the restricted version of (UK), as well as the relevant alternatives theory, is their ability to safeguard against the possibility of knowledge by luck. At the stage (2) of the barn example, the agent's belief could have easily been false, and so, according to (UK), his true belief fails to be knowledge. It is worth noting that resistance to luck, considered as an adequacy condition on any proper account of knowledge, has no analog in the case of theories of justification which is why even a restricted version of (UJ) lacks intuitive plausibility.

6.2 Arguing for underdetermination principles

The proceeding remarks were intended to show that, due to their crippling effects on epistemological theorizing, underdetermination principles lack initial credibility. However, for all that has been said, they may in fact be true. In this section, I shall consider arguments that have been adduced in their defense. These arguments are either directly targeted at establishing their legitimacy, or, rather, proceed to reach the same conclusion via the indirect route of showing how they can be derived from other principles that seem to be initially plausible. Starting with direct arguments, I shall try to show that none holds water. I will be focusing on (UJ).

6.2.1 Direct plausibility arguments

There are two related direct arguments for the validity of (UJ). The first argument proceeds to argue for (UJ) by considering a special case of the principle where the alternative to the target proposition ϕ is its own negation using epistemic supervenience as a premise.

> Consider the special case when the same person is identically epistemically situated with respect to two propositions p and $\sim p$. Then according to the supervenience principle he is either justified in believing both p and $\sim p$ or neither. If we assume the first alternative, trouble will ensue: The person would be justified in believing each of a pair of incompatible properties. But if so, he would be justified in believing the conjunction of these two propositions and hence an inconsistent proposition. Since this is not acceptable, the only alternative is to say that he is justified in believing neither p and $\sim p$. Generalizing from this case to cases where there are more than two incompatible propositions we arrive at [UJ]. (Yalcin 1992, pp. 11–12)

But there are a number of problems with this argument. First, as already noted, the theses of epistemic supervenience and (UJ) do not sit well together. Second, the argument focuses on a special case involving explicitly contradictory beliefs where one might as well have reasoned for the desired conclusion without invoking the claims that are being assumed in the argument. It provides no clue as to how one can generalize this case to other cases involving merely incompatible hypotheses.

Moreover, the argument seems to assume the so-called "conjunctive" principle according to which if e is sufficient to justify the subject's beliefs that ϕ and ψ, then e is sufficient to justify his believing "$\phi \& \psi$." However, as Foley has shown, this assumption is invalid (Foley 1979). Suppose someone has very good (but not perfect) evidence for believing ϕ and has equally good evidence for believing ψ. But he might not have as good evidence for believing their conjunction. This is because, not being perfect, the evidence makes the subject liable to some risk of error. Accordingly there is a serious possibility that he would be prone to an even greater risk of error when coming to believe the conjunction of ϕ and ψ. Now the likelihood of error might reach a point where there is not evidence sufficient to justify a belief in the conjunction. So the argument from failing to justifiably believe the conjunction of two inconsistent propositions to the failure of justifiably believing each individual belief does not work.

A more elaborate argument in support of (UJ) has been proposed by Cohen who claims that the plausibility of (UJ) derives from the following more basic and "intuitively plausible" principles about evidential favoring (FAV) and incompatible hypotheses (INC) (Cohen 1998).

(FAV) For all S, ϕ, ψ, if S's evidence does not favor ϕ over φ and S's evidence justifies ϕ, then S's evidence justifies ψ.

(INC) For all S, ϕ, ψ, if S's evidence justifies ϕ, and ϕ entails $\sim\psi$, then S's evidence does not justify ψ.

Granting that the conjunction of (FAV) and (INC) entails (UP), it is clear that (FAV) just gives expression to the supervenience thesis according to which there is no difference in the justified status of the same type of beliefs without a difference in their evidential grounds. So everything hangs on the credibility of (INC) which simply states that one's evidence cannot justify two incompatible propositions. Is it valid? To see this, let us begin by recalling that on a truth-conducive conception of justification truth conducivity is normally characterized in terms of a probability relation between the truth of a belief and its grounds. Thus, to assess the validity of (INC), it would be instructive to begin by construing it in terms of the notion of mere evidential support or confirmation, and then see if our conclusion also holds for the level of evidential support that is generally thought to be sufficient in rendering a proposition (belief) justified.

Construed in terms of the notion of evidential support, (INC) is equivalent to one of the consequences (c) of Hempel's adequacy conditions on any proper account of confirmation, namely, the consistency condition according to which unless an observation report is self-contradictory, it does not confirm any hypotheses which contradict each other (Hempel 1965, pp. 33–5). It is, however, widely thought that (c) is false, that there is nothing wrong with a piece of evidence confirming competing hypotheses. Counter-examples abound. Suppose we know that one of the three people (John, Jim, and Jill) working in a government office is a spy. We subsequently find out that Jill is not a spy. This observation report raises the likelihood of the two incompatible hypotheses "John is a spy" and "Jim is a spy." Or, consider the evidence that many observed birds of many species had the same color as other birds of its species. This would concurrently confirm both "All ravens are black" and "All ravens are white." Approaching the question from a Popperian perspective, one might also say that any unsuccessful attempt to find a red raven would corroborate both "All ravens are black" and "All ravens are white."

We may now proceed to raise the evidential support between evidence and a hypothesis to a level sufficient for its justification (as in Cohen's (INC)). But (INC) still seems to be false. Again, counterexamples abound. Consider the following case. Hypothesis H takes the variables x and y to be related to one another by the equation $y = (1 \pm r)x$ while H′ represents them by the equation $y = (1 \pm r)\{x + (x - 1)(x - 2)\}$ where r is a small constant. Suppose every time x is given the value 1 (to a high degree of approximation) we find out that y also has the value 1 (to a high degree of approximation). These observations tend to justify both hypotheses despite their being inconsistent.[4] For real life examples we may turn to science. All the known evidence supporting (to a degree strong enough for the justification of) Newton's theory of gravitation is also evidence justifying Einstein's theory of gravitation despite the two hypotheses being incompatible (Popper 1977, p. 374). So it seems that there is nothing absurd in the idea of evidence justifying a pair of incompatible hypotheses—bearing in mind that justification does not entail truth (Lycan 1988, pp. 176–7). It might be pointed out that, if true, the evidence would, ipso facto, justify an inconsistent proposition, namely, their conjunction which is certainly implausible. But this contention presupposes the truth of the controversial "conjunctive principle." I conclude therefore that, *pace* Cohen, (INC) is far from being "intuitively plausible" and that he consequently fails to authenticate (UJ) in the manner he suggests. I shall now turn to certain indirect attempts to establish the plausibility of (UJ).

6.2.2 Indirect plausibility arguments

Instead of substantiating (UJ) in a direct manner, indirect arguments try to reach this goal by showing that the credibility of (UJ) derives from the principle of closure which is widely admitted to be initially plausible. In this section, I set out to examine and eventually reject two such attempts that seek to show that (CJ) entails (UJ). The first argument is due to Brueckner who makes the stronger claim that (CJ) and (UJ) are equivalent. But as Cohen notes his reasoning is fallacious. So I shall focus only on his argument (as articulated by Cohen) that (CJ) entails (UJ) (Cohen 1998). To see how the argument proceeds, it is convenient to consider the following (equivalent) versions of (CJ) and (UJ).

(UJ′) For all S, ϕ, ψ, if S's evidence justifies ϕ, and ϕ and ψ are incompatible, then S's evidence favors ϕ over ψ.

(CJ') For all S, ϕ, ψ, if S's evidence justifies ϕ, and ϕ and ψ are incompatible, then S's evidence justifies $\sim\!\psi$.

To complete the argument, all we need to do is to show how (CJ), in conjunction with the antecedent of (UJ'), entails the consequent of (UJ').

(1) If S's evidence justifies ϕ, and ϕ and ψ are incompatible, then S's evidence justifies $\sim\!\psi$. [(CJ')]
(2) S's evidence justifies ϕ, and ϕ and ψ are incompatible. [antecedent of (UP')]
(3) S's evidence justifies $\sim\!\psi$. [from 1, 2]
(4) S's evidence justifies ϕ and S's evidence justifies $\sim\!\psi$. [from 2, 3]
(5) S's evidence favors ϕ over ψ. [from 4]

The argument is obviously formally valid. The crucial step concerns the move from (4) to (5). Why is it valid? Here Cohen invokes the following principle which he takes to be a necessary truth (NT).

(NT) For all S, ϕ, ψ, if S's evidence justifies ϕ, and S's evidence justifies $\sim\!\psi$, then S's evidence favors ϕ over ψ.

Since (NT) is supposed to hold for all ϕ and ψ, it would also hold when the propositions in question are incompatible yielding the following instance.

(NT') If S's evidence justifies ϕ, and ϕ and ψ are incompatible, and S's evidence justifies $\sim\!\psi$, then S's evidence favors ϕ over ψ.

Now (NT') looks very similar to (UJ') with the only difference that the antecedent of (NT') also includes the sentence "S's evidence justifies $\sim\!\psi$." Consequently, (NT') appears epistemically and semantically too close to (UJ') to count as a logical truth underwriting the plausibility of (UJ'). Put differently, those who find (NT') intuitively obvious would, in all probability, have the same attitude toward (UJ'). This is, of course, no accident because (UJ') in fact trivially entails (NT'). It is a logical truth that $(X{\rightarrow}Y) \models (X\&Z){\rightarrow}Y$ *whatever* Z maybe (be it "S's evidence justifies $\sim\!\psi$" or whatever). Thus, if anything, the plausibility of (NT') derives from (UJ') rather than the other way round (just as Cohen himself claimed that the plausibility of (UJ') derives from (FAV) and (INC) because it is logically entailed by them). I conclude therefore that the Brueckner/Cohen indirect argument fails to lend any credibility to (UJ).

Another attempt in the same direction is due to Vogel who invokes a different assumption in his argument (Vogel 2004). Vogel mostly works with the knowledge version of the underdetermination principle, but, for the sake of uniformity, I shall reformulate his discussion in terms of (UJ) while using his own wording of the principle in the following manner.

(UJ*)   If ϕ and ψ are incompatible, then one can be justified in believing ϕ only if one can non-arbitrarily reject ψ.

Vogel's notion of "non-arbitrary rejection/acceptance" of a proposition is effectively the same as our old notion of favoring one proposition over another as he articulates it in terms of the concept of "epistemic merit," in turn, construed in terms of the notion of evidential support: "Suppose S non-arbitrarily accepts P. By definition, P is greater in epistemic merit (for S) than any of its competitors, and, therefore, (ii) S can non-arbitrarily reject that competitor" (Vogel 2004, fn.17). In discussing his argument, however, I shall stick to his formulation. He begins the argument by assuming that to reject a proposition is to accept its negation. So, if S can non-arbitrarily reject ψ, then S can non-arbitrarily accept $\sim\psi$. However, to show that (CJ) entails (UJ*) he makes a further assumption (JN).

(JN)   If S is justified in believing ϕ, then S can non-arbitrarily accept ϕ.

His argument can then be summed up as follows.

(1)   If S is justified in believing ϕ, and ϕ and ψ are incompatible, then S is justified in believing $\sim\psi$. [from (CJ)]
(2)   If S is justified in believing $\sim\psi$, then S can non-arbitrarily accept $\sim\psi$. [from (JN)]
(3)   If S is justified in believing ϕ, and ϕ and ψ are incompatible, then S can non-arbitrarily accept $\sim\psi$. [from 1 and 2]

Since, for Vogel, to nonarbitrarily accept a proposition is to reject its negation, (3) is none other than the underdetermination principle (UJ*) which is what we wished to establish.

It seems to me, however, that the argument trades on an ambiguity involving the sense of "non-arbitrary acceptance/rejection." Taken one way,

(a)   it makes (CJ) and (UJ*) equivalent, thereby, rendering the argument redundant. Taken another way,
(b)   it endangers the argument with circularity.

Let us begin with the first reading (a). As we have seen the "non-arbitrary" qualifier in "non-arbitrarily accepting ψ" involves having reasons or evidence favoring ψ. Furthermore, it is safe to assume that the notion of "acceptance"—as used in this context—refers to the attitude of belief. Thus, "non-arbitrarily accepting ψ" would amount to "justifiably believing ψ." Let us now recall what (CJ) says: If S's evidence justifies ϕ, and ϕ and ψ are incompatible, then S's evidence justifies $\sim\psi$. It is, on the other hand, obvious that if one *is* justified in believing a proposition, then one *can* justifiably believe that proposition. It then follows from (CJ) that if S is justified in believing ϕ, and ϕ and ψ are incompatible, then S can justifiably believe $\sim\psi$. Thus, given Vogel's assumption that the notions of "justifiably rejecting ψ" and "justifiably accepting (believing) $\sim\psi$" are identical, (CJ) turns out to be roughly equivalent to (UJ*) rendering Vogel's argument redundant.

Moving to the second reading, (b), suppose we take "non-arbitrarily rejecting ψ" as meaning that one's evidence (e) is strong enough to rule out ψ. This would be a natural interpretation in the light of Vogel's formulation of the underdetermination principle. However, thus understood, Vogel's crucial assumption (JN) becomes problematic. For what it now says is that if e justifies ψ, then one can non-arbitrarily reject, or, in our current terminology, rule out $\sim\psi$. But to be able to rule out $\sim\psi$, e should be strong enough to rule out the members comprising the class it represents. To take a simple example, suppose ψ is the proposition "This (pen) is red" and our justifying evidence (e) is something like "being appeared to redly." Then, what (JN) states is that if e is to discharge its justification-conferring function, it should be able to rule out that the object is not red. Given that, normally speaking, a non-red object is either blue, green, and the like, e should be strong enough (which in this case is) to rule out such *mundane* alternatives to the object being red. However, once the size of the class in question is so determined, then the conjunction of (CJ) and (JN) fails to give us (UJ*) which recognizes no such restriction on the alternatives to the target proposition.

On the other hand, if, as in the preceding example, the class representing $\sim\psi$ is allowed to include such alternatives as the object's being white but lit by red light, then e would no longer be able to rule out those alternatives. However, if (JN) is understood as requiring that one's evidence be strong enough to rule out *all* the alternatives to a target proposition if one is justified in believing it, then (JN) would simply collapse into (UJ*) rendering Vogel's argument viciously circular. I conclude, therefore, that Vogel's indirect argument for the plausibility of (UJ*) fails for it helps itself with the highly contentious assumption (JN).

He himself seems to acknowledge the controversial nature of (JN) though he fails to see how it might affect his argument, thereby, underestimating its impact: "I think that the soundness of [UJ*] depends on whether non-arbitrary acceptance is necessary for knowledge [justification]" (Vogel 2004, p. 435).

It is interesting to note that, despite seeking to defend the underdetermination thesis, Vogel's other observations about the nature of skeptical arguments tend to undermine it. It is widely thought that skeptical arguments from certainty are implausible because of imposing too strong a requirement on the concept of knowledge. Vogel concurs: "[W]e don't ordinarily recognize such a requirement, and instead embrace some kind of fallibilism" (Vogel 2004, p. 439). But he defines "being certain that p" as "[being unable] to be wrong about p" (Vogel 2004, p. 438). Now, one may wonder whether the invoking of (UJ*) is actually not tantamount to imposing the certainty requirement on the concepts of knowledge or justification. For if knowing ϕ, as in Vogel's version of (UK), requires the ability to "non-arbitrarily reject" all competitors to ϕ, does this not inevitably insure us against the possibility of error? After all, to be in error about ϕ is to accept one of its alternatives. Subjecting our concepts of knowledge and justification to the underdetermination requirements automatically rules out such possibilities of error. Thus if the certainty requirement is to be rejected on the ground of being too severe, so are the underdetermination principles which is precisely why we earlier concluded that they usher in epistemic stalemate. In other words, the same sorts of considerations that tell against the certainty requirement also tell against the unacceptably high standards of (UK). I conclude therefore that none of the arguments adduced in support of the underdetermination thesis succeeds in yielding it the required credibility.

6.3   Explaining away the intuitive appeal of (UJ)

Despite the preceding negative observations and misgivings about (UJ), it cannot be denied that it initially strikes one as an intuitively appealing thesis. One way to resolve the tension is by explaining away the intuition in question. It seems to me the reason why we find (UJ) intuitively appealing is because we tend to confuse it with a superficially similar but entirely distinct principle which *is* plausible as it concerns not the status of our *individual* beliefs but, rather, the epistemic status of the *comparative* content of those beliefs. We may thus distinguish between the following principles.

(UJI) If the subject's evidence for believing ϕ does not favor ϕ over ψ, then he lacks justification for believing ψ.

(UJC) If the subject's evidence for believing ϕ does not favor ϕ over ψ, then he lacks justification for believing "ϕ *rather than* ψ."

(UJI) is concerned with the justification of *individual* beliefs (ϕ or ψ) while (UJC) is concerned with the justification of the *comparative* content of those beliefs "ϕ rather than ψ." We can definitely say if the subject's evidence does not favor ϕ over ψ, then he lacks justification for believing "ϕ rather than ψ."

The point can best be illustrated in the dramatic settings of the familiar Twin Earth scenario. Suppose there is a planet, Twin Earth, which is an exact duplicate of Earth except for the fact that the colorless liquid that the Twin Earthians call "water" and falls from the sky and quenches their thirst, and so on, and is superficially indistinguishable from water is not H_2O but has a different microstructure, *XYZ*. Consider now an agent, Smith, who, without his knowledge, has for some time been undergoing a series of switches back and forth between Earth and Twin Earth remaining on each planet long enough to acquire the concepts of their respective inhabitants. Suppose further that, whenever looking at the lakes in each planet, Smith forms the belief that "This liquid is water" on the basis of the indistinguishable superficial properties of the liquids filling the lakes on those planets. It is quite plausible to say that the beliefs formed on each planet are justified. On the other hand, if externalism is true, they have a different content. One is about water, the other about twater ("twater" being the translation of "water" into Smith's language on Earth). Let us assume however that Smith finds out about the switching plot. He then finds himself in front of a lake not knowing which planet he is on. Being aware of his plight, he wonders whether "this liquid is water rather twater." It is obvious that the evidence consisting of the superficial properties of the liquid in the lake which was earlier sufficient to justify the pertinent individual beliefs is no longer able to justify the (comparative) content of the latter thought. These observations clearly justify the distinction between (UJI) and (UJC). But we need not have to go to such extremes to illustrate this point. Think of the familiar cases where people have made mistakes, taking, for example, facades for entire houses, holograms for real objects and so on. Under such circumstances one lacks justification for the comparative content of the relevant competing beliefs such as "This is a real barn rather than a fake barn," "I see a red book rather than a white book lit by red light" and so on because, by hypothesis, one's evidence cannot discriminate between those beliefs. On the other hand, as we have seen, we have been presented with no reason as to why *individual* beliefs cannot be justified under these conditions.

We have already noted the similarities between the notions of justification and confirmation and compared some of their consequences. It is interesting to note that an analog of the above confusion is also present within the confirmation theory. In the heydays of the debate over the paradoxes of confirmation a number of accounts of the nature of confirmation were proposed with a view to solving the Hempel's paradox. One such account was suggested by Scheffler who called the resulting notion of confirmation "selective confirmation" (Scheffler 1963). To confirm a hypothesis, he said, is not to show it to be likely to be true, but to add to the likelihood of its truth more than to that of its rival. Confirmation, he said, is always confirmation against a rival. Selective confirmation is clearly a comparative notion (much in the same way that (UJC) is concerned with the idea of the epistemic status of beliefs comparative contents). However, it was pointed out against Scheffler that selective confirmation was no longer what Hempel's paradox was concerned with (see Swinburne 1973). Hempel was concerned with what confirming a hypothesis consists in, in the sense of rendering it (with a given background knowledge) more likely to be true than does the background knowledge alone. It is true that the result of testing a hypothesis is relevant to the status of its rivals. But, surely, the point of selective confirmation is confirmation (in Hempel's sense). The difference between the Hempelian theory of confirmation and the theory of selective confirmation is rather analogous to the difference detected between (UJI) and (UJC) (considered as constraints on the notion of justification). Indeed, Cohen's principle (INC)—which he took to underlie (UJ)—functions pretty much like Scheffler's thesis of selective confirmation. It can be thought of as giving expression to a notion of "selective" justification requiring that if the subject's evidence is to justify ϕ it should fail to justify (disconfirm) its rivals.

I suggest therefore that any appeal attached to (UJ) results from confusing it with (UJC). This means that as far as Cartesian-style skeptical arguments are concerned, the skeptic's best bet still lies with the arguments that exploit the initially plausible principle of closure rather than the underdetermination thesis.

Part III

Meeting the Skeptical Challenge?

Skeptical arguments, especially of the Cartesian variety, have loomed large in our discussions in Chapters 5 and 6. Opinions differ, however, as to how best one should approach such arguments. There are, on the one hand, those philosophers who are generally dismissive in regard to the merits and significance of the arguments that are often presented in defense of skepticism, and there are, on the other hand, those epistemologists who are pessimistic about the prospect of solving the problem of skepticism. Stroud expresses this sentiment when he says that "[w]ithout some independent way of establishing that [the] possibility [of our being victims of an evil scientist] does not obtain, I find there is a necessary condition of knowledge that I can never fulfill. That is what seems to make the prospect of knowledge hopeless once that possibility is taken seriously" (Stroud 2000, p. 48).

As my discussions in Part II show, I am in general agreement with the view that historically prominent skeptical arguments cannot be easily dismissed on the ground of making obvious mistakes such as being self-refuting, committing some sort of performative contradiction and so on.[1] Recent years have, however, witnessed a number of powerful anti-skeptical responses that have aimed at rebutting the Cartesian arguments by seeking to undermine, in particular, their categorical premise, namely, the claim that we do not know we are not victims of a demon or a mad scientist. Unlike some philosophers who seem to be generally content with a summary dismissal of such anti-skeptical arguments, I think one needs to show why they fail. For one thing, there is much to be learnt about the nature of the central concepts of epistemology by a careful study of those arguments.[2] This part of the book deals with some of the most prominent of such anti-skeptical responses assessing their merits. As mentioned earlier, these responses generally seek to undermine the categorical claim in the Cartesian arguments, to the effect that we may be radically mistaken about our environment, by either trying to show that the hypothesis that there is an external world is the best explanation of our sense experiences, or that its truth is actually a necessary condition of their possibility, and that, therefore, our commonsense beliefs are justified. Alternatively, they take the more direct route of attempting to establish that beliefs are, by nature, largely true or justified and that, in virtue of the argument provided, constitute knowledge. In the following chapter, I examine one of these latter attempts, namely, Davidson's argument from the nature of belief and the principle of charity.

7
Argument from the Principle of Charity

In a number of influential papers Donald Davidson has argued that it is a necessary condition of successful interpretation that the interpreter must assume that the objects of interpretation, by and large, believe what (he thinks) is true. He has further claimed that this assumption, known as the principle of charity, has some significant epistemological ramifications (Davidson 1973, 1977, 1981, 1982). According to Davidson the inherently charitable nature of interpretation rules out the possibility that we are radically mistaken about the external world.

The claim has, however, proved to be quite controversial generating a large body of conflicting responses. In particular, some of Davidson's ideas, like that of an omniscient interpreter playing the role of a field linguist, have largely been greeted with incredulity. In this chapter, I propose to consider the debate in a new light by reconstruing the principle of charity as a supervenience thesis. This would explain, I claim, why Davidson has proposed a set of seemingly unconnected ideas under the rubric of charity, and whether charity per se has the anti-skeptical consequences it is said to have. I will then provide an alternative explanation as to why the principle of charity seems to be forced on us in the circumstances that Davidson envisages. Finally, I shall examine whether the sort of considerations that Davidson adduces as evidence for the necessity of charity can endow it with the required epistemic potentials. The overall conclusion will be that Davidson's semantical argument fails.

7.1 Charity explained and applied

An adequate semantic theory for a language should, according to Davidson, be such that if a person comes to know the theory, he would, partially, understand the language. It is well known that for Davidson such a theory should take the form of a Tarski-style truth theory, and, consequently the bulk of his writings on this topic is taken up with enunciating the conditions of adequacy for such theories. Very roughly, he takes the evidence for the semantic theory to consist in the conditions under which speakers hold sentences true. The holding of a sentence to be true by a speaker turns out, however, to be a function of both what she means by that sentence as well as what she believes. This means that belief cannot be inferred without prior knowledge of the meaning, and meaning cannot be deduced without the belief. It is here that the principle of charity enters the scene. We can solve the problem of the interdependence of belief and meaning "by holding belief constant as far as possible while solving for meaning. This is accomplished by assigning truth conditions to alien sentences that make native speakers right when plausibly possible, according, of course, to our own view of what is right" (Davidson 1973, p. 137).

Unlike Quine however who adopts the principle of charity as regulative maxim in choosing between empirically adequate translation manuals without, at the same time, thinking that it would reduce the amount of indeterminacy involved, Davidson takes the principle to be constitutive of intentional ascription (Hookway 1988). A theory of meaning which fails to show that the speakers' beliefs are largely true is inadequate. The principle entitles the interpreter to take the speaker to believe what he observes to be the case about his environment.

Davidson claims that the charitable nature of radical interpretation has significant epistemological consequences for certain forms of traditional skepticism which recognize the intelligibility of massive error. For if a subject is to be interpreted at all, we must, as just noted, assume that his beliefs are by and large true. So if the skeptic grants that beliefs are interpretable, then it is hard to see how one's beliefs could fail to be generally correct. The principle of charity, thus, rules out the possibility of global error. However, as Davidson himself recognizes, this argument is too quick. For all that the principle of charity requires is the maximization of truth by the interpreter's own lights. But, for all we know, the interpreter's beliefs might very well be mistaken. Mere consistency between the beliefs of the speaker and those of the interpreter fails to ensure their truth. In response, Davidson suggests two, loosely related, arguments both of which have faced stiff resistance. The first argument appeals to the idea of an omniscient interpreter, and the second exploits certain claims about the nature and means of identification of beliefs.[3] I shall consider both arguments in turn.

As we saw the method of interpretation with its constitutive principle of charity only ensures that there is a good deal of agreement between the interpreter and the speaker. To add some epistemic bite to the anti-skeptical argument that exploits this principle, Davidson introduces into the picture the idea of an omniscient interpreter who believes all and only truths. Suppose now that this omniscient being were to interpret the speaker by maximizing agreement between himself and the latter. Since the interpreter is, by hypothesis, omniscient, to be in agreement with him is to believe largely in truths. This means that the interpretee cannot be radically mistaken about her environment. Many theorists have found this to be a strange argument. Even some of those sympathetic to Davidson's general strategy against skepticism tend to regard it as "more of a hindrance than help to the Davidsonian cause" (Malpas 1994, p. 180). Moreover, it has been pointed out, for example, by Foley and Fumerton that the earlier argument, at best, establishes the following subjunctive conditional: If there were an omniscient interpreter employing Davidson's method of interpretation he would believe that most of what the interpretee believes is true (Foley and Fumerton 1985). This conditional is true if in the closest possible world in which there is an omniscient interpreter employing Davidson's method of interpretation he would believe that most of what the interpretee believes is true. But, they say, the closest possible world in which there is an omniscient being might be very different from the actual world, and so the interpretee's beliefs may fail to be true.

Davidson's second strategy against skepticism relies heavily on his views about the nature of belief which commits him to, what he calls, the inseparability of the speaker's environment from his utterances and his beliefs. Beliefs are identified, he says, by matching them with the facts in the world that prompt them. They are, therefore, essentially (largely) veridical.

> What stands in the way of global skepticism of the senses is, in my view, the fact that we must, in the plainest and methodologically most basic cases, take the objects of a belief to be the causes of that belief. And what we, as interpreters, must take them to be is what they in fact are. (Davidson 1981, pp. 317–18)

This means that we have to interpret the utterances of the inhabitants of the Cartesian demon world or a vat world as referring to, say, the brain's computer environment regardless of the experiences that it is induced to have.

This hard-line response to the possibility of skepticism has prompted a number of theorists to charge Davidson with simply shifting the focus of skeptical doubt from the question of truth to that of content.[4] Thus, Brueckner (1986), Klein (1986), and Craig (1990) have, among others, objected that while the Davidsonian strategy might be able to establish that most of our beliefs are true, it achieves this feat only at the cost of undermining our knowledge of the content of our beliefs. Davidson himself has recognized this problem (Davidson 1987a). So although the brain in a vat, on Davidson's construal of its predicament, holds (generally) true beliefs, it does not know that it is actually referring to the states of a computer when thinking about, say, the color of the sky. Davidson's suggestion about the way the content of a belief can be read off the world presupposes some of the very knowledge that the skeptic denies we possess.

> Unless I can claim to know what my beliefs' contents are, I cannot claim to know that I am not a brain in a vat but rather a sitting, embodied human. And I cannot claim to know what my beliefs' contents are unless I claim to know what their causal determinants are. To claim the latter knowledge is to beg the question against the skeptic. (Brueckner 1986, p. 267)

Despite the severity of the opposition, Davidson has not, however, been without supporters. Addressing Brueckner, Klein, and Craig's objection, Jeff Malpas, for example, has argued that Davidson does indeed have the resources to defeat skepticism (Malpas 1994). He claims that not only our beliefs are true but also we generally know what they are about. This conclusion follows, he thinks, from Davidson's holistic account of the mental which he characterizes as saying that "beliefs, desires and the rest [of attitudes] are differentiated and individuated, and therefore constituted, by the relations between them" (Malpas 1994, p. 172). Holism, claims Malpas, requires that those beliefs and attitudes be consistent with one another. The requirement of consistency extends, however, beyond first-order beliefs. Second-order beliefs (speaker's knowledge of what she means and believes) are equally subject to such a constraint. Now, by the requirement of overall consistency, the second-order beliefs must be consistent both with other second-order beliefs and with first-order beliefs.

But since second-order beliefs concern the content of first-order beliefs, if second-order beliefs are to be consistent with first-order beliefs then those second-order beliefs must generally be true—we must know what we mean and believe if our beliefs about what we mean and believe are to be consistent with what we actually do mean and believe. (Malpas 1994, p. 173)[5]

But it does not seem to me that this argument succeeds in establishing the claim that we generally know what we mean and believe. All that it ensures, if anything at all, is that the agent's second-order beliefs are *correct* rather than *justified* (or being instances of *knowledge*). Moreover, Malpas's argument also suffers from the following problem. Assuming his version of holism, what his remarks establish is that my second-order beliefs are consistent with my first-order beliefs. From this it does not follow that I know what I mean and believe. To acquire such knowledge I should also *know* that my set of beliefs is consistent. That is, I should be able to *determine* whether my second-order beliefs are consistent with my first-order beliefs. Assuming that detecting the consistency and coherence of our belief sets is a possible feat,[6] the performance of the task presupposes the very knowledge that the skeptic is out to deny that we possess. For to determine whether my beliefs about what I believe and mean are consistent with "what I actually do believe and mean," I should first find out what I actually believe and mean. And this, in turn, requires knowing what has prompted those beliefs which is precisely what the skeptic denies.

Thus, none of the earlier strategies appear to succeed in ruling out the possibility of massive error. Davidson's semantic and metaphysical ploys seem to manage to thwart the threat of skepticism only for it to reappear at a different level. What seems to have contributed to the obscurity of the debate, however, is that Davidson's anti-skeptical strategies are all being put forward under the name of the "principle of charity." As was noted, the principle was initially intended to function as an adequacy constraint on theories of meaning. Davidson's suggestion was if a theory of meaning satisfies a number of constitutive constraints on interpretation, like the principle of charity, it will be interpretive. Later on however, seeking to link his account of meaning and belief attribution with a theory of knowledge, he claimed that the principle has significant epistemological implications, making it particularly impossible that we could be in massive error. But as we saw, Davidson had already realized that the principle, formulated in terms of agreement in belief between interpreter and speaker, allows for the possibility of "speaker and interpreter understand[ing] one another on the basis of shared but erroneous beliefs" (Davidson 1981, p. 317).

To rule out this possibility and allow truth to get a foothold, he then introduced the idea of an omniscient interpreter, and further required that the objects of belief be taken to be their causes, thereby, strengthening the principle of charity. Apart from failing to undermine skepticism, these later additions, as we have seen, were largely greeted with hostility. An initial reaction of many philosophers to Davidson's idea of an omniscient interpreter was one of puzzlement and disbelief. What has seemed puzzling to many is how the omniscient interpreter and the nature-of-belief strategies relate to the principle of charity and to one another. Foley and Fumerton (1985), for example, entitling their article "Davidson's Theism?" call the argument involving an omniscient interpreter "curious" (p. 84), and Malpas describes the idea as "possibly misleading, and certainly contentious" (Malpas 1992, p. 218). Sosa, on the other hand, professes not to understand "exactly how [Davidson's anti-skeptical strategies] intertwine" (Sosa 1986, p. 395). In the section that follows, I shall suggest one way of making sense of Davidson's gradual refinement of the principle of charity.

7.2   Charity and supervenience

As was just noted, the application of the principle of charity, formulated in terms of agreement and understanding between the interpreter and the speaker, does ensure truth and consistency of the speaker's beliefs and attitudes to a large extent, but this is truth and consistency by the interpreter's own lights, as he sees it. It does nothing to guarantee the truth of the beliefs of either. It is at this point that Davidson resorts to the strategies discussed above, namely, the introduction of the idea of an omniscient interpreter, and the thesis that the objects of beliefs are their causes. As I have already remarked, apart from the question of the success of these strategies, what has seemed puzzling to many is to see how their adoption is prescribed by the principle of charity. That is, to understand the moral behind the transition from the early version of the principle of charity that requires only agreement and mutual understanding to the later versions which involve such exotic ideas as an omniscient interpreter playing the role of a field linguist. In what follows, I shall argue that the best way to make sense of the transition is by reformulating the relevant theses as supervenience claims. This would enable us to see the extent to which the transition in question has been guided by epistemological concerns.

The core idea of supervenience is that things that are indistinguishable with respect to the base or subvenient properties (B) must be indistinguishable[7] with respect to the supervenient properties (A). Thus, moral properties are said to supervene on natural properties if and only if there could be no difference of a moral sort without a difference of natural sort. Once the natural properties are fixed, moral properties are fixed as well. The core idea admits, however, of a number of interpretations, depending on whether it is within the same world or across different possible worlds that things are being compared. Thus, Kim has distinguished between weak and strong supervenience (Kim 1993). Let A and B be two nonempty sets of properties. Then to say that A weakly supervenes on B is to say that necessarily, if anything has some property F in A, there exists a property G in B such that the thing has G, and everything that has G has F ($\Box \forall x \forall F(Fx \rightarrow \exists G(Gx \& \forall y(Gy \rightarrow Fy)))$). To say A strongly supervenes on B, however, is to say that necessarily, if anything has some property F in A, there exists a property G in B such that the thing has G, and *necessarily* everything that has G has F ($\Box \forall x \forall F(Fx \rightarrow \exists G (Gx \& \Box \forall y(Gy \rightarrow Fy)))$). The definition of strong supervenience, thus, contains one more occurrence of the "necessarily" operator.[8] As noted earlier, A and B stand for nonempty sets of properties. So to say, for example, that mental properties (M) supervene on physical properties (P) is just to say that, necessarily, if anything has some property M_i in M, there exists a property P_j in P such that the thing has P_j, and necessarily, everything that has P_j has M_i. This is, however, quite compatible with M_i having P_k as its base property. Supervenience is thus quite compatible with multiple realizability. The property of, say, being in pain can be multiply realized by various physical properties (e.g., brain processes of certain types).

Now going back to our question regarding the anti-skeptical potentials of the principle of charity, we can formulate the relevant theses in terms of various supervenience relations. To begin with, Cartesian skepticism is the position that asserts that, for all we know, we might be hallucinating or be brains in vats thinking wrongly that there is an independently existing external world which prompts our various beliefs. This follows, as we have seen, from, among other things, the recognition of the possibility that there are worlds (vat worlds, Cartesian demon worlds, etc.) which are radically different from the actual world, but in which our experiential evidence remains intact. So what Cartesian skepticism denies, to state in the supervenience jargon, is the following thesis.

(R) Facts about the world (i.e., truth) supervene on facts about our sensory evidence or experience.

The supervenience in question should be understood as strong (logical) supervenience, meaning that it is logically impossible for there to be situations which are indiscernible with respect to sensory evidence but distinct with respect to facts about them. The possibility of a vat or demon world is thus ruled out by (R) because such a world describes a situation in which our sensory experiences remain intact while facts about our environment undergo radical change. (Note that all (R) says is that by fixing facts about our sensory experience, facts about the world are automatically determined. This is compatible with the latter facts having various sensory bases, just as mental properties can be said to be multiply realizable by various physical properties while supervening on them.)

Now if, as Davidson claims, the principle of charity is to refute Cartesian skepticism, it should, in effect, be able to establish (R). The principle requires the radical interpreter to maximize agreement between himself and the speaker by assigning to the latter the same type of beliefs on the basis of the same type of sensory evidence. So what the principle says can be formulated as the following supervenience thesis.

(CHe) Beliefs supervene on (sensory) evidence.

Consonant with Davidson's requirements, all that (CHe) says is that in every possible world in which cognizers are confronted with the same sensory evidence, they should be assigned the same type of beliefs.[9] This is what guarantees agreement and mutual understanding between the interpreter and the interpretee. What it expresses therefore is a *weak* supervenience thesis. It only requires that in every possible world in which a cognizer is assigned a belief (b) on the basis of some evidence (e), the same type of belief should be assigned to any other cognizer in that world who is also acquainted with the same evidence.[10] It does not rule out the possibility of a world where an individual forms a different type of belief (c) on the basis of the same sensory evidence (e). (CHe), thus, guarantees only intra-world agreement rather than cross-world agreement. It lacks, in other words, the modal force of a strong supervenience thesis. It also says nothing about truth. It does not require that the ascribed beliefs be true. It only requires the ascription of same type of beliefs to individuals (in the same world) on the basis of the same type of evidence.

With these points in mind, let us return to Davidson's claim that (CHe) refutes Cartesian skepticism. If this is to be the case, (CHe) must be able to establish (R)—which is the denial of the basic assumption of

Cartesian skepticism. But this is puzzling. (R) is a strong supervenience thesis which involves truth, whereas (CHe) is a weak supervenience thesis which is concerned only with the type of attributed beliefs rather than their truth value. (CHe) lacks, in other words, both the modal and verific force of (R). And both these features are needed if Davidson is going to make claims of the following sort; "Once we agree to the general method of interpretation I have sketched, it becomes *impossible* correctly to hold that anyone could be mostly *wrong* about how things are" (Davidson 1981, p. 317, emphasis added). What can then be done to elevate (CHe) to the rank of (R)? Well, to make up for the absence of the modal and verific force of (CHe), we can adopt either of the following two strategies. We might, for example, postulate that there is a necessarily existing omniscient interpreter playing the role of a field linguist. Being a necessary existent, it is guaranteed that every possible world with belief-forming agents is a world with an omniscient interpreter. Being omniscient, however, it ensures that those agents are generally correct about their immediate environment. By postulating such a being we can provide (CHe) with the modal and verific force that it requires in order to refute skepticism.

Alternatively, we might look in another direction for the missing features. We might, for example, shift the focus of our attention from the believer (interpreter) to the nature of belief itself. We might say, with Davidson, that "in the plainest and methodologically most basic cases, [we must] take the objects of a belief to be the causes of that belief. And what we, as interpreters, must take them to be is what they in fact are." This would insure that "beliefs are by *nature* generally *true*" (Davidson 1981, p. 319, emphasis added). Beliefs are essentially (largely) true because we assign content to them on the basis of the facts in the world that cause them. It is clear that reference to both the nature and truth of a belief (in the above remarks) provides us, respectively, with the required modal and verific force. This in fact suggests a new version of the principle of charity requiring us to assign the same type of beliefs to agents when and only when they happen to share the same (type of) causal bases. This can be expressed as the following supervenience thesis.

(CHc) Beliefs supervene on their causes.[11]

It seems to me that the characterization of charity as a supervenience thesis allows us to follow and understand the gradual development of Davidson's argument against skepticism. It has the merit of explaining a number of puzzling features of the argument and the ensuing debate. In the remainder of this section I will try to justify this claim.

Earlier we noted how Davidson's anti-skeptical strategies prompted a generally hostile reaction among epistemologists. I believe much of the incredulity generated by Davidson's arguments is justified. The idea of an omniscient interpreter who is supposed to interpret speakers in every possible world, thereby, guaranteeing the "impossibility … that anyone could be mostly wrong" is indeed odd, especially when it is proposed by someone within the mainstream Quinean tradition. Moreover, it is not obvious how this is related to the principle of charity and also to the argument from the content of belief. But much of the confusion can be cleared, I believe, once we look at Davidson's arguments from the perspective I have provided. The supervenience perspective enables us to see how Davidson's epistemological concerns led to the later refinements and additions to the principle of charity. When reacting to the question of why it could not be the case that speaker and interpreter understand one another on the basis of shared but erroneous beliefs, he says "this can, and no doubt often does, happen. But it cannot be the rule" (Davidson 1981, p. 317). He then proceeds to explain why his proposed strategies "stand in the way of global skepticism" without making it clear how they relate to one another and to the principle of charity.

But the supervenience perspective brings out the connections to the surface. Both the omniscient interpreter and nature-of-belief strategies are actually intended to make up for the missing modal and verific force of the principle of charity (CHe)—if it is to have anti-skeptical consequences. They are also closely related to each other because they are intended to play the same function, namely, provide modal and verific support for (CHe). Their difference seems to consist only in the fact that while one strategy is geared toward the believer, and, thus, postulates an omniscient interpreter, the other picks out the nature of belief, and, thus, proposes to identify the objects of beliefs with their causes.

The supervenience perspective is also able to explain why Davidson's argument from the content of belief has been criticized for failing to be a genuine response to the threat of skepticism, merely shifting the focus of doubt from the question of truth to the question of content. All that the argument shows, says Brueckner, is that no matter whether or not I am a brain in a vat, my beliefs are true (when appropriately interpreted). It does nothing to dispel the doubt that my world might be a vat world, and that, for all I know, I might be a brain in a vat. I think our supervenience gloss on Davidson's thesis about the content of a belief can explain why his attack on skepticism meets only with partial success.

For all that his thesis, as seen through (CHc), says is that beliefs supervene on their causes. It says nothing about the *nature* of the causes involved. My belief that there was a car crash yesterday may have either been caused by that very event or through appropriate computer stimulations. That is why the application of (CHc) fails to rule out the possibility that I am a brain in a vat. It only guarantees that my beliefs are true while keeping silent about the nature of objects that prompt them. The identity of causes does not, and, in fact, cannot enter into the content of (CHc). For any attempt at identifying the causes would inevitably invite the charge of begging the question against the skeptic. The description "the cause of that belief" in the formulation of (CHc) is, if you like, used only attributively (Donnellan 1966). So what (CHc), in fact, says is that beliefs supervene on their causes, whatever they are. So while Brueckner and others have rightly criticized Davidson's argument from the content of belief for failing to have enough anti-skeptical firepower, our supervenience perspective explains why it *cannot* have that power. Let us now see if we can make sense of other salient features of the principle of charity in the light of preceding remarks.

7.3   The necessity of charity

As we saw a theory of meaning, on Davidson's account, is a Tarski-style truth theory which for each object language sentence (s) gives a meta-language sentence (p) which is true if and only if that object language sentence is true. The theory thus yields theorems (T-sentences) of the form "s is true iff p" providing the truth conditions (meaning) of the sentence mentioned: "when the interpreter finds a sentence of the speaker the speaker assents to regularly under conditions he recognizes, he takes those conditions to be the truth conditions of the speaker's sentence" (Davidson 1981, p. 316). The idea is, thus, to assign meaning to the speaker's utterances, at least in the methodologically most basic cases, on the basis of the objects and events in her environment, or, to put it differently, to infer the meaning of those utterances from the environmental circumstances that prompt them. But the transition is not that simple. The speaker's assent to a sentence is due to both what that sentence means and what the speaker believes (the interdependence of belief and meaning). Thus the fact that a sentence is assented to under certain environmental circumstances does not warrant taking the latter as constituting the truth conditions (meaning) of that sentence, for the sentence might have either truth-value in those circumstances. To break into the closed circle of belief and meaning, the interpreter has to assume that the speaker perceives her environment roughly as he does and, consequently, comes to form similar beliefs. This is what grounds the necessity of charity, making it inevitable for the process of interpretation.

I shall now try a different route to the necessity of charity by restating the question of meaning within the supervenience framework (here, I shall focus on Davidson's favored version of charity as expressed by (CHc)). The idea of radical interpretation is to establish semantic hypotheses from non-semantic starting points by recovering the meaning of sentences from the relationships they bear to the environmental circumstances in which they are uttered. We want sentences that are uttered in response to the same circumstances be assigned the same meaning. We are, in other words, requiring that meanings be supervenient on appropriate environmental circumstances. How can we show this to be the case?

Well, it is easy to show that the meaning of a sentence supervenes on the content of the belief that would be expressed by an utterance of that sentence. When two individuals hold the same (type) of belief, this implies, given the standard account of propositions, that sentences to which they are assumed to be similarly related have the same content or meaning (i.e., meanings supervene on the relevant beliefs).[12] But we want meanings to supervene on the appropriate environmental circumstances. Now, having shown that the meanings of sentences supervene on beliefs that are expressed by uttering those sentences, all we have to do to get the required supervenience thesis is to assume that beliefs equally supervene on environmental circumstances that cause them, that is, (CHc). For with meanings supervening on the relevant beliefs and beliefs supervening on the circumstances that cause them, it follows, given the transitivity of the supervenience relation, that meanings, after all, supervene on the appropriate circumstances that prompt the relevant utterances, thus the required thesis. The supervenience framework, thus, offers a way of thinking about (an explanation of) the alleged necessity of charity, namely that it acts as a bridge to connect the meaning of sentences to the world, and as such, I suppose, not a particularly deep feature of radical interpretation as it is generally made to appear on the Davidsonian approach. I shall now proceed to investigate the consequences of seeing the principle of charity as a supervenience constraint on belief attribution for the logical status of the principle itself.

7.4 Charity: methodological and constitutive

While Quine views the principle of charity as a methodological and regulative maxim in choosing between empirically adequate translation manuals, Davidson takes the principle as being constitutive of such concepts as belief, desire, meaning, and soon, by allowing it to govern their application. In the hands of Davidson charity becomes constitutive of correctness rather than a merely methodological maxim. Of course it is one thing to say what Davidson intends with the principle, it is another to see whether he has the resources to realize that aim. To get a better grip on the question, let us restate it within the supervenience framework.

One of the main functions of charity, as we have seen, is that it enables the interpreter to maximize the consistency and coherence of his beliefs and those of the interpretee, thus, bringing about agreement and mutual understanding. Sometimes this is stated by saying that the point of charity is to make the agent as rational as possible, but, for Davidson, the rationality of beliefs, and of attitudes and behavior in general, consists in their coherence, and "coherence is nothing but consistency." Thus, the main purpose of charity, construed as an interpretive constraint, is to ensure that the agent is as consistent and coherent as possible. Consistency and coherence are the hallmark of a successful interpretation of an agent's linguistic and nonlinguistic behavior. Now it is instructive to note that this function is equally discharged by our alternative construal of the principle of charity as a supervenience constraint on belief attribution, providing further support for the conclusions reached so far. For consistency and coherence are precisely the features that are usually associated with claims that certain properties supervene on others. Let us recall how Richard Hare argues for the supervenience of moral on natural properties.

> Suppose that we say "St. Francis was a good man." It is logically impossible to say this and maintain at the same time that there might have been another man placed exactly in the same circumstances as St. Francis, and who behaved in exactly the same way, but also differed from St. Francis in this respect only, that he was not a good man. (Hare 1952, p. 145)

As we have already seen in Chapter 5, The idea is that if we deny moral supervenience, we are committed to the absurd idea that two objects could differ in respect of the property of goodness, but be indistinguishable in respect of their natural properties. Rather, on pain of being inconsistent, we ought to treat like cases alike. Moral supervenience can, thus, be seen as a consistency constraint on moral attribution. The same sorts of considerations, as noted before, have been adduced in support of the thesis that epistemic properties supervene on non-epistemic ones (Van Cleve 1985).

Now, going back to our discussion of charity, if we construe the principle as a supervenience constraint, then that would ensure the consistency of our belief ascripions. We will be required to attribute the same type of beliefs to agents on the basis of the same type of evidence or causes. If charity is not assumed, there will be room for inconsistent belief ascriptions which is as implausible as was the case of inconsistent moral attributions. The principle of charity, construed as a supervenience constraint, thus, governs the application of such concepts as belief, desire, and so on, much in the same way that moral supervenience is intended to govern the application of the concept of good. And that is precisely what Davidson requires of charity as an interpretive constraint.

> The point of the principle is to make the speaker intelligible, since too great deviations from consistency and correctness leave no common ground on which to judge either conformity or difference. ... What needs emphasis is only the methodological necessity for finding consistency enough. (Davidson 1981, p. 316)

The standard view of charity and our alternative construal, thus, turn out to be functionally equivalent. It might be objected that charity ensures the consistency and coherence of the interpreter's beliefs *and* those of the interpretee, whereas supervenience constraints, as in the case of the moral, only require the consistency of (moral) *attributers*. But this difference is only apparent. It is true that the application of charity ensures general agreement between *two* parties (interpreter and the interpretee), but, as Davidson and Quine have both emphasized, charity begins at home. The interpreter's beliefs are as much subject to the constraint of charity as are the beliefs of the interpretee. While throwing some light on the nature and function of the principle of charity, the supervenience construal of charity also highlights some of its hidden features that would sharpen the question of its status as well as its alleged epistemological potentials. I close this chapter by a brief consideration of the issues involved.

As emphasized by Klagge, one should distinguish between ascriptive and ontological supervenience (Klagge 1988). The ascriptive version of supervenience only involves *judgments*, and says that an agent's judgments of a certain (supervening) kind about things cannot differ unless judgments of other kind about the things differ. By contrast, ontological supervenience involves a relation between two classes of *properties*, saying that a set of properties, *A*, supervenes on another set of properties, *B*, when and only when there could be no difference of sort *A* without some difference of sort *B*. As Klagge points out, one cannot infer ontological supervenience from ascriptive supervenience, for from the fact that our judgments are subject to a certain constraint, nothing follows about the internal constitution of the world. Hare's position, in fact, clearly illustrates this point. Although he argues for moral supervenience, being a moral antirealist, he cannot be interpreted as being committed to the ontological version of moral supervenience.

A similar situation arises for the principle of charity (construed as a supervenience constraint). The principle can either be considered in an ascriptive sense, thus, involving judgments about belief attribution, or in an ontological sense identifying a connection between two non-empty sets of properties. These two senses of charity seem to correspond to Quine and Davidson's attitudes toward the principle. Quine is inclined, as we saw, to use the principle of charity in a regulative, pragmatic sense to help us live with translational indeterminacy. This is roughly the use of charity as involving a relation of ascriptive supervenience. For Davidson, however, the principle is a constitutive thesis. He takes the psychological realm as being governed by a requirement of overall coherence and consistency. If the concepts of belief, desire, and the like are not applied in accordance with the principle of charity, there is no reason, he says, to take them as applying at all. Davidson is, thus, using the principle in a sense that involves a relation of ontological supervenience between certain kinds of properties. Indeed, that is how the principle should be understood if it is to have significant ramifications for the truth and veridicality of our beliefs, that is, if it is to say something about the world (as opposed to merely involving our judgments about the world).

This, however, raises the following question. Does the sort of consistency considerations that Davidson adduces for the legitimacy of the principle of charity suffice to establish it as a constitutive thesis? The question can be paraphrased using the supervenience jargon: Does the imposition of a consistency constraint on belief attribution establish the principle of charity as expressing a supervenience thesis in the ontological sense? Consistency considerations (of the relevant sort) do seem to suffice for ascriptive supervenience, but, as we saw, the inference from the latter to ontological supervenience is illegitimate. From the fact that it is reasonable to subject our belief attributions to a consistency constraint, nothing follows about the constitution of such properties as belief and desire, and, in particular, their purported supervenience on the environmental causes of attitudes of that type. Indeed, there are positions within psychology, resembling Hare's attitude toward morality, which happily endorse the imposition of a charity constraint on belief ascription, but which nonetheless advocate some version of an antirealist stance toward propositional attitudes.[13] This provides a more general reason than those already advanced for being suspicious of the epistemic potentials of the principle of charity.

8
Argument from Epistemic Conservatism

It has been suggested that the stability of one's belief system is a cognitive virtue, an end toward which cognitive agents should strive. While sticking dogmatically to one's beliefs is epistemically preposterous, it would be equally unreasonable, it is said, to change them in the absence of any good reasons. This position known as epistemic conservatism seems to have had a distinguished line of advocates among the likes of Quine and Chisholm. Although, it has been claimed that epistemic conservatism has informed and resolved various positions and problems in epistemology from foundationalist theories of justification to problems such as the underdetermination of theories by data, one can primarily regard it as an anti-skeptical strategy whose most widely held form upholds that the mere holding of a belief confers justification on that belief.

The argument from epistemic conservatism, thus, has only modest aims. It does not seek to establish that our commonsense beliefs are true. It is only intended to show that some of our beliefs are justified. Our goal in this chapter is to see whether this minimalist strategy is successful. Looking at the literature on this topic though, it is difficult to single out an account as definitely representing the thesis of epistemic conservatism. Sometimes the thesis is formulated in terms of the requirement that one be justified in holding on to a theory even when faced with competing but evidentially equivalent hypotheses. And sometimes, as just noted, it is claimed that mere belief in a proposition is sufficient for its justification, and so on. In general, what one finds is that various principles are being employed under the rubric of conservatism often without sufficient attempt being made to establish their credibility beyond mentioning certain pragmatic considerations.

In this chapter, I begin by expounding the thesis of epistemic conservatism and its alleged applications. Having shown that the applications in question are far from being genuine, I highlight the disparate and largely unconnected attempts that have been made to establish conservatism. The diversity, I shall argue, is mainly due to the fact that the theorists are actually concerned with different and non-equivalent versions of epistemic conservatism. Having distinguished between different varieties of conservatism, I set out to determine their credibility and anti-skeptical potentials by evaluating various arguments that have been offered or may be considered in their defense. While finding the arguments generally wanting, it is important, I believe, not to opt for a wholesale rejection of the conservative theses as the arguments offered in their defense vary in their structure. The burden of this paper is, therefore, to assess the merit of each argument on its own as it is geared toward establishing a distinct thesis. I close, however, by arguing that those versions of the thesis of epistemic conservatism that survive critical scrutiny fail to live up to the aspirations of the thesis as a substantive anti-skeptical canon of rationality.

8.1   Varieties of epistemic conservatism

According to the thesis of epistemic conservatism, it is unreasonable to subject our belief system to revision or change without any good reasons. Not only would this incur an unnecessary utilization of resources and energy on the part of the cognizer, it would also fail to bequeath the agent's cognitive system any epistemic benefit. Thus, epistemic conservatism views the stability of one's belief system as an epistemic virtue, something that, on certain accounts of the thesis, has survival value and is the product of the optimific process of natural selection. Epistemic conservatism comes in many forms, the most basic of which asserts that the mere possession of a belief confers justification on that belief. So an agent is justified in holding a belief simply in virtue of the fact of holding it.

Although the proponents of conservatism are quick to point out that the epistemic credibility that it bestows on a belief is only prima facie and minimal, one cannot help feeling that there must be something unsatisfactory about a thesis that takes the mere holding of a belief to endow it with epistemic worth. And, in general, would not the conservative policy of encouraging stability and retaining the status quo in one's belief repertoire hinder the course of inquiry by undermining our motivation to break new grounds? The advocates of conservatism, however, reject these charges as being superficial. In turn, they highlight the cases where conservatism has supposedly informed and shaped a number of prominent contemporary philosophical views such as those of Quine and Chisholm (Quine 1951; Chisholm 1980). It is further claimed that conservatism helps us to deal with a number of intractable quandaries in philosophy such as the problem of the underdetermination of theories by data, the problem of keeping track of the justifications of one's beliefs, and so on. And, as was briefly noted, some even go as far as suggesting an evolutionary story of why it features so prominently among our purported canons of theory choice. It is, they say, a good thing in cost–benefit terms that we maintain stability in our belief system. In fact, this is what Nature has designed us to do: "[It] would not want us to change our minds capriciously and for no reason" (Lycan 1988, p. 161).

Despite such enthusiasm, doubts about the epistemic legitimacy of conservatism linger on. Such doubts become if anything stronger when, on close inspection, one realizes that some of the applications and uses of the conservative policy are rather contrived and superficial than genuine. For example, in some cases the conservative thesis just does not sit well with the views that allegedly exploit it. Conservative principles are primarily principles of justification and reasonableness of holding beliefs and, as such, they seem to be at odds with those views, such as Quine's, that seek to eschew the most distinctive feature of traditional epistemology namely, its normativity altogether replacing it by descriptive psychology.[1] And sometimes, where a particular conservative principle—as a norm of rationality—is claimed to be at work (as in the case of Sklar's principle), it turns out that what is really doing the job is some disguised form of a holistic coherentism or another theory of justification. To substantiate this claim, I shall examine some of the cases where the thesis of epistemic conservatism is said to be operative.

The first case involves the use of conservatism in dealing with the problem of underdetermination. For the sake of concreteness, I shall focus on Foley's account of the story. According to Foley some philosophers suggest that when confronted with a number of incompatible but otherwise equivalent hypotheses, "it is more rational for a person to believe the hypothesis which conflicts with the smallest number of his beliefs than to believe the other hypotheses" (Foley 1982, p. 166). What lies behind the legitimacy of this advice, he claims, is the thesis of epistemic conservatism: "As far as I can see, *if* such questions are to be given a fully epistemic answer, it must be in terms of a principle similar to the [conservative] principle which Chisholm endorses" (Foley 1982, p. 166). The principle says "anything we find ourselves believing may be said to have *some* presumption in its favor—*provided* it is not explicitly contradicted by the set of other things that we believe" (Chisholm 1980, pp. 551–2). But that cannot be the whole story. As I shall explain later, Chisholm's principle is just one expression of the thesis that takes the bare fact of holding a belief to confer justification on that belief. As such, the principle would be of no help in deciding which of the hypotheses to believe. For, by assumption, all competing hypotheses are evidentially equivalent and (by Chisholm's principle) should enjoy an equal degree of presumption in their favor. Rather, what seems to be doing the work, in Foley's account of the story, is the appended consistency condition to the principle requiring the new belief not to induce an explicit contradiction in the cognizer's belief repertoire. So one can see Foley's suggested policy in regard to choosing between evidentially equivalent hypotheses as really being underpinned by a straightforward consistency requirement, rather than a conservative principle like Chisholm's, to the effect that one should minimize inconsistency in one's belief system when deciding to add new beliefs. Moreover, it would be quite futile to try to implement the policy if it turns out that all the competing hypotheses are equally consistent with our background beliefs.

Foley's other example of the use of epistemic conservatism involves a position, called "Maximalism," which he attributes to Goldman, and takes it to be in conformity with the Quinean conception of epistemology. Foley quotes Goldman on the nature of Maximalism: "It invites us to employ *all* our antecedent beliefs whenever we wish to appraise our cognitive methods. A Maximalist argues that there is likely to be little or no basis for choice among methods unless we employ a prior corpus of belief. And if *some* prior beliefs are allowed, why not allow them all" (Goldman 1979, pp. 29–30). However, those prior beliefs which the cognizers happen to hold cannot be used in the appraisal process of their cognitive methods unless we assume that they "have some favorable epistemic status" themselves. But to assume this, says Foley, is to involve the thesis of epistemic conservatism for we are, in effect, assuming that those prior beliefs acquire their favorable epistemic status in virtue of being held by the cognizers.

But this is not really a good example of epistemic conservatism in action, for Foley quotes only part of what Goldman says about Maximalism. Maximalism would indeed presuppose conservatism if the "prior corpus of belief" had its epistemic worth conferred on it only in virtue of being held by the agent. But Goldman is quite explicit about the source of justification of these prior beliefs. They owe their positive epistemic status to the fact that they are adequately grounded or reliably produced. Immediately after the last sentence in the above quote, Goldman goes on to delimit the scope of allowable prior beliefs by adding the following qualifiers:

> Or at least the more confidently held among them, or those arrived at by methods which, until now, we regard as most reliable? ... Given the present state of science, we have a rich set of beliefs about the physical world. ... According to Maximalism, all this information can legitimately be used in commending new cognitive strategies, or appraising the ones we have. (Goldman 1979, p. 30)

Goldman contrasts Maximalism with Minimalism, a position that holds that "the appraisal and choice of cognitive procedures should *antecede* acceptance of scientific beliefs, and hence must not appeal to any such beliefs" (Goldman 1979, p. 29). So it is quite clear that the prior corpus of belief that, according to Goldman, should be employed in the appraisal of cognitive methods consists mostly of scientific beliefs and, in general, beliefs that are obtained reliably. It is because of the way these beliefs are produced or obtained that they enjoy favorable epistemic status and not because of the bare fact that they are held by agents. Regardless of whether it is an epistemically credible position, Maximalism does not presuppose epistemic conservatism.

The preceding remarks are not intended to count as a wholesale denial of the epistemic utility of the thesis of epistemic conservatism. Perhaps some versions of the thesis can have some legitimate application in our cognitive practices. But they should, at least, admonish us against describing it as an overarching anti-skeptical strategy in our cognitive endeavors. However, what compounds the problem is that discussions of the thesis tend to switch back and forth between what seem to be different and often nonequivalent versions of the thesis of epistemic conservatism. Apart from the ensuing confusions, this makes it difficult to ascertain the validity of the arguments that have been suggested in its defense, for an argument that is designed to defend one version of the thesis may turn out to be quite irrelevant to the validity of another. My aim in the rest of this chapter is, therefore, to isolate different varieties of epistemic conservatism and evaluate their merits individually on their own.

Looking at the literature on epistemic conservatism, one is struck by the various guises under which the thesis of conservatism appears. Sometimes we see a theorist adopting a differential attitude, choosing to focus on one version of conservatism to the exclusion of others, and sometimes we see another theorist taking all versions on board implying that what he says about one version is equally true of others. In neither case, however, is any attempt made to explain the uniformity of the adopted methodology or its lack thereof. Here are some examples.

In an early statement of the thesis of epistemic conservatism, or "methodological conservatism" as it is called there, Sklar opens his remarks by dismissing what he regards as a strong version of the thesis according to which "the very fact that a proposition is believed can serve as warrant for some attitude to be rationally maintained in regard to believing it" (Sklar 1975, p. 375). Instead, he opts for a more "modest" principle of methodological conservatism which requires us not to reject a hypothesis once believed just because we come to know of an evidentially equivalent alternative to it. This is also the line that is taken by both Vogel and Adler in their discussions of epistemic conservatism (Adler 1990b; Vogel 1992). By contrast, Chisholm articulates and makes use of a variant of the version of epistemic conservatism that Sklar had earlier rejected for being too strong.

Gilbert Harman initially defines conservatism as the view that a proposition can acquire justification simply by being believed, but officially defends a version of conservatism according to which "one is justified in continuing fully to accept something in the absence of a special reason not to" (Harman 1986, p. 46). (He gives a slightly different but closely related formulation of conservatism when expounding his Principle of Positive Undermining.) William Lycan, on the other hand, mentions all the aforementioned theses under the rubric of epistemic conservatism, and seems to think that they are all legitimate although, for the most part in his discussion, he focuses on his significantly anti-skeptical "Principle of Credulity" according to which one is required to accept at the outset propositions that seem to be true (Lycan 1988). Likewise, David Christensen, to give one last illustration, declares that the thesis of epistemic conservatism takes many forms and claims, without offering an argument, that all these forms share the basic idea that the mere fact of believing a proposition confers some justification on that proposition, and is, thus, a significant tool against skepticism (Christensen 1994).

As the preceding remarks show, one is faced with many and often seemingly nonequivalent versions of the thesis of epistemic conservatism. This is not just because of the fact that some theorists are keen to accept one version of the thesis to the exclusion of others, but also because the arguments that are adduced to substantiate epistemic conservatism are usually tailored toward defending one specific version of the thesis and are ineffective to support others. So in order to evaluate the feasibility of epistemic conservatism, it would be necessary to isolate different varieties of conservatism. I think one can discern three types of conservative principles which nevertheless share varying degrees of anti-skeptical potentials because, if true, they underwrite the justificatory status of one's beliefs.

Generation Conservatism (GC)	Holding a belief is sufficient for its justification.
Perseverance Conservatism (PC)	One should stop believing a proposition whenever one positively believes one's reasons for believing that proposition are no good.
Differential Conservatism (DC)	One is justified in holding on to a hypothesis (belief) despite coming to know of evidentially equivalent alternatives.

(GC) can be particularly associated with Chisholm while (PC) and (DC) have been respectively defended by Harman and Sklar. In what follows, I shall evaluate (in reverse order) the credentials of each of these principles in the light of the arguments and considerations that have been offered in their favor.

8.2   Differential conservatism

Differential conservatism has been prominently defended by Sklar. As was just noted, he begins his discussion of epistemic conservatism by considering what we have called the principle of "generation conservatism" (GC) and dismisses it as being too strong for it would seem to have the consequence that any belief whatsoever could be deemed as rational. Sklar, thus, opts for "more modest" principles of conservatism whose distinguishing mark, he says, is that they are not actually concerned with positive warrant for a belief, but, rather, with its justificatory status once it is held. He offers the following principle as truly reflecting the content of the thesis of methodological conservatism which is just a long-winded version of what we have called "differential conservatism" (DC).

> (DC)   If you believe some proposition, on the basis of whatever positive warrant may accrue to it from the evidence, a priori

plausibility, and so forth, it is unreasonable to cease to believe the proposition to be true merely because of the existence of, or knowledge of the existence of, alternative incompatible hypotheses whose positive warrant is no greater than that of the proposition already believed. (Sklar 1975, p. 378)

Sklar immediately notes the difference between (DC) and (GC), saying that (DC) "does not commit us to the believability ... of a proposition merely because it is believed. ... All it commits us to is the decision not to reject a hypothesis once believed simply because we become aware of alternative, incompatible hypotheses which are just as good as, but no better than, that believed" (Sklar 1975, p. 378). What this means is that the evidential source of a belief in (DC) is different from that which is specified in (GC), namely, the bare fact of holding that belief.

Is (DC) warranted? Before turning to this question, let us consider a commonly made objection that is intended to call into question the coherence of (DC) (Goldstick 1971). According to (DC) if an agent believes *p* on the basis of evidence *e*, he is justified in believing that *p* despite coming to recognize that an incompatible hypothesis, *q*, is equally supported by *e*. Now, consider two individuals coming to believe *p* and *q* respectively on the basis of evidence *e*. By (DC) they are both justified in their beliefs despite the beliefs being incompatible, and this, says the objection, is absurd. Sklar, however, denies that there is anything absurd about this, and gives the example of two societies that are organized on different social systems that serve equally well in bringing about identical social ideals. Under these circumstances, he says, there is no need to change one system and replace it by another. However, as Sklar recognizes, this is not a particularly good analogy as the notion of "correctness" (i.e., truth or falsity) is not really applicable in the case of alternative political systems and this may be said to be responsible for the coherence of the idea of their coexistence. Not so in the case of alternative but evidentially equivalent hypotheses. He thus offers a different analogy much closer to home. Consider a case where two agents form incompatible beliefs on the basis of *different* observational evidence. There is no doubt that they can be both rational. Sklar goes on to conclude that

> if it is *logically coherent* to maintain that two parties who differ in their evidence can both be rational even though their beliefs are incompatible, then it is logically coherent to maintain that they are equally rational in their incompatible choices even though their

different warrant for their beliefs is based solely on the fact that they *do* believe different incompatible hypotheses and each adopts a principle of conservatism which tells him not to change his belief unless there is some reason to do so. (Sklar 1975, p. 385)

But this argument is not compelling. For, to begin with, Sklar cashes out the notion of the "evidential source of a belief" in terms of the conservative principle (GC) whose credibility he had rejected earlier as when he describes the warrant for beliefs as being "based solely on the fact that [the agents] *do* believe different hypotheses." Moreover, it is not at all clear why the coherence of maintaining the rationality of incompatible beliefs in the case where those beliefs are based on different observational evidence should be equally carried into the case where incompatible beliefs are based on the same (type of) evidence. In any event, the resemblance of the two cases (vis-à-vis their coherence) is what we are supposed to show rather than assume.

However, recalling our discussion in Chapter 6, I go along with Sklar in maintaining that there is nothing absurd about two incompatible beliefs being equally rational. But perhaps that is not what lies behind the above objection to (DC). Indeed, it seems to me that the underlying worry is that (DC) contravenes the thesis of epistemic supervenience according to which the justification of a belief supervenes on certain non-epistemic properties of that belief (e.g., being part of a coherent belief system, being reliably produced, being adequately grounded, etc.). This would mean that when two beliefs share the same subvening property and one is justified, so is the other. Suppose now two scientists S_1 and S_2 who, faced with the task of explaining the same data, come up with incompatible but evidentially equivalent hypotheses H_1 and H_2 respectively. Suppose further that the hypotheses in question become known to both some time later during a meeting where S_2, for some reason of his own, gives up H_2 and follows S_1 in believing H_1. Now, according to (DC), S_2 should have stuck with H_2. His belief that H_1 is, thus, unjustified while S_1 is justified in believing H_1 and rejecting H_2. So, assuming that (DC) is normatively correct, we are faced with a situation in which while believing H_1 is rational (justified) for S_1, another token of the same belief fails to be rational (justified) for S_2 despite the two tokens sharing the same subvening justification-conferring property, and this contravenes the thesis of epistemic supervenience.

Further on in his discussion, Sklar speculates that perhaps those who are wary of conservatism are actually reacting to its apparent "arbitrariness," for (DC) seems to require one to prefer the first-born hypothesis to others. But any of the alternatives could have had that status and this introduces an implausible degree of arbitrariness into our canons of rationality. Sklar dismisses this objection. We would not reject Newton's inference to his theory of spacetime as irrational, he says, because it was the data involving absolutely accelerated objects that first caught his attention and not the results of the Michelson–Morely experiment which were not yet available. But this example is one where the adopted hypotheses are prompted by different rather than the same evidence. Given Newton's evidence, his inference to his spacetime theory was quite rational and nonarbitrary, but the objection seems to be concerned with cases where two hypotheses' competition for the rationality status is decided solely on the basis of the fact as to which one is the first-born despite both being evidentially on a par.

It seems to me that what lies behind the worry that Sklar discusses can, once again, be spelled out in terms of the violation of the supervenience constraint on the notion of rationality (justification). To see this we should not construe "arbitrariness" in temporal terms, in terms of the time of inception of a hypothesis. Rather, if our account of the failure of supervenience in the context of (DC) is correct, what the worry seeks to accentuate is that conservatism has the consequence that like cases fail to be treated alike. That is, with the failure of epistemic supervenience, we are prepared to ascribe the property of justification to one belief while refraining from treating another belief as justified despite both beliefs sharing the same subvening justification-conferring property, and this introduces an element of arbitrariness into our canons of rationality.

Now, leaving aside the implausible consequences of (DC), what can be said in its favor? The first thing to note is that (DC) is lacking in intuitive plausibility. The idea is that when an agent, say, a scientist, proposes a hypothesis H_1 to account for a set of available data, and it then comes to light that another alternative H_2 is equally capable of explaining the data, this revelation should, intuitively speaking, shake the scientist's confidence in her hypothesis. Under the new circumstances, she is no longer entitled to give the same credence to H_1 that she initially awarded it. The availability of an alternative should, at least, give her a pause. It would be quite irresponsible of her to go on to develop her theory and completely ignore the alternative explanation in her research (cf. Adler 1990b; Vogel 1992). Let us now turn to the arguments that have been proposed in support of (DC).

The first type of argument is of a pragmatic nature, and it is broad enough to cover all varieties of the conservative thesis. Both Lycan and

Sklar offer such arguments (though Sklar does not give it much weight). The idea, in a nutshell, is that changing one's mind for no good reason is a waste of time, effort, and resources on the part of the cognizer. So adhering to conservatism is a good thing because it saves the energy and effort that would be wasted in changing one's mind. This argument suffers from the weakness of all pragmatic arguments when they are intended to make an epistemic point. Adhering to conservatism may be a good thing from the point of view of saving energy and resources, but what we are interested in (in this context) is whether it is a good thing from the *epistemic* point of view of maximizing truth and minimizing falsity in one's body of belief. Pragmatic considerations, however, do not speak to such concerns. Lycan realizes this problem but his attitude toward the concept of epistemic justification is quite ambivalent and equivocal. First he acknowledges that he is not "suggesting that our customary canons of theory-preference [which includes conservatism] are *epistemically justified* by the adaptive utility of our habit of using them" (Lycan 1988, p. 159). This raises the expectation that he will have something positive to say about why the thesis is epistemically justified. But he goes on to state that "[c]onservatism as a canon of theory-preference has no justification in the epistemological sense" (Lycan 1988, p. 166). I conclude, therefore, that, as far as epistemic justification of (DC) is concerned, pragmatic considerations fail to lend it any support. Let us then turn to non-pragmatic defenses of (DC).

One such argument for (DC) has been offered by Sklar. He bases his defense on a model of epistemic justification he calls the "local theory of justification" according to which all epistemic justification is relative to a body of an assumed, unchallenged background belief. He thinks this precludes foundationalism with its postulated ultimate beliefs that require no reference to other beliefs for their justification because there cannot be any global justification of our beliefs taken "all at once"—I think Sklar's reasons here trade on the ambiguity between "being justified" in holding a set of beliefs and the "activity of justifying" those beliefs, but we can safely ignore this point for our purposes here. The local theory of justification, however, raises the specter of a problem that is usually associated with coherence theories of justification: There can be incompatible total belief structures all equally rational from the point of view of local justification. To thwart such a possibility, Sklar invokes (DC) which requires us to stick with what we have despite becoming aware of competing alternatives (in this case total belief structures). As Sklar himself points out, this argument is of a transcendental type seeking to show that "without conservatism there could be no rational belief at all."

Sklar's argument, however, is unsuccessful. For it has either to assume the version of conservatism (GC), that Sklar himself rejects, or else let the local theory of justification collapse into the (holistic) coherence theory of justification. Either way, it fails to establish (DC). Consider the first horn of the dilemma. According to the local theory of justification, "we justify the beliefs we take to be in need of justification 'one at a time' using all the resources of our unchallenged background beliefs in the process." But this immediately gives rise to the following problem. These background beliefs must themselves have some epistemic worth in order to justify the target belief, and the question is how they acquire their positive epistemic status. With the rejection of foundationalism, these beliefs cannot be the basic beliefs of the foundationalist. One way of getting round this problem is to invoke the generation version of conservatism (GC) according to which beliefs acquire positive epistemic status merely in virtue of being believed in so far as there is no good reason against them. And this is roughly how Sklar justifies the use of background beliefs: "We are warranted in using them to decide upon the acceptance and rejection of new hypotheses only because their own status is at the time not under scrutiny or challenge" (Sklar 1975, p. 398).

To avoid this horn of the dilemma, Sklar might choose to say that the background beliefs acquire their epistemic status just like the rest of the members of the agent's corpus of belief, namely, by belonging to a coherent belief system. Opting for this alternative, however, makes the local theory of justification collapse into a (holistic) coherence theory of justification according to which beliefs acquire their justification in virtue of belonging to a coherent belief system. And it is no wonder that Sklar finds himself compelled to tackle the alternative coherent systems objection that is usually raised in the context of coherence theories of justification. But by taking this route, Sklar's argument is stripped of its transcendental character, thus, failing to establish (DC). For now, the invoking of (DC) is not the only way of retorting to the alternative systems objection as there are a number of coherentist responses available to such challenges. Let us now turn to another variety of conservatism, namely, what I have called, "perseverance conservatism" (PC).

8.3   Perseverance conservatism

According to (PC) one is justified to continue to hold a belief as long as there are no good reasons against it. (PC) is most explicitly defended by Harman (1986). He considers it in the context of his theory of reasoned belief revision, and his guiding light in the course of his discussion is the phenomenon that may be called "lost justification." The idea is that people do not usually keep track of the justification relations among their beliefs. It so happens that many of an agent's beliefs are such that although they were initially based on adequate evidence, and, thus, justified, the agent subsequently forgets what that evidence was. We have all had experiences in which we justifiably form a belief about something on the authority of some source even though we no longer remember the source despite having retained the belief. This failure to keep track of one's justifications is thought to be a natural consequence of the limitations of our memories and, in general, our brain. There is a limit to the set of things one can store or retrieve. This cognitive failing seems to explain the phenomenon that cognitive psychologists call "belief perseverance in the face of evidential discrediting." Well-documented experiments have shown that people tend to retain many of their beliefs despite having been informed of the inadequacy of their original evidential source. The reason for the perseverance is said to be the fact that they no longer remember what the evidential source of their belief was, that the discredited evidence was the reason that prompted the belief in them in the first place.

Harman claims that the fact that people fail to keep track of the justifications of their beliefs (i.e., the phenomenon of lost justification) directly impinges on our arbitration between two main competing theories of belief revision, namely, the foundations theory and the coherence theory, thus, allowing us to determine the viability of epistemic conservatism. According to the foundations theory one is justified in continuing to believe a proposition if one has a special reason to continue to hold that belief, while on the coherence theory one is so justified in the absence of any special reason to change it. It is clear that on the foundations theory one ought to keep track of one's original reasons for one's beliefs if one is to be justified in them, whereas no such requirement is needed in the case of the coherence theory. It seems that the foundations theory is normatively implausible because, given the phenomenon of lost justification, it would imply that people are unjustified in almost all their beliefs. Harman concludes that it is the coherence theory that is normatively correct. He identifies the normative elements of the foundations and coherence theories, respectively, in terms of the following principles (Harman 1986, p. 39).

Principle of Positive Undermining (PPU)	One should stop believing p whenever one positively believes one's reasons for believing p are no good.

Principle of Negative Undermining (PNU)	One should stop believing p whenever one does not associate one's belief in p with an adequate justification.

As was pointed out, given the phenomenon of lost justification, Harman argues that it is (PPU) rather than (PNU) that is correct. Harman further points out that this result supports epistemic conservatism because, unlike the foundations theory, the coherence theory is a conservative principle, for it requires change in one's belief system only if there is a special reason to do so. ((PPU) is in fact what we have called "perseverance conservatism" (PC).)

I shall now turn to the question whether Harman's argument succeeds in showing that it is (PPU) that is the correct normative principle of belief revision, or, to put it differently, whether it commits us to epistemic conservatism as he claims. The first thing to find out is which version of conservatism is purportedly supported by Harman's argument from lost justification. Harman himself is not quite clear what kind of conservative principle he has in mind. He initially construes conservatism as the view that "a proposition can acquire justification simply by being believed" (Harman 1986, p. 30). This shows that it is (GC) that he has in mind. Later on, however, he offers a different formulation of the thesis. According to the principle of conservatism, he says, "one is justified in continuing fully to accept [believe] something in the absence of a special reason not to" (Harman 1986, p. 46). This is more or less equivalent to (PPU) which we have called the "perseverance conservatism." In fact Harman's latter construal of epistemic conservatism turns out to be identical to another formulation of (PPU) that he offers in a later part of his book: "[A] principle of positive undermining ... takes any current belief to be justified as long as there is no special reason to give it up" (Harman 1986, p. 117).

So, as far as exegetical considerations are concerned, the type of conservative principle that Harman seems to associate with his favored theory of belief revision is, despite occasional lapses, (PC) (i.e., (PPU)). In fact it is easy to see that (GC) is inconsistent with the considerations he adduces to support the coherence theory of belief revision. Why? According to (GC) mere believing of a proposition renders it justified. Now, if the bare fact of holding a belief were to constitute a source of justification for that belief, then there would be no room for the phenomenon of lost justification. For as long as an agent holds a belief, that belief remains justified. There would be no way the agent could lose track of the justification of her belief as long as mere believing is allowed to constitute the source of the justification of that belief. So, consonant with exegetical considerations, (GC) cannot be what Harman's argument from lost justification seeks to establish. Let us now see how the argument fares vis-à-vis the principle of (PC). To answer this question, consider the following concrete example (provided by Christensen).

Suppose I currently believe that the population of India is greater than that of the US, remembering to have learnt it from some source though I no longer recall what it was. According to (PC), I am justified in continuing to believe this proposition in the absence of undermining evidence. David Christensen has argued that one can explain the reasonableness of maintaining this belief without invoking epistemic conservatism. To explain, he gives a somewhat similar example where an appeal to conservatism is intuitively unattractive. Suppose I flip a coin which lands out of my sight. Without going over to look, I decide that it has landed "tails" up. Intuitively speaking, the fact that I now believe the coin has landed "tails" up does not justify me in maintaining my belief that it has landed tails up. What, then, is the difference between these two cases? According to Christensen, "[i]n both cases, I have a belief for which I am unable to cite any grounds. ... Yet in one case, maintaining the belief seems quite reasonable; while in the other, ... unreasonable" (Christensen 1994, p. 74). The difference, he says, can be accounted for in a way that also shows why the invoking of conservatism is not needed in the India case. The idea is that in the case of my belief about the population of India, I have some other beliefs to persuade me that the belief in question is accurate despite my forgetting its original evidential source. These beliefs include, among others, the belief that I initially formed my belief about the population of India on the basis of some reliable source, that, despite India being a common topic of family conversation, I have not yet encountered contradictory evidence, and so on. These background beliefs constitute the reason for maintaining my belief about India's relative population size. But, says Christensen, these are precisely the kind of beliefs that are absent in the coin case which explain why I am not justified in continuing to believe that the coin has landed "tails" up.

However, Christensen's argument fails on several counts. To begin with, his argument is actually targeted at the generation version of conservatism as is made clear by the structure of his coin example and his query whether, in that case, mere believing is sufficient for the justification of the belief that the coin has landed "tails" up. But, as I have emphasized, it is (PC) that is the target of Harman's argument from lost justification. Second, the coin case is not really analogous to the India case. It is true, as Christensen says, that "in both cases, I have a belief for which I am unable to cite any grounds," but in the coin case this statement owes its truth to the fact that there *are* no grounds to cite, not that there are grounds but I have now lost track of them. My belief that the coin has landed "tails" up, unlike my belief about the population of India, is completely ungrounded and this is something that I *know*.

Moreover, the India case is not really pertinent to Harman's argument, for it is not a case in which an agent loses track of the justifications of his belief by failing to recall its evidential ground. Given Christensen's way of setting up the example, I know *enough* about the evidential ground of my belief regarding India's population to render it justified. I know, among other things, that "I was once told by my mother, or a teacher, or some other reliable source, and I (quite rationally) accepted the source's word for it" (Christensen 1994, p. 74). What seems to be lacking, then, is just my knowledge of who told me this, my mother, John, or Jane. But surely the name or identity of my source would be irrelevant to the justification of the belief in question. The belief was not, say, that "My mother told me that India is more populous than the US" so that the case described would count as one where justification is lost. Rather, the belief in question is about the relative size of India's population, and what we know about its origin is quite sufficient to render it justified. So this is not a genuine case where one's justification for a belief is lost. For the example to count as pertinent to Harman's argument, it is essential that the original evidential source be genuinely lost. Suppose, a few years ago, I read in *The Guardian* that India is more populous than the US. I then justifiably formed a belief about India's population. Suppose I still retain the belief but no longer recall the original evidential source. Nevertheless, it is still justified because it was acquired in an epistemically proper manner, and that is exactly what (PC) maintains.[2]

To provide further support for the above contention, recall that Harman uses the fact of losing track of one's justification to explain the "phenomenon of belief perseverance in the face of evidential debriefing" where, as studies seem to show, agents still hold on to their beliefs despite being told that their (original) evidential source was inauthentic: "They continue to believe things after the evidence for them has been discredited because they do not realize ... that the discredited evidence was the *sole* reason why they believe as they do. They do not see they would not have been justified in forming these beliefs in the absence of the now discredited evidence" (Harman 1986, p. 38). Now, surely, in

Christensen's example, if there were to be a debriefing, the agent would no longer persist in his belief about India's population. Once he is told that, for example, he got his belief from an unreliable source, then he would give the belief up. This further shows that Christensen's India example is not really pertinent to Harman's argument.

So we are still left with the question whether Harman's argument from lost justification shows that his brand of epistemic conservatism, that is, (PC), is normatively correct. One thing that Harman's argument effectively shows is that, given the phenomenon of lost justification, the foundations theory of belief revision is not normatively correct. It shows, in other words, that it is not the case that one should stop believing a proposition whenever one does not associate one's belief in that proposition with an adequate justification, that is, that (PNU) is false. But to show that (PNU) is false is not, ipso facto, to show that (PPU)— that is, (PC)—is true. In fact, (PPU) seems also to be undermined by the phenomenon of lost justification. According to (PPU), one should stop believing a proposition whenever one positively believes *one's reasons* for believing that proposition are no good. But this requires, at least, that one should be able to recall one's reasons for a belief, something which seems to be at odds with the phenomenon of lost justification. However, as I noted, Harman is not quite consistent when formulating (PPU) or his considered version of the conservative thesis. Sometimes, he formulates it in a way that is no longer susceptible to the above problem as when he says that "according to the principle of positive undermining, one is justified in continuing to believe a proposition as long as there is no special reason to give it up." Is this modest version of (PC) plausible?

To answer this question, let us recall that Harman's perseverance brand of conservatism concerns cases where an agent is initially justified in believing a proposition but later loses track of his reasons. It is necessary that the agent be initially justified in his belief, for otherwise one could hardly make sense of him losing track of the *justification* of that belief. Thus, assuming that people generally fail to keep track of the justifications of their beliefs, it would be reasonable to continue to hold them provided there is no undermining evidence. So this version of (PC) is plausible, but it is questionable whether it really deserves to be seen as canon of rationality (in virtue of being a conservative principle) as it seems that one may explain its plausibility by invoking certain innocuous assumptions about the concept of epistemic justification.

To see this, we may begin by assuming that "being justified" is an objective property of a belief which, as we noted, supervenes on certain non-epistemic (but equally objective) properties of that belief (e.g., being adequately grounded, being reliably produced, etc). We may also distinguish between "being justified" in holding a belief and the "activity of justifying" that belief, assuming that one can be justified in believing a proposition without being able to show that one is so justified, just as one can be said to have a moral virtue without being able to show that one is in possession of that virtue (Alston 1989). In the light of these assumptions, it would be plausible to maintain that if an agent is initially justified in holding a belief but later loses track of her reasons, the belief in question remains justified, or, to put it differently, she remains justified in holding that belief (provided, of course, that the justification in question is not undermined by her cognitive state at any time[3]). The agent's losing track of the grounds of her belief does not affect the fact that the belief was initially prompted by adequate justification-conferring grounds and, thus, came to instantiate or possess the property of justification. What it *does* affect, however, is that, under the new circumstances, the agent is no longer able to *show* that she is justified in holding the belief in question, but, as was emphasized, performing the latter task is not a necessary condition of the agent's being justified in holding that belief. We can thus view our modest version of (PC) as being underpinned by certain plausible assumptions regarding the concept of justification rather than drawing on some general idea of epistemic conservatism. Let us now turn to our third and final version of epistemic conservatism.

8.4   Generation conservatism

While the two varieties of conservatism we have considered so far are concerned with the justificatory status of a belief *after* its conception and acquiring positive epistemic value, (GC), as the name implies, is concerned with the *initial* stage of a belief-forming process where the produced belief comes to acquire its epistemic worth. In this sense (GC) is the most fundamental type of epistemic conservatism. In its most widely used formulation, it says that a proposition acquires positive epistemic status simply by being believed by an agent. So, if true, (GC) would prove to be an effective tool in combating skepticism. But, as we have seen, (GC) has also been regarded as the most controversial version of epistemic conservatism, even by those who are favorably disposed toward other varieties of the conservative thesis.

Despite its controversial character, however, a number of theorists have defended some version of (GC). Lycan, for example, has advocated a version of (GC), which he calls the "Principle of Credulity," according to which one should "accept at outset each of those things that seem to be true" (Lycan 1988, p. 165). Another version has been endorsed by Chisholm who proposes it as an assumption that has to be made if one is to construct a viable foundationalist theory. Chisholm's principle seems to be the most promising version of generation of conservatism as it is intended to avoid the over-permissive character of the original formulation, and will thus be, for the most part, the focus of my attention in this section. As we have mentioned repeatedly, part of theorists' ill-disposition toward (GC) is the ease with which it allows any belief to pass as rational. In order to avoid this consequence, Chisholm qualifies (GC) by requiring that the mere believing of a proposition endows it only with some presumption of rationality: Anything we find ourselves believing may be said to have some presumption in its favor (*provided* it is not explicitly contradicted by the set of other things that we believe). On Chisholm's construal, (GC) occupies the lowest epistemic level in the hierarchy of justification; " 'Certainty' [constitutes] the highest degree of epistemic justification and 'having some presumption in its favor' the lowest" (Chisholm 1980, p. 547). Chisholm's characterization of "reasonability" in terms of the "general requirement to try to have the largest possible set of logically independent beliefs which is such that the true beliefs outnumber the false beliefs" is precisely how "justification" is generally understood in terms of the aim of maximizing true beliefs in one's belief system (Chisholm 1980, p. 546).

I think, however, that Chisholm's principle should be qualified along one further dimension in order to provide a tighter safeguard against the problem of over-permissiveness. (GC) tended to make the justification of a belief independent of the fact that beliefs are responsive to the cognizer's environment and the world in general. This would then allow any belief that a cognizer happens to hold (irrespective of how it is acquired) as possessing some rationality. Consequently, we may qualify (GC) along the following lines: Any proposition an agent comes to believe as a response to his (relevant) environment has some presumption of rationality (provided it does not explicitly contradict the rest of what he believes). But even this version of (GC) is far from being ideally clear as it fails to provide us with an account of the boundaries of the notion of rationality it involves. So the thesis needs some filling out. However, before attending to this task, I wish to examine some objections of Foley's which are intended to demonstrate that even this modest version of (GC) is too strong (Foley 1982, 1987).

Foley's general strategy is to propose certain test cases through which he hopes to highlight some of the implausible consequences of

Chisholm's version of (GC). As an example, he considers a case where an agent *S* comes to believe a proposition *h* (not explicitly contradicted by the set of his beliefs) whereas, given his circumstances, it is more reasonable for him to believe its negation (~*h*). According to Foley such cases are surely possible though they are ruled out by Chisholm's conservative principle which he describes in the following terms: "[I]f *S* believes *h* and *h* is not explicitly contradicted by anything else *S* believes, then proposition *h* ... is a proposition which is more reasonable for *S* to believe than to disbelieve" (Foley 1982, p. 173). But this objection is not convincing. First a dialectical point. Foley's example need not be taken as discrediting Chisholm's principle. For we can consider the principle, as described by Foley, as a norm of reasoning and belief formation (a canon of rationality), and regard the agent's knowledge of such norms as constituting his reasoning competence. We can then make a distinction between performance error and competence error, that is, between mere mistakes or lapses and systematic violations of the norms in question. Nothing in what Foley says shows that the type of case he mentions is a systematic and persistent phenomenon (he describes it as a "possible situation"). We may then say that such divergences from the norm are performance error, and not really indicative of the agent's reasoning competence failing to match those norms. Of course this is a large task, but the point is that, even if one concedes the coherence of Foley's cases, there are ways of redescribing them that may leave the coherence of the corresponding norms intact.

Moreover, one may ask, in Foley's example, what makes ~*h* more reasonable for *S* to believe than *h*. This might be the case because ~*h* is better supported by *S*'s total evidence, but then we are assuming that *S* has in his possession some independent evidence which supports ~*h* rather than *h*. If so, then there would be no need to apply Chisholm's principle for it is a principle that concerns cases where an agent's justification in believing a proposition has its source in the bare fact of its being believed by that agent. If, on the other hand, we are not assuming that *S* has independent evidence that favors ~*h*, then, on pain of begging the question against Chisholm, it is not clear how ~*h* is more reasonable for *S* to believe than *h*. This is a charge that Foley himself recognizes might threaten his arguments: "Constructing [those] counterexamples ... does not amount to constructing a non-question begging argument against conservative positions" (Foley 1982, p. 179). These considerations are also pertinent to Foley's other counterexamples. Given the basic nature of the principle of (GC), the most promising procedure for its evaluation is, I think, to try to draw the contours of the notion of rationality it involves, for it is only then that one would be able to judge whether it really lives up to the expectations that a principle of conservatism, as a canon of rationality, generates. Here is how I propose to do this.

It seems to me that the following considerations, involving Davidson's principle of charity, can be used to lend some support to Chisholm's principle, and concurrently reveal its epistemic potentials through giving content to the notion of rationality it aspires to invoke. We may recall from our discussion in Chapter 7 that a theory of meaning, on Davidson's account, is a Tarski-style truth theory that for each object language sentence (s) gives a metalanguage sentence (p) which is true if and only if that object language sentence is true. Such *T*-sentences provide the truth conditions (meaning) of the object language sentence. Thus when an interpreter finds a sentence of the speaker which the speaker assents to regularly under conditions he (the interpreter) recognizes, he takes those conditions to be the truth conditions of the speaker's sentence. But, as we saw, this is, by no means, a straightforward feat. Because of the interdependence of belief and meaning, the interpreter has to assume that the speaker perceives his environment roughly as he does and, consequently, comes to form similar beliefs. This is what grounds the necessity of the principle of charity in getting the process of interpretation going. Accordingly, the principle of charity requires the maximization of truth by the *interpreter's own lights*. It requires, in other words, the interpreter to maximize agreement between himself and the speaker by assigning to him the same type of beliefs as his.

Now, if belief ascription is constrained by the principle of charity, then this goes some way toward supporting our qualified version of (GC). For, as was emphasized, the process of charitable belief ascription is characterized by the aim of maximizing truth and minimizing falsity in the speaker's belief system, which is, as we have seen, how epistemic justification is generally characterized, namely, in terms of the aim of the maximization of truth and minimization of falsity in an agent's body of belief. So once belief ascription is seen as constrained by the principle of charity, this would automatically provide some "presumption of rationality" for the ascribed belief which is precisely what (GC) claims. Note that the distinction between the belief ascriber and the believer is not really epistemically significant in the context of our discussion for, as noted before, charity begins at home. The interpreter's beliefs are as much subject to the constraint of charity as are the beliefs of the interpretee.

Now, to what extent are the ascribed beliefs rational, or, to put it differently, what notion of rationality is at work in the case of belief ascription to a speaker? I said that the charity constraint on belief ascription provides the belief in question with some "presumption of rationality." The use of the quoted phrase was deliberate, as I wanted to use the very term that had appeared in Chisholm's formulation of (GC). But, given the mechanism of the interpretive process, we can now be more precise about its content and import. We are now familiar with the fact that, initial impressions notwithstanding, the principle of charity is not an epistemically potent thesis for all that it requires is maximization (minimization) of agreement (disagreement) between the interpreter and the speaker. The ensuing agreement, at best, ensures that the beliefs of the interpreter and speaker form a coherent set without guaranteeing their truth since, for all we know, the interpreter's beliefs might be mistaken and ill-formed.

So, in a sense, in the course of the interpretive process we do not seem to be leaving the web of belief. Of course, these beliefs *might* be true but all that the argument from interpretation guarantees is coherence, and coherence is not, for familiar reasons, necessarily conducive to truth. (As noted before, it is for this reason that Davidson appends the argument from charity with two loosely related strategies, namely, the invoking of the idea of an omniscient interpreter and a particular brand of externalism about the nature of belief to give the argument some epistemic bite.) All that can be deduced from these considerations is that the kind of rationality that results from the interpretive process is rationality-from-the-point-of-view-of-the-agent alone (taking the interpreter and the interpretee to be one and the same person), a conception of rationality that takes it to be exclusively a function of how things appear from an agent's perspective. We have already ruled out such accounts on the ground of failing to do justice to the truth-conducive character of epistemic justification (see our discussion of Foley in Chapter 1). This is consonant with Chisholm's claim that his generation principle occupies the lowest level in the hierarchy of justification. The point I wish to make is only that if we take the charity constraint on belief ascription to underwrite the thesis of (GC), then the epistemic limitations of the principle of charity will equally determine the epistemic strength of the conservative thesis itself in drawing the boundaries of the notion of rationality it involves.

In the light of the preceding remarks, it would be safe to say that to the extent the thesis of (GC) is plausible, it is of limited (anti-skeptical) potential. This is also true of Lycan's version of (GC), namely, the principle of credulity, according to which the seeming plausibility (truth) of beliefs is sufficient for their acceptance. This principle renders, what Lycan calls, "spontaneous beliefs" (i.e., beliefs not inferred from other beliefs but produced by such sources as perception, memory, etc.) prima facie justified (Lycan 1988, ch. 8). This is an interesting and substantial epistemic principle. But just when the conservative thesis begins to look interesting, Lycan weakens it to make it plausible. He realizes that his principle, indiscriminately, warrants both, what he calls, "lovable" as well as "wild" spontaneous beliefs with the former category involving perceptual, memory beliefs, and the like, while the latter category is supposed to include religious, superstitious beliefs, and the like. To exclude wild spontaneous beliefs, he imposes a number of constraints on his principle of credulity: logical consistency and consistency with previously justified explanatory beliefs. But he also requires that our total body of beliefs and theories be able to provide an explanation of how the spontaneous belief in question was produced in us.

Although the above-mentioned constraints might be able to exempt wild spontaneous beliefs from the reach of the principle of credulity, the resulting conservative principle faces, at least, two problems. First there is the problem whether these constraints can be satisfied even in the case of the so-called "lovable" spontaneous beliefs. Consider the first two consistency constraints. Lycan is not ideally clear about their import. He seems to require that we should be able to determine whether such beliefs are consistent with other spontaneous beliefs as well as with all "previously justified beliefs or with explanatory beliefs conjoined with other spontaneous beliefs" (Lycan 1988, p. 167). But given the size of these background beliefs and in view of our so-called "finitary predicament"—limitations of our cognitive resources—this is a rather daunting task to perform (Cherniak 1986). And in any case, the consistency of an agent's set of beliefs may not be accessible to that agent even on careful reflection (recall, as an example, Frege's acceptance of the axioms of the Basic Laws).

Second, it is not quite clear whether Lycan's third "explanatory" constraint is really able to rule out, what he regards as, "wild" sponta-neous beliefs. For consider someone who claims to have received direct communications from heaven. Surely, he does possess, on the basis of his total body of beliefs, an explanation of how the spiritual beliefs were produced in him. Indeed, Lycan (1988) goes on to admit that "[t]here are many interesting border line cases here" (p. 169), and he includes logical intuitions and religious beliefs among them. This further erodes the value of his conservative principle as a substantive canon of ration-ality (at least, by his lights). Moreover, the imposition of Lycan's third constraint runs the risk of reducing his conservative norm to a variant of the more familiar standard of rationality, namely, the reliability norm.

Given a spontaneous belief, he requires that our "total body of beliefs and theories yield an idea of how that spontaneous belief was produced in us—perhaps even a mechanical explanation of how it was. Finally suppose that according to this idea or explanation, the mechanism that produces the belief was (as we say) a reliable one, in good working order. Then, I submit, our spontaneous beliefs are fully justified" (Lycan 1988, p. 168). Although he says he does not require the believer to have a full knowledge of "the reliable mechanism," he maintains that the agent should "be aware of the source of the belief and recognize that the source is a generally trustworthy one" (Lycan 1988, p. 169). But now his principle of credulity seems too close to a version of the reliability account to count as an independently legitimate and substantially conservative thesis.[4]

As our investigation shows certain plausible versions of (PC) and (GC) survive critical scrutiny. However they are epistemically very modest (in the sense of having anti-skeptical potentials), thus, falling short of the aspirations of the thesis of epistemic conservatism as a substantive canon of rationality. To conclude, to the extent that principles of conservatism are epistemically promising, they are not plausible. To the extent that they are plausible, they fail to function as effective means in combating skepticism.

9
Argument from Inference to the Best Explanation (IBE)

We often form our beliefs against the background of a set of alternatives all of which lay some claim to explaining the phenomena we are confronted with. We tend to believe those hypotheses that are, in certain respects, superior to the other members of the set. While this seems to be a rather fair description of the mechanism of belief formation in areas such as commonsense, science, and philosophy, it is also the source of a great many puzzles. The main question that it raises concerns the nature of the inferential mechanism that is thought to underlie these cases of belief formation. Recent tradition has identified this mode of inference as "abduction" or "inference to the best explanation" (IBE). The idea being that when faced with a set of competing hypotheses all covering the data (evidence), the hypothesis that best explains it is the one more likely to be true.

The defenders of IBE take it to be a fundamental form of inference, and some, like Harman, have even gone as far as claiming that all inductive inference is really just IBE (Harman 1965). That IBE has informed the views of many theorists in areas as diverse as metaphysics, epistemology, science, and so on, is no exaggeration. Chomsky's poverty of stimulus argument for the innateness of knowledge of grammar as well as Quine's indispensability argument for mathematical Platonism both involve the use of IBE (Field 1989). So does Armstrong's defense of universals (Armstrong 1978). The problem of (commonsense) realism is often handled by appealing to IBE, and the existence of God is inferred to as the best explanation of the existence and order of the universe. Within epistemology IBE has been put to a variety of uses. BonJour, for example, appeals to IBE to show that his coherence theory of justification retains its link with truth (BonJour 1985). And while Haack (1991) and Moser (1991) have, in their own ways, made use of IBE to resolve the problem of nondoxastic justification, namely, the problem of showing how sensory experiences, lacking propositional content, can confer justification on beliefs they give rise to, Lycan (1988) goes further and claims that all justified reasoning is fundamentally explanatory reasoning. In science, the main reason for postulating theoretical entities is often thought to be that they are the best explanation of the observable phenomena while philosophers of science defend scientific realism on the ground that it is the best explanation of the instrumental reliability of science (Boyd 1983).

Despite its prevalent application, however, IBE has not been without its critics. It has especially come under fire from van Fraassen (1980), Fine (1984), Cartwright (1983), and Railton (1989), to mention but a few names. Although these theorists formulate their attack on IBE against the background of different philosophical persuasions, they are all united in calling into question the alleged truth-conducive character of IBE, that is, its legitimacy as a rule of inference. This question actually splits into two questions. (1) What makes one explanation a *better* explanation than another? This is a request to identify the canons of theory choice. (2) Why does a theory's possessing these explanatory virtues make it more likely to be true? Answers to question (1) have often been formulated in terms of such largely unanalyzed notions as simplicity, parsimony, non-ad hocness, and the like, prompting theorists to either forgo their truth-conduciveness by declaring IBE a purely methodological principle, or to resort to such equally unclear metaphysical assumptions as the simplicity and uniformity of nature.

In this chapter, I shall first deal with the problem of the nature of explanatory virtues, and then proceed to distinguish between the legitimacy and effectiveness of IBE. It will be argued that while IBE is a legitimate form of inference, its effectiveness depends on whether the background theory of knowledge which it assumes can discharge its function. Let us then begin by addressing the question of the nature of explanatory virtues. I approach this question however via an extensive discussion of one of the most appealing applications of IBE, namely, in inferring the existence of the physical world as the best explanation of our sensory experiences. This is, in fact, directly related to our discussion of the Cartesian skeptical argument for, if valid, its application would undermine the second premise of the argument and, thus, undermine its skeptical import. Moreover, studying IBE in such an epistemically barren context will enable us to have a better grasp of its possible limitations as a rule of inference, and its epistemological significance in general.

9.1   IBE and commonsense realism

IBE has widely been used to defuse skepticism about the external world by, among others, Russell, Slote, Bennett, Mackie, and, more recently, by Alan Goldman, Vogel, BonJour, Aune, and Lycan. The general idea is as follows. The patterns of our sensory experiences exhibit a remarkable degree of constancy and coherence. For example, when I enter my room I am confronted with a visual experience of seeing a desk before me, followed by other visual and tactile impressions as I move around the room. These impressions disappear and reappear depending on how I am located vis-à-vis the objects in the room. Even if these regularities fall short of having a lawlike character, they are structured enough to require an explanation. The standard explanation is that they are actually produced by an independently existing world of objects that is stable enough to produce them. It is at this point that the skeptic enters the debate by highlighting some of the alternative hypotheses that seem equally to account for the course of our sensory experience.

The most widely discussed alternatives, as we have seen, are those of the Cartesian demon hypothesis, and, its hi-tech version, the brain in a vat hypothesis. According to these hypotheses, there is no real world of familiar objects, but we are deceived into thinking that there is such a world by an evil demon or a superscientist who induces in us the same patterns of sensory experience that would be produced were there such a world. To show that the standard explanation is true, the realist appeals to IBE claiming that since the standard account is a better explanation than its competitors, it is more likely to be true. Attempts to defend the standard explanation can be broadly divided into two groups. The first group seeks to establish the superiority of the standard explanation by showing that it best satisfies the usual criteria of theory choice, while assuming that the explanatory advantages are truth-conducive. The second group tries to achieve the same thing in the course of showing that IBE is a legitimate form of inference.[1] In this section I try to show that none of these attempts succeed and that their failure is symptomatic of a more serious problem. A more in-depth analysis of IBE's ability to support the standard account (or other alternatives) shall be attempted later once we get a grip on its structure.

Starting with the first group, some of its representatives have ruled out the skeptical hypotheses on the ground that they are impoverished in richness of detail when compared with the standard account. Alan Goldman, for example, has claimed that these explanations "leave further natural questions about the nature and motivations of the superbeings [of the skeptic's imagination] unanswerable" (Goldman 1988, p. 197). This remark can be taken in two ways. It is either a complaint about these explanations failing to provide us with reasons as to why such sequences of appearances are produced or it is a remark about their lack of originality. In either case, it is difficult to see how they bear on the issues in question. First, it is not clear why a coherent story cannot be told about the motivations lying behind the skeptical hypotheses. Furthermore, once the request for explanation is pushed further and further up (to ultimate grounds), it is not obvious that the standard account would do any better. The charge of derivativeness and lack of originality has also been made by Aune who gives his use of IBE a Bayesian slant (Aune 1991, p. 200). What it amounts to is that the skeptical explanations are parasitic upon the standard explanation. We can identify their predictions only by reference to the predictions that would be made on the basis of the standard hypothesis. But as Alston correctly points out, it may well be true that *we* need the standard hypothesis to work out the patterns of sensory experiences that are supposed to be induced in us in the skeptical scenarios, but there is no reason why the demon or the superscientist should be saddled with the same restrictions (Alston 1993a, p. 79).

The most commonly cited ground for preferring the standard explanation is, however, its alleged simplicity or economy. Yet, it has turned out to be notoriously difficult to make these notions sufficiently precise. Simplicity is often understood in terms of the number of entities, or, rather, the number of different kind of entities that the explanatory hypotheses postulate. But it is not evident that the standard account would fare better in this regard. Indeed, the skeptical alternatives seem to be committed to the existence of only a few objects or kinds of objects. A more recent attempt at analyzing the notion of simplicity along a more acceptable line is that of Vogel (1993). According to Vogel a skeptical hypothesis has to satisfy a number of constraints to be able to match the standard account in explanatory adequacy. It should both invoke items corresponding to the elements of the standard hypothesis, and should posit, as holding of these items, a pattern of properties, relations and explanatory generalizations matching those of the standard account. Having satisfied these constraints, the resulting hypothesis would then have an explanatory structure completely isomorphic to that of the standard hypothesis.

As an illustration, Vogel picks up the brain in a vat hypothesis to show that, by failing to satisfy some of these constraints, it is inferior to the standard hypothesis on simplicity grounds. He specifically considers spatial properties whose ascription to physical objects does explanatory work within the standard account. Having ascribed locations to objects, we discover the principle that no two objects can be at the same place and at the same time. Since the vat hypothesis is supposed to be isomorphic to the standard account by mimicking its explanatory structure, it should equally ascribe different pseudo-locations to things it posits (pieces of the computer disk storing the information about the object to be simulated). Now while this principle naturally follows from the nature of the objects posited in the standard account, the idea that within the vat hypothesis no two objects are to be assigned the same pseudo-locations requires some explanation, that is, some principle barring two objects having the same coordinates within their files. This, says Vogel, burdens the vat hypothesis with an extra empirical regularity to which no regularity in the standard hypothesis corresponds, thus, resulting in a loss of simplicity.

It is not however obvious that the postulation of such extra principles would disrupt the isomorphism between the explanatory structures of the two hypotheses. All it shows is that the set representing the explanatory structure of the standard hypothesis (containing as elements propositions about the identity of objects, their locations and explanatory generalizations) is only a subset of the set representing that of the vat hypothesis. But this does not undermine their isomorphism since we can generate an *infinite* number of truths about the objects within the standard hypothesis (say, about their relative distance from one another). This infinite set of truths must find an echo within the vat hypothesis regardless of whether or not extra empirical principles are required to explain them. Once the sets representing the explanatory structures are infinite, the fact that one is a subset of the other does not upset their isomorphism, and, so long as simplicity is construed in terms of the isomorphism of explanatory structures, the standard hypothesis cannot be said to be superior over the skeptical one on the ground of simplicity.

The prospect for choosing between the competing explanations of our sensory experience on the basis of explanatory virtues, thus, seems poor. Even if one could detect some genuine differences among them, it would simply not be obvious how this is going to bear on the problem of their choice when these differences are considered in isolation from their purported truth-conducive character. One philosopher who conducts his explanationist defense of the standard hypothesis against the background of a detailed discussion of the legitimacy of IBE is William Lycan (1988). His defense of commonsense realism does not add anything to the previous attempts and, in fact, his reasons for rejecting the skeptical hypotheses are no different from those advocated by Goldman and Aune. But if his argument for the legitimacy of IBE is sound, that would, at least, show that, by identifying some explanatory differences among alternative hypotheses, we would eventually be in a position to settle the realism issue. It seems to me, however, that this argument is seriously flawed for reasons that will shortly be adduced.

According to what Lycan calls "explanationism," it is the explanatory contribution of a belief that grounds its justification. He regards IBE, with its customary canons of theory choice (simplicity, etc.), as being the basic mode of inference that underlies this explanationist strategy. The first question that is taken up by Lycan concerns the alleged justification-conferring character of the explanatory virtues or, as he himself puts it, the "reason [we] have to think that these humble conventional virtues are really what control our intuitions about the justified-unjustified distinction" (Lycan 1988, p. 157). This is how he responds.

> Just as a logician starts with a set of intuitively valid inferences and a set of intuitively invalid ones, the epistemologist starts with a set of intuitively rational theory choices and a set of (actually or counter-factually) irrational ones ... If the explanatory virtues seem after exhaustive reflection to be what all justified theory choice has in common, that is as good evidence as one could have that they do in fact underlie all justified belief. (Lycan 1988, pp. 105–6)

To begin with, Lycan's analogy with inferential rules is not convincing. Lacking clear cut intuitions about valid rules of inference, we initially start with what we regard as plausible rules and accepted inferences. They are then brought into continual interaction with each other, modifying and reinforcing each other, until they reach a state of reflective equilibrium (Goodman 1973). This is not, of course, to suggest that this mechanism provides conclusive justification for our inferential rules. The point is, rather, that it is the lack of precise intuitions about the validity of rules and inferential practices that necessitates the reaching of an equilibrium position. But this is not the mechanism that Lycan suggests with regard to the justification of the customary canons of theory choice. And in any event, unlike the case of inferential rules, no consensus has so far been reached on how best to construe theory change, and scientific methodology in general. There have not only been significant differences in regard to principles that are supposed to govern the process of theory choice, the very rationality of this process has also been called into question.[2]

The main problem, however, is that Lycan's proposed explanation of the justification-conferring character of explanatory virtues is viciously circular. For if a hypothesis's being the best explanation of certain phenomena (by possessing the familiar explanatory virtues) is supposed to justify our belief in it, then the question of why these virtues are justification-conferring is just the question of IBE's legitimacy. Lycan's argument is that because all justified theory choice has these virtues in common, then that is a good evidence that they underlie all justified belief. But this is itself of the form of an IBE argument. It claims that explanatory virtues are justification-conferring because that is the best explanation of why all intuitively rational theory choice has these virtues in common.[3] Lycan's response, thus, presupposes the legitimacy of the very inference he seeks to establish.

Another question discussed by Lycan concerns the purported truth-conducive character of explanatory virtues, namely, "Why does a theory's being simple make it more likely to be true?" (Lycan 1988, p. 147). He has this to say in response.

> The immediate answer is that it does not, at least not in any straight-forward way ... Actually, I *reject* it as stated for two reasons. (1) ... appeal to simplicity is in fact a fundamental epistemic method ... no further question can arise regarding its "connection to truth" ... (2) For that matter, I do not in the first place accept the a priori assumption that epistemic justification must be a matter of quantitative relation to truth. (Lycan 1988, pp. 147–8)

This latter statement explains why the question of truth-conducive nature of explanatory virtues is different from the previous one which involved their justification-conferring character. The two questions would collapse into one another if we take justification to be essentially linked to truth, but, as the earlier quotation shows, Lycan does not. This creates some tensions within his explanationist account to which I shall now turn.

On Lycan's account, truth is an extrinsic or external feature of epistemic justification, for he goes on to say "In the beginning, 'rational' is a primitive term used to evaluate epistemic acts; particular principles are later seen to 'tend toward truth', because the beliefs they produce are rational—not the other way round" (Lycan 1988, p. 156). But now it looks as if, with these added qualifications about the role of truth, one could use his explanationist strategy to render truth an intrinsic feature of justification by setting up an argument analogous to the one he himself suggested to show that explanatory virtues are justification-conferring.

It would go like this. The satisfaction of the canons of theory-preference would issue in justified beliefs which are "later seen to tend toward truth." Since truth is what all justified beliefs have in common, then "that is as good evidence as one could have" that epistemic justification is essentially truth-linked. Moreover, with the concept of justification detached from truth and taken as a primitive, it is not clear how Lycan is able to identify the corpus of justified beliefs relative to which he could identify justification-conferring virtues.

Another point where Lycan's views on the nature of justification affect the conclusion he wishes to draw from the application of IBE is in his defense of commonsense realism. The reason for believing in the existence of the familiar objects, he says, is that this belief is entailed by the most plausible explanation of our sensory experience. But given the fact that, for Lycan, justification or rationality is not to be understood as "likely to yield truth," it is not clear how the explanationist strategy could yield a realist picture. For all that follows from his defense of realism is that it is more rational or justified to accept the standard hypothesis than the skeptical ones, in a sense of "justified" that has no clear connection to truth. He cannot therefore conclude that the standard hypothesis is *true* (or more likely to be true than its alternatives) which is what realism demands. Note that it is not open to Lycan to say that, like other cases of theory choice, the belief in the standard hypothesis is later seen to "tend toward truth," for at a level this basic there is simply no way one could test the theories for their truth. All competing hypotheses are equally compatible with our experience.[4]

In view of the earlier considerations, it is fair to conclude that the appeals to IBE in establishing commonsense realism have not been sufficiently convincing. Indeed, given the lack of any consensus on the nature and function of simplicity and other virtues, it would have been surprising that attempts to either exploit or justify them could have had any other outcome. This is actually indicative of a deeper problem. For what all these IBE arguments seem to have in common is that they conceive of explanatory virtues as some sort of abstract, structural, and global principles that guide our inductive practices regardless of their subject matter or context. This view of the matter has been forcefully challenged in some recent studies by Elliott Sober (Sober 1988, ch. 2, 1994). In the section that follows I shall summarize and elaborate on Sober's account, preparing the ground for an assessment of IBE's ability to justify commonsense realism and its epistemological significance in general.

9.2 Simplicity and parsimony: the structure of IBE

Approaches to the principles of simplicity and parsimony can be divided into two groups; those which view the use of simplicity and parsimony as resting on such metaphysical assumptions as nature's being simple, and those which take them as purely methodological principles. Both groups, however, regard the principles as being sufficiently abstract to guide our inductive practices in any field of inquiry. Hume's idea that our extrapolation from observed to unobserved cases requires the principle of the uniformity of nature can be seen as a precursor to the claims upheld by the first group. This approach has been subjected to severe criticisms by the representatives of the second group. They point out that the idea of nature's being simple and uniform is not only too vague and imprecise, it is also not even true that nature is uniform in all respects. We should rather regard simplicity as involving no assumptions at all about the way the world is, viewing it as a purely methodological principle guiding the way we allow observations to bear on our judgments about the plausibility of hypotheses.

While sympathizing with the methodological critique of the Humean approach to simplicity, Sober believes that Hume was right in thinking that some extra ingredient is needed to bring the observations to bear on hypotheses. Where he went wrong was when he thought that the missing link is one single uniformity principle. Sober's reason for denying that simplicity is a presuppositionless concept is founded on his views about the nature of confirmation. Following Good, and, *pace* Hempel, he takes confirmation to be a three-place relation between a hypothesis, observation, and a background theory. Whether an observation confirms, disconfirms, or is irrelevant to a hypothesis depends on what else one believes. A black raven, for example, could disconfirm "All ravens are black" given a suitable background theory. As he succinctly puts it: "Only in the context of a background theory do observations have evidential meaning" (Sober 1994, p. 171). The same is true of differential support: Observations support one hypothesis better than another only relative to a set of background assumptions. How are these remarks related to the question of the nature of simplicity? Simplicity has often been thought of as having an epistemological function, namely, taking us from observations to hypotheses. It is supposed to allow us to choose the "best" explanation among a set of competing hypotheses which all account for the relevant observations and data. Now, from what was said about the nature of confirmation, it follows that whenever simplicity performs this function, it actually embodies empirical assumptions about the world.

> Whenever observations are said to support a hypothesis, or are said to support one hypothesis better than another, there must be an empirical background theory that mediates this connection. It is important to see that this principle does not evaporate when a scientist cites simplicity as the ground for preferring one hypothesis over another in the light of the data. *Appeal to simplicity is a surrogate for stating an empirical background theory.* (Sober 1988, p. 64)

In order to be clear about the epistemic import of Sober's denial of the presuppositionless character of simplicity, it would be helpful to look at a recent interpretation of his view which seem to reduce it to a mere triviality. According to Day and Kincaid, Sober's remarks about simplicity highlight the contextual character of IBE arguments (Day and Kincaid 1994). But this feature, they argue, also holds of other forms of reasoning such as arguments from infinite regress. The mere presence of an infinite regress does not establish its conclusion. Some further assumptions are required to explain why that regress is not acceptable in a particular context. For example in "the first cause argument," the repeated application of the principle that every event has a cause that is itself another event generates an infinite regress. But whether this regress is sufficient to establish that there is a first cause depends entirely on how the notion of "causal connection" is understood: "Thus, as with simplicity, evaluating regress arguments requires looking case by case at the substantive assumptions that do the work" (Day and Kincaid 1994, p. 285).

But this grossly misrepresents Sober's contentions about the use of simplicity and parsimony. What the authors claim is the trivial point that whether the premises of an argument support its conclusion depends on how the concepts involved are intended to be used. Thus, whether an infinite regress of causes leads to a first cause depends on how the notion of "causal connection" is intended to be used in that particular argument. But, surely, the soundness of *any* argument depends on how the notions involved in its premises are used or understood by the proponents of that argument. For example, whether Quine's famous indeterminacy argument renders meaning indeterminate depends on, among other things, the plausibility of his (behavioristic) assumptions about the notion of meaning and semantic facts in general. In saying that the use of simplicity involves substantive background assumptions, Sober is not making the general claim that our use of this concept, like other concepts, is guided by *some* theory. For the way his opponents use this notion is equally informed by a theory, namely, that it is an abstract and presuppositionless concept. He is, rather, propounding a *specific* proposal saying that its use must be seen as "carry[ing] with it substantive implications about the way the world is" (Sober 1988, p. 65).

Moreover, the fact that conceptions of "causal connection" or "simplicity" vary from one representative user group to another, does not render regress or IBE arguments contextual, for any concept could be subject to a multitude of interpretations. What gives rise to the contextual character of IBE arguments, on Sober's account, is the fact that while the background empirical assumptions that the use of simplicity involves in one context might be justified, this may not be true of another set of assumptions that its use involves in another context (dealing with a different subject matter). Day and Kincaid seem to have confused the context-relativity of "simplicity" with the user-relativity of its conception. Sober's construal of the role of parsimony and simplicity may be compared with the functional analysis of mental concepts. Unlike Hume who identified simplicity with a single assumption underlying all inductive inferences (compare with type identity theories of mental states), he believes that simplicity is just a surrogate for stating a background theory that varies with context (compare with token identity theories). Yet what all these instances have in common is the function that use of simplicity plays in these contexts, namely, allowing observations to bear on competing hypotheses. Having obtained a clearer insight into the structure of IBE, let us now proceed with assessing its ability in grounding commonsense realism and its possible limitations.

9.3 IBE, realism, and the grades of epistemic involvement

Before enunciating my own appraisal of the problem, it would be helpful to consider Sober's views on this matter as it would indicate where I depart from him on the question of the epistemic significance of IBE. He introduces and defends a position he calls "Contrastive Empiricism" whose main difference with the previous forms of empiricism is that it is about problems, not propositions. While previous empiricisms sought to discriminate between statements involving observables and those involving unobservables and treat them differently, Contrastive Empiricism requires no such distinction. It denies that there is any significant epistemic difference between, say, "This is a black raven" and

"Space-time is curved," but retains an important empiricist element by denying that we can solve "discrimination *problems* in which experience makes no difference."

Consider, for example, the problems of discriminating between (H1) "All emeralds are green" and (H2) "All emeralds are green until the year [2005], but after that they turn blue" and between (H'1) "There is a printed page before me" and (H'2) "There is no printed page before me; rather, an evil demon deceives me into thinking that there is one there." According to Contrastive Empiricism, the second problem, unlike the first, is insoluble. Why? On a Bayesian approach the comparison between two hypotheses, both accounting for the same set of data, comes down in the end to comparing their likelihoods [Pr(O/Hi)], and their prior probabilities [Pr(Hi)]. In neither of these problems do the contrasted hypotheses differ in their likelihoods, but there is, according to Contrastive Empiricism, an important difference.

> [In the first problem] I may have an empirical theory about minerals (developed before I examined even one emerald) that tells me that emerald color is very probably stable. This theory allows me to assign (H1) a higher prior than (H2), [thus, providing a ground for preferring (H1)]. (Sober 1994, p. 129)

But why can we not equally appeal to some background assumption in the case of the second problem to assign a lower prior to the demon hypothesis? Indeed, that is exactly what BonJour does by making an assumption about the likelihood of the sort of desires that a demon can have, thus, assigning an extremely low prior probability to the demon hypothesis: "[A] demon is capable of having *any* set of desires and purposes, thus making the quite special set of desires and purposes which would lead him to produce a coherence-conducive set of observations ... unlikely" (BonJour 1985, p. 185). Sober does not elaborate on why we cannot appeal to such background assumptions to discriminate between (H'1) and (H'2). He is satisfied to say that "no defensible reason can be given for assigning empirically equivalent theories different priors" (Sober 1994, p. 129). Does this mean that BonJour's assumption about the nature of demon's desires is not a "defensible reason"? Well, that depends on what is meant by "defensible reason." Does it mean something that is not speculative? But then this should equally preclude the assumption about the stability of emerald color given the way it is said to have been conceived, namely, "before examining even one emerald." Does "defensible" mean "known to be true"? Of course the assumption about the nature of demon's desires is not known to be true, but neither is the assumption about emerald color.

The nearest we can get to a plausible interpretation of Sober's remark is that, unlike the assumption about emerald color, the one about the demon *cannot* be known to be true on the ground that it makes no difference to experience whatsoever. But to say this is to hark back to the old discredited concern with *propositions*, something the rejection of which was supposed to mark the departure of Contrastive Empiricism from its predecessors. Indeed, if that is what is supposed to differentiate between defensible and nondefensible theories, why not appeal to it in the first place to rule out the demon hypothesis (H'2) on the ground that it makes no difference to experience, and do away with the *problem* of contrasting competing hypotheses and all its Bayesian complications.

Here I depart from Sober in my assessment of the epistemological significance of IBE, while following him in seeing the use of simplicity and parsimony as involving background assumptions about a relevant subject matter. Unlike Sober, I do not think that it is the nature or status of these assumptions (discriminated, say, on verificationist grounds) that decides whether they can be used to ground our preferences. What decides the matter is whether we have the *right* to appeal to them given the kind of epistemic situation we find ourselves in. To put it differently, what sanctions the use of these assumptions has, rather, to do with, what we may call, the "grade of epistemic involvement" of our doxastic situation. It is the grade of epistemic involvement that decides the kind of assumptions that one is allowed to make use of in grounding one's preferences.

For example, if we are in a scientific context trying to adjudicate between competing hypotheses on ground of their simplicity, then our appeal to simplicity would involve certain empirical assumptions about the subject matter under discussion. Invoking such assumptions in this context would not be unjustified because such contexts do not generally impose strict epistemic constraints on what can be said to be known. They allow, in other words, a high degree of epistemic involvement. By contrast, certain contexts possess such a low degree of epistemic involvement that every assumption is automatically called into question, thus, shrinking the size of the allowable assumptions to a bare minimum. The context of establishing the standard hypothesis is precisely such a context. Here our predicament is precisely the Lockean one where we are barricaded behind the impenetrable wall of ideas having direct access only with the contents of our minds. At a level this basic, we are, on pain of begging the question, precluded from appealing to background assumptions about the subject matter in question (be it the external world, the demon or whatever). This is because, in such a context, *all* we are justified to appeal to are facts about our sensory experience on the basis of which we are supposed to infer to external facts, of some sort, to explain them. So if appeals to simplicity are to be seen as involving background assumptions about a particular subject matter, IBE cannot be put to use to ground our preference for the standard hypothesis (realism) or other competing explanations for that matter.[5] Having got some insight into the structure of IBE and its limitations as a rule of inference, we can finally embark on evaluating its epistemological significance, a task to which I shall now turn.

9.4   The epistemological significance of IBE

As we saw, anti-realists and those unsympathetic to realism (such as van Fraassen and Fine) have been, to varying degrees, skeptical of IBE's legitimacy. But this attitude is not confined to anti-realists. Philosophers of a generally realist persuasion like Cartwright, Railton, and Day and Kincaid have also been critical of the use of IBE in settling the disputes over scientific realism (see also Ben-Menahem 1990). It should, however, be noted that these attitudes are by no means uniform. Van Fraassen, for example, seems to accept the use of IBE when its conclusion does not postulate unobservables, while rejecting such inferences to theoretical conclusions. Cartwright endorses only abductive inferences to the most likely cause. Day and Kincaid adopt a qualified attitude but are keen to point out that IBE is more successful in, say, scientific contexts than in philosophical ones. How can we explain these ambivalent attitudes? My feeling is that both the defenders and critics of IBE are guilty of confusing the *legitimacy* of IBE with its *effectiveness*, the latter being the measure of its epistemological significance. Let me explain.

We have seen that the main reason that frustrated attempts seeking to establish the truth-conduciveness of explanatory virtues, and thus the legitimacy of IBE, was their mistake in regarding those virtues as some sort of abstract and presuppositionless concepts. However, once we note, *a la* Sober, that appeals to, say, simplicity are actually surrogates for stating a background empirical theory allowing observations to bear on hypotheses, the question of IBE's legitimacy is immediately resolved. For, being guided by a background theory, our grounds for choosing the best explanation would then be firmly anchored in truth. For instance, when we cite our reasons for choosing the hypothesis that the sun will rise tomorrow as the best explanation of our observations, our well-confirmed theory of planetary motion features prominently among them. Or, to give a more mundane example, imagine the following scenario. We see a person (S) entering a house, a knife in his hand and, after an hour, leaving with a suitcase and looking particularly nervous. Subsequently we find the stabbed body of the owner of the house and find out that her jewelry is missing. S's fingerprints are all over the place and a subsequent search of his room by the police recovers both the knife and the suitcase containing the jewelry. We naturally form the belief that S is the culprit. When asked why we find this the best explanation of our observations rather than, say, the hypothesis that the detectives fabricated the evidence in order to frame S, we appeal to our background empirical assumptions about the way thefts are usually committed, the reliability of circumstantial evidence, the unlikelihood of the police attempting to frame someone of no particular significance, and so on. Of course all these assumptions may further be challenged. The point, however, is that, being informed by empirical considerations, our canons of theory-preference evolve with the body of empirical knowledge turning IBE into a legitimate form of inference.

But being a legitimate form of inference is not the same thing as being an epistemically effective one. All we are entitled to draw from the preceding considerations is that the best explanation (properly understood) is more likely to be true. But "best" is a relative term indicating that the "best hypothesis" is usually identified against a range of alternatives. Let us consider the hypothesis p and define the "contrast class" (CC) as the class of situations that are necessarily eliminated if p is the case. (CC) would include both the mundane and esoteric alternatives to p as well as those designed specifically to be empirically equivalent to it. Faced with such a large class, our background theories and assumptions may fail to pick out the best hypothesis, thus, rendering IBE ineffective. IBE's effectiveness (*not* its legitimacy) therefore depends on the choice of a *proper* contrast class within which it can discharge its function. But how are we to identify this proper contrast class? IBE itself is impotent to do the identification for it can only operate on an already given contrast class. Here we need a substantive *theory of knowledge* to select the proper contrast class. So while IBE is a legitimate form of inference, its effectiveness depends on the sort of background theory of knowledge that can help it discharge its function. One such theory that might (temporarily) do the job and, as I shall suggest shortly, seems to be able to account for some of the conflicting attitudes toward IBE is the so-called relevant alternatives theory of knowledge (Dretske 1981). (To emphasize, I am not endorsing the relevant alternatives theory. I am rather using it as an illustration of how a background theory of knowledge can, in the contexts where IBE is applied, help it to discharge its function.)

According to the relevant alternatives theory not all members of (CC) are relevant to the issue of making knowledge-claims. To know that a hypothesis (p) is true, one need not rule out all the alternatives to p, but only those that are relevant. To paraphrase it in our current terminology; to know that p is true, by showing that it is the best explanation of our evidence, one need not contrast it against all the alternatives but only against those that are relevant. Once we identify this "relevance class" [(RC), a subset of (CC)], IBE can then be called upon to determine whether p is true by finding out if it better explains the evidence than the rest of the members of (RC). The crucial question that arises at this point concerns the identity of the factors that decide which alternatives should be included in (RC). This is, as we saw in Chapter 5, a big question for the relevant alternatives theory and one that has so far resisted a satisfactory resolution. As our aim here is mainly illustrative, I shall proceed by assuming an intuitive understanding of the pertinent notion of relevance. I have already commented on the failure of IBE to establish the commonsense realist thesis about the external world. The preceding suggestion as to how IBE actually functions supports this conclusion: The relevant alternatives theory, as we have seen, does not have the resources to show that such alternatives as the demon hypothesis are irrelevant in the context of the realism debate. Let us now see if our proposed mechanism can account for some of the ambivalent attitudes toward the effectiveness of IBE in less esoteric and more mundane contexts. Let us pick up some examples.

According to van Fraassen IBE is legitimate when its conclusion involves only observables, but when it says something about unobservables no conclusion about its truth value should be drawn. He gives an example of what he calls an "ordinary case" where IBE is legitimate: "I hear scratching in the wall, the patter of little feet at midnight, my cheese disappears—and I infer that a mouse has come to live with me ... Not merely that all the observable phenomena will be as if there is a mouse; but that there really is mouse" (van Fraassen 1980, pp. 19–20). Van Fraassen's decision to confine the use of IBE to observation contexts and, thereby, render its legitimacy context-relative, has struck many people as unprincipled and arbitrary.

How can we explain van Fraassen's differential attitude toward the legitimacy of IBE in observational and theoretical contexts? It seems to me that our distinction between the legitimacy and effectiveness of IBE can help explain his ambivalent position. It is not, *pace* van Fraassen, the legitimacy of IBE that varies with context but its *effectiveness*, and this is because what the background theory of knowledge delivers varies from context to context. In the example he gives, van Fraassen describes an "ordinary situation" where, according to the relevant alternatives theory, certain possibilities are irrelevant (e.g., an invisible Martian mimicking the behavior of a mouse, etc.) while others are relevant (the presence of a mouse, a cat, a rabbit, etc.).

This is because, under *ordinary* circumstances, some alternatives, like the Martian hypothesis, are, intuitively speaking, irrelevant. Having ruled out the disturbing hypotheses, an application of IBE (involving our well-confirmed background beliefs about the behavior of animals) among the members of the relevance class would choose the mouse hypothesis as the best explanation of our evidence. But this is achieved only after the relevant alternatives theory has done its job in trimming the size of the contrast class. It is thus the background theory of knowledge that turns the situation into one involving observable entities by ruling out the disturbing hypotheses such as the invisible Martian. The effectiveness of IBE does not depend on the observation/theory distinction, but on whether the background theory of knowledge can rule out the problematic alternatives. This explains both what lies behind van Fraassen's judgment in regard to his "ordinary" example, and, at the same time, why people have found his reference to observation/theory distinction as grounding his differential attitude unconvincing and guilty of epistemic double standards.

The same sort of considerations underlie the positions of those who, despite having mixed views on the legitimacy of IBE, are nevertheless impressed with what they see as its successful implementation in scientific contexts. For example, Day and Kincaid, while adopting a Soberian approach to simplicity and parsimony, develop a qualified position on the legitimacy of IBE: *"[W]hen and where* IBE is warranted may vary. As we argued IBE has no automatic warrant ... just what sort of inferences it warrants may vary greatly depending on the kind and the extent of the relevant background knowledge" (Day and Kincaid 1994, p. 282). But they go on to make the following remark.

> [Although] anti-realist attacks on IBE do carry real weight when IBE arguments are alleged to answer skeptical challenges ... in other contexts, arguments for realism can forcefully appeal to IBE. Physicists argue over realism as well—for example, they argue whether a given piece of data warrants postulating an entity ... Consequently, they are arguments to the best explanation. Yet they do not beg the question. (Day and Kincaid 1994, pp. 290–1)[6]

Peter Lipton also expresses the same sentiment when, after criticizing the so-called "miracle argument" for scientific realism, goes on to say "If I were a scientist, and my theory explained extensive and varied evidence, and there was no alternative explanation that was nearly as lovely, I would find it irresistible to infer that my theory was approximately true" (Lipton 1991, p. 184).

Again, it is not the legitimacy of IBE or its warrant that varies with context but its effectiveness. The authors rightly highlight the success of IBE in scientific contexts, where scientists often seem to be able to converge on what to regard as the best explanation of the data, but are at a loss to identify the reason behind it. The reason for the effectiveness of IBE in scientific contexts, should, once again, be sought in the way the background theory of knowledge (e.g., the relevant alternatives theory) functions in such contexts. One factor that is often appealed to in order to determine the relevance class, in a specific context, is the shared presuppositions of the participants in the discourse (resulting in the formation of an epistemic community).[7] So what seems to underlie the effectiveness of IBE in scientific contexts is the fact that the presuppositions shared by the members of the community (scientists) trim the size of the contrast class by ruling out irrelevant and disturbing hypotheses, thus, paving the way for IBE to finish the job by finding the best explanation among the members of the relevance class.

To conclude, both the defenders of IBE (like Boyd) and its critics (like Fine and van Fraassen) seem to have failed to appreciate the difference between its legitimacy and effectiveness. The reason why the dispute shows no sign of abating is that, in the course of their arguments, both sides switch unconsciously between the legitimacy of IBE and its effectiveness, thus, continuing to talk at cross-purposes to each other. They both ignore the role of the background theory of knowledge that provides IBE with something like an epistemic engine. IBE is a legitimate form of inference, but its effectiveness depends entirely on whether the background theory of knowledge on which it rides piggyback is able (in the light of the context) to rule out the disturbing alternatives. *Only in the context of a background theory of knowledge does inference to the best explanation have epistemological significance.* However, in so far as the use of IBE in defeating radical skeptical hypotheses is concerned, the end result, as we have seen, has been a glaring failure.

10
The Epistemological Significance of Transcendental Arguments

Another popular attempt to rebut Cartesian arguments has involved appealing to Kantian transcendental arguments. The topic of transcendental arguments has had a rather checkered history ever since it was introduced into philosophical literature by Immanuel Kant. He utilized these arguments in order to uncover the necessary conditions of the possibility of experience, and, thus, undermine Cartesian skepticism about our knowledge of the external world. The existence of objects in space, Kant claimed, is a necessary condition of the possibility of experience whose obtaining is recognized even by the skeptic.

The past few decades have witnessed a revival of interest in transcendental arguments. Many theorists, most notably Peter Strawson, saw them as powerful means to combat varieties of skepticism, and, thus, sought to extract and save what, they regarded, as the most defensible elements of the Kantian enterprise. This optimism, however, gradually waned as many of these arguments turned out, on examination, to deliver much less than it was originally thought. It has been claimed, by Stroud, for example, that a transcendental argument, at best, shows that we must *believe* a certain proposition to be true, rather than that proposition being actually true, if experience or language is to be possible (Stroud 1968). These and other objections prompted some of the most ardent exponents of transcendental arguments, such as Strawson, to concede their impotence as a general anti-skeptical strategy, and go as far as saying that they can only be used to reveal "the connections between the major structural features or elements of our conceptual scheme" (Strawson 1985, p. 23).

Despite the now widespread pessimism about the epistemic significance of transcendental arguments, there is still no consensus on their nature or internal structure. Transcendental arguments have been described as disclosing the necessary conditions of the possibility of phenomena as diverse as experience, self-knowledge, and language. They have been thought of as some sort of practical reasoning "no different from Peircean abduction" that justify the replacing of one conceptual scheme with another, or as being no more than some kind of "parasitic" arguments showing the skeptic's conception of the world to be parasitic on more conventional notions, and so on (see, e.g., Rosenberg 1975; Rorty 1971). In this chapter, I seek to advance a unified account of the nature of transcendental arguments, one that incorporates, as much as possible, some of the intuitions expressed about them in the literature. This would, in turn, clarify the question of the epistemic potentials of such arguments. To this end, I shall first try to justify Stroud's claim with respect to both language and experience, and then proceed to present a consistent account of some of the seemingly disparate aspects of the controversy.

However, before proceeding to delineate the general contours of the debate, the following caveat is in order. As these initial remarks indicate, my main preoccupation in this chapter is to assess the epistemological significance of transcendental arguments against the background of contemporary concern with the topic. So although I shall be looking at Kant's main argument in the Deduction, I shall restrict myself to one version of the argument (as seen through Strawson's gloss), and the responses that Strawson's own work has generated. No doubt many of these arguments involve issues, such as the question of the conditions of the possibility of language, which are quite distant from what Kant had intended in the Deduction. But, given the aims of this chapter, a discussion of recent attempts at reconstructing "Kantian" transcendental arguments would be inevitable.

10.1 Skepticism and varieties of transcendental arguments

The kind of skepticism that is the target of Kant's attack in his *Critique of Pure Reason* is the familiar Cartesian one which questions our claim to knowledge of the external world: Our having the experiences we ordinarily take to be of the physical objects around us is compatible with the possibility of there being no such objects, where these experiences are being induced in us by, for example, a (Cartesian) evil genius. Against this, Kant launches his project of transcendental deduction that aims to establish, what he calls, the "objective validity" of the categories. The idea being that, once we reflect on the possibility of (self-conscious) experience, we would realize that the truth of the propositions about the external world, which the skeptic denies, is itself a necessary condition of that possibility. So the skeptic cannot consistently admit that he is the subject of experiences and, at the same time, deny that there are physical objects.

This is what underpins Kant's argument in the Transcendental Deduction of the Categories. He argues, very roughly, that if experience is to be possible, one's experiences must belong to a unified consciousness. But since the latter would only come about if these experiences are experiences of objects, it follows that there are, contrary to the skeptic's claim, physical objects. Kant's argument, however, involves a commitment to transcendental idealism, something which recent advocates of transcendental arguments, such as Strawson, flatly reject.[1] For Kant it is the world of appearances, as opposed to the world as it is in itself, that answers to the requirements for the possibility of experience. Strawson, however, finds any reference to transcendental idealism completely superfluous. For him transcendental arguments, when properly understood, will tell us something about the real world as it is in itself.[2] He thus tries to reconstruct Kant's main argument in the Deduction (usually referred to in the literature as the "objectivity argument") within a realist framework (to which I shall return later in this chapter).

Thus far we have characterized transcendental arguments as involving premises which deal with the possibility of experience. Due to influential writings of Barry Stroud, however, it has now become fashionable to include the possibility of language as another starting point for running a transcendental argument (Stroud 1968). The idea is to show that the truth of what the skeptic denies, for example, that there are physical objects, is a necessary condition of the meaningfulness of that denial. But since the skeptic could always get out of the trap by denying that talk about physical objects makes any sense, Stroud takes the starting point of a transcendental argument to be the possibility of language in general rather than the meaningfulness of any restricted class of statements. For no one can, on pain of self-referential incoherence, deny that there is language. We thus arrive at the following general schema for representing a transcendental argument.

(TA) There is experience or language; a necessary condition of the possibility of experience or language is the truth of P; therefore P.

Not everybody, of course, shares the same intuitions about how best this core conception of a transcendental argument should be interpreted. In addition to those who opt for the standard Kantian reading of (TA), there are also theorists who tend to view the project in a rather different light as, say, a piece of practical reasoning, or as displaying the relations of presupposition among concepts and so on (Moltke 1971; Rorty 1971; Rosenberg 1975; Bennett 1979; Genova 1984). What is particularly striking is the assimilation of (TA)-type reasonings, on some views, with such seemingly different inferences as abduction or inference to the best explanation. I shall return to the question of interpretation at the end of this chapter. For now I wish to examine some of the main objections that have usually been directed against transcendental arguments.

Among the many criticisms that have been made of these arguments, three objections feature prominently, and have been widely discussed in the literature. One is a demand for clarification and concerns the status of the modality involved in the claim that certain conditions are neces- sary for the possibility of language or experience. One wants to know what this alleged necessity really consists in. The other objection, often called the "uniqueness objection," was emphasized by Korner and has been restated by Mackie and Rorty among others (Mackie 1974, ch. 4; Rorty 1979; see also Forster 1989; Walker 1989).

> [E]ven if we grant the possibility of showing that *some* categorical framework must be employed in everybody's objective thinking, we do not for this reason have to grant that the accepted categorical framework is the *only* available, or possible, categorical framework. (In a similar manner, we grant the possibility of showing that we must drink some liquid if our thirst is to be quenched, without granting that lemonade is the only available, or conceivable, liquid.) The transcendental deduction of a categorical framework thus presupposes – or, if we prefer, includes – a demonstration of its uniqueness. (Korner 1971, pp. 214–15)

Korner's suggestion is that Kant was too wedded to the science of his day. What he took to be the necessary conditions of the possibility of experience were merely the presuppositions of the Newtonian science, some of which have since been discarded in current scientific theories. What underlies the uniqueness objection is that, when propounding a transcendental argument, philosophers often tend to proceed to establish the necessity of the truths of certain specific kind, for example, that there are physical objects, by ruling out what they conceive to be the most likely alternatives. But this says more about the limits of our imagination than those of the reality. There is no reason to think that the alternatives considered exhaust all that there is in the logical space. Reasonings of this sort, thus, fail to make good on their uniqueness claims.

Another objection, attributed to Stroud, that seems to have gained wide acceptance is that, to discharge their anti-skeptical function, transcendental arguments need to rely on some version of the verification principle. We saw that, for Stroud, a transcendental argument must find the necessary conditions of the possibility of language or meaningful discourse. So he first designates a class of propositions as the "privileged class" consisting of those propositions whose truth is required for the possibility of language, and then goes on to make the following claim (which we may call the "Doxastic Hypothesis").

[F]or any candidate S, proposed as a member of the privileged class, the Skeptic can always very plausibly insist that it is enough to make language possible if we *believe* that S is true, or if it looks for all the world as if it is, but that S needn't actually be true. (Stroud 1968, p. 128)

The claim is that the conclusion of a transcendental argument can only be a belief or doxastic state of an appropriate kind. Such an argument, at best, shows that it is necessary to possess certain concepts or hold certain beliefs if meaningful discourse is to be possible. It carries no implications for the truth (or justification) of those beliefs or the applicability of the concepts. To endow the conclusion with anti-skeptical bite, we must assume that one could not have a belief or possess a concept without knowing how to determine whether the belief is true or false, or whether the concept is instantiated. But to assume this, is to assume the verification principle. Reliance on the verification principle, however, says Stroud, would make the transcendental argument completely superfluous, for we could reject the skeptic's claim straightaway on the ground that it violates the principle.

It is important however to distinguish between Stroud's claim, that is, the Doxastic Hypothesis and his verification objection. As far as the latter is concerned, Stroud presents no argument to show that all successful transcendental arguments need to rely on the verification principle. He does consider some particular transcendental arguments (due to Strawson and Shoemaker) and shows that they tacitly assume the verification principle. But this obviously falls short of being a general objection to the effect that *all* transcendental arguments require some version of the principle for their validity.[3] Stroud seems to think that, given the truth of the Doxastic Hypothesis, we are bound to rely on the verification principle if we are to defeat Cartesian skepticism, for the latter involves truth and knowledge rather than mere belief. The problem, however, is that nowhere in his paper does he make any attempt to justify the Doxastic Hypothesis. It is, therefore, of great significance to see if the hypothesis is true, for, in addition to making the verification charge stick, it promises to disclose some important facts about the nature and scope of transcendental arguments. This is indeed what I am going to attempt in the section that follows. But before proceeding to take up this task, it is necessary to take note of the following point.

The point is that, having identified (TA) as the basic form of transcendental arguments, we can plausibly distinguish between the validity (soundness) of a transcendental argument and its epistemic effectiveness vis-à-vis the question of skepticism. Some of the objections that have been raised against transcendental arguments (e.g., Stroud's verification charge) actually concern their epistemic effectiveness rather than their validity. They provide no basis for thinking that it is impossible to find a proposition (*P*) whose truth is necessary for the possibility of language or experience. It might, nonetheless, be the case that *P* fails to have any significant implications for the question of skepticism. But this is only to say that, as far as the question of the refutation of skepticism is concerned, transcendental arguments are epistemically ineffective. These objections are, in other words, actually reflections on a particular *use* of transcendental arguments (whose form is given by (TA)) rather than their validity. Let us now examine the credibility of Stroud's Doxastic Hypothesis, and explore its consequences for the question of the epistemic import of transcendental arguments.

10.2 The epistemic import of transcendental arguments

To find out what sort of conclusions can be derived from a transcendental argument, I propose to deal separately with arguments that seek to identify the necessary conditions of the possibility of language and those that are concerned with the possibility of (self-conscious) experience. That these phenomena call for separate treatments is prima facie plausible especially in view of there being no convincing proof for the (controversial) thesis that experience requires linguistic capacity. One can also discern a general tendency among theorists writing on transcendental reasoning to deal with these phenomena individually. Brueckner, for example, when discussing the verification objection, remarks that "Kantian transcendental arguments deal with the conditions for the possibility of *self-conscious experience*, whereas the kind of transcendental argument which was the object of Stroud's criticism dealt with the conditions for the possibility of *meaningful discourse*" (Brueckner 1983, p. 556). And Cassam, despite his claim that transcendental arguments involve a conceptual component delineating a particular distinction, admits that Kant's (objectivity) argument "does not speak explicitly of the drawing of a certain distinction or the application of a certain concept being required for experience" (Cassam 1987, p. 361). So it is wise, I think, to try to identify the purported necessary conditions of the possibility of language and experience one by one. I begin with language.

Stroud, as we saw, claims that for any sentence *S*, whose truth is thought to be necessary for the possibility of language, the skeptic can always insist that all that this possibility requires is we *believe* that *S* is true. And, after examining some recent transcendental arguments for the existence of physical objects and other minds, he concludes by saying that "the most that could be proved by a consideration of the necessary conditions of language is that ... we must *believe* that there are material objects and other minds in order for us to be able to speak meaningfully at all" (Stroud 1968, p. 129). As mentioned earlier, Stroud does not argue for this claim but one may determine its credibility by considering it in the context of a more general question: What is required for the possibility of meaningful discourse? This question, however, constitutes the core of Davidson's truth-theoretic semantic theory (which was extensively discussed in Chapter 7). Let us recall, very briefly, its salient features.

For Davidson a theory of meaning for a language *L* is a Tarski-style truth theory, which should enable us to understand the language. Such a theory should yield theorems (T-sentences) connecting each object language sentence with a metalanguage sentence which is true if and only if that object language sentence is true. Davidson then seeks to spell out the conditions of adequacy for such theories, taking, as evidence for the semantic theory, the conditions under which speakers hold sentences true. This gives rise to the problem of the interdependence of belief and meaning whose resolution, as we saw, involved the introduction of the principle of charity as a necessary condition of the possibility of interpretation and communication.

> [C]harity is not an option, but a condition of having a workable theory of [radical interpretation]. ... Charity is forced on us; whether we like it or not, if we want to understand others, we must count them right in most matters. If we can produce a theory that reconciles charity and the formal conditions for a theory, we have done all that could be done to ensure communication. (Davidson 1974, p. 197)[4]

With the necessity of charity for the possibility of interpretation and meaning, we have, at our disposal, a general strategy to argue for and support Stroud's claim that "the most that could be proved by a consideration of the necessary conditions of language is that ... we must believe that there are material objects." For what charity requires, as we have repeatedly emphasized, is that we assume the speaker, by and large, shares our beliefs. No anti-skeptical consequences, however, necessarily follow from the application of charity. It ensures, in other words, a good deal of agreement between the interpreter's beliefs and those of the speaker without requiring the truth of the either, and that is in accord with Stroud's claim that transcendental arguments have to rely on the verficationist principle in order to establish the truth of common sense beliefs. As noted in Chapter 7, it is primarily for this reason that Davidson himself augments his principle of charity with some additional theses to endow it with enough epistemic bite to refute skepticism (i.e., the idea of an [infallible] omniscient interpreter supplemented with a claim about the nature and means of identification of beliefs, according to which the objects of beliefs are their causes).[5] I shall now turn to the question of what a transcendental argument can deliver when it is the possibility of experience that constitutes its starting premise.

As we noted earlier Kantian transcendental arguments are more concerned with the necessary conditions of the possibility of experience. To delineate the scope of such arguments and what they can impart, I turn to Strawson's version of Kant's argument in the Deduction—the so-called "objectivity argument"—which seeks to establish "by analysis of the concept of experience in general ... the conclusion that a certain objectivity and a certain unity are necessary conditions of the possibility of experience" (Strawson 1976, pp. 31–2). The question that I shall be concerned with is whether one can argue to the objective order of things from the possibility of experience.

Strawson's reconstruction of Kant's argument proceeds as follows. It begins with the "fundamental premise ... that experience contains a diversity of elements (intuitions) which, in the case of each subject of experience, must somehow be united in a single consciousness capable of judgment, capable, that is, of conceptualizing the elements so united" (Strawson 1976, p. 87). The idea seems to be that experience requires unity in a single consciousness capable of conceptualization, that is, capable of being recognized to have some general character or falling under some general concepts. Recognition, however, implies the "*potential* acknowledgement of the experience into which recognition necessarily enters as being one's own" (Strawson 1976, p. 101). But this self-ascription—this is mine—can only make sense against a background of items that can be described as being not-mine. It implies, says

Strawson, that experience should be self-reflective, that it should allow for an is/seems distinction, that is, for a distinction between "how things objectively are" and "how things are expressed as being." But such a distinction is possible only if experience is (partly) of an objective realm, thus, the conclusion of the objectivity argument. It is primarily on this ground that both Kant and Strawson reject the alternative, the hypothesis of the purely sense-datum experience, according to which an experience is simply an awareness of a series of disconnected impressions like flashes, tickling sensations, colors, smells, and so on. Such an account allows no room for an is/seems distinction.

This transcendental argument seems to offer an attractive way of neutralizing some extreme forms of skepticism. But is it successful? Does an analysis of what constitutes or counts as experience have the ability to yield a conclusion about the existence of physical objects? To answer this question, I approach it, as in the case of language, from a more general perspective, that is, by considering it within the context of the internalism/externalism debate about mental content. As we saw in Chapter 3, the debate is about the existence and identity conditions of mental states, and whether contextual facts enter into the individuation of those states. While internalism takes mental content to be essentially independent of social and physical environment, externalism holds that facts external to a thinker's skin are relevant to the individuation of *certain* of his mental contents. The claim, therefore, is not that all the thinker's mental contents are environmentally determined, but that some of them are.

Recall Putnam's twin earth thought experiment. Oscar lives on earth while Toscar lives on twin earth (an exact duplicate of earth except for the fact that the liquid twin earthians call "water" and is superficially indistinguishable from water is not H_2O but has a different chemical composition, XYZ). Now, the widespread intuition is that when both Oscar and Toscar utter the words "Water is wet" they express different thoughts for "water" in their mouths refers to different entities. Such thought experiments seem to lend support to the view that certain thought contents (concepts) are individuation-dependent on the relevant entities they are about. Ignoring a number of subtle issues surrounding the externalist thesis, let us take it, for our purposes here, as roughly implying that, for example, no water-thoughts can exist in a world where there is no H_2O (McLaughlin and Tye 1998). McGinn calls this sort of externalism "strong externalism" to contrast it with weak externalism. If a given mental state is weakly external, then it requires the existence of some item belonging to the nonmental world, whereas if it is strongly external it would require "the existence *in the environment of the subject* of some item belonging to the nonmental world, and ... its identity [would turn on] that item" (McGinn 1989, p. 7).

Now, given the lessons of Putnam's twin earth cases, it seems that strong externalism is true of concepts with indexical components (like natural kind concepts). The environment seems to make a definite contribution to the content of natural kind thoughts. The reason, primarily, is that the identity of a natural kind is not determined by its appearance (to us). Two different natural kinds (water and twin water) can be experienced in the same way as colorless, tasteless, and the like. The question that is directly pertinent to the topic of this section is whether strong externalism is also true of perceptual content. For if this is the case, one could then argue from the existence of perceptual content to the worldly entities that constitute that content.

When we have perceptual experience the world appears to us to be in a certain way. So the content of experience is a matter of how things *seem* to us (perceptual seemings) consisting of the way the world appears to us. Is strong externalism true of such content? In other words, is it the case that "its seeming to [us] that the world is thus and so depends upon its being environmentally thus and so" (McGinn 1989, p. 58). The answer seems to be in the negative. And the reason, as is widely believed, is that we do not seem to be able to construct a twin earth case for perceptual content. What made the running of a twin earth thought experiment in the case of natural kind concepts possible was that the identity of natural kinds is not fixed by their appearances. That is why we could keep the appearance of water and twin water constant despite their being distinct kinds.

But we cannot do that in the case of the contents of experience. Suppose while on earth square things produce in us experiences as of square things, on twin earth these very same experiences are produced by round things. Our twins then apply the predicate "square" to their world on the basis of these experiences. But, as McGinn says, this is not enough to make it the case that, whereas our experiences are as of something square, theirs are as of something round. Despite different distal causes of these experiences on earth and twin earth "square" still means square, not round, on twin earth. This is because it is the introspectible character of perceptual states, not their external causes, which determines their content. What distinguishes the case of perceptual content from that of the content of natural kind thoughts is that in the former, unlike the latter, there is "no conflict or rivalry between how things seem and how they are" (McGinn 1989, p. 61). In the case of perceptual seemings, in other words, there is no room for an is/seems distinction. Perceptual content is, thus, not strongly external.

Now how is the status of perceptual content vis-à-vis the internalism/ externalism debate (about mental content) going to bear on the question of the validity of the objectivity argument? Well, if the foregoing remarks are correct, then we have, at our disposal, an effective way of identifying the epistemic import of arguments that proceed by delineating the individuation conditions of what is to count as experience, or, to put it in the Strawsonian terminology, that seek to draw the contours of what counts as "a truly intelligible description ... [of the] general structure of experience" (Strawson 1976, p. 15). (*Pace* Strawson, however, the absence of an is/seems distinction, as our discussion of mental content shows, does not signal the incoherence of a certain conception of experience, but its failure to have a strongly external content.) To see this, let us remind ourselves of the structure of the skeptic's argument. According to the skeptic since we cannot rule out the possibility that we are, say, brains in a vat and being fed with precisely the same experiences and perceptual seemings we currently enjoy, we cannot claim to know what we ordinarily take ourselves to know about our environment. Now, if strong externalism were true of the contents of our experience, it would seem that our experiences would not be the way they are unless there was a reality with which they corresponded. But, as we have seen, strong externalism fails to be true of the contents of our experiences. It therefore follows that we cannot conclude on the basis of having, say, an experience as of a square thing that the environment contains square things. Thus a transcendental argument, in the manner of the objectivity argument, moving from premises involving the nature and identity conditions of experiences does not necessarily lead to a conclusion about the way the world is.

Moreover, ignoring the question of the epistemic import of transcendental arguments, in so far as the skeptical potentials of strong externalism is concerned, even if it is assumed that strong externalism *is* true of perceptual seemings, we will still be unable to refute the skeptic. For now the skeptical focus will be shifted to the content of our experience; that of knowing whether our seemings are really such. Our experiences become introspectively opaque. I will not know my representational contents unless I know the reality those contents are supposed to represent. This shifting of the skeptical focus is precisely what followed, as we saw, when Davidson (whose concern was with the nature of belief rather than experience), gave an externalist slant to the principle of charity (by taking the objects of beliefs to be their causes) in order to add epistemic bite to it (see Chapter 7; McGinn 1989, pp. 107–17). Both strategies are epistemically impotent against the skeptical threat. It, therefore, follows that transcendental arguments which start by delineating the contours of experience cannot be expected to deliver any epistemically significant results. Having dealt with the epistemic significance of transcendental arguments, I now turn to the question of their structure in order to see if there is a way of accounting for the conflicting intuitions that have been expressed about them.

10.3   The structure of transcendental arguments

I have already emphasized that the validity of a transcendental argument (TA) should be distinguished from its epistemic effectiveness, if it has significant anti-skeptical implications. We were then led to investigate the epistemic import of transcendental arguments trying to specify the extent to which their conclusions can be epistemically significant. Bringing together the results of these investigations with our metaphilosophical reflections, we are now in a position to assess the credibility of the claims made on behalf of and about transcendental arguments. What seems to have clouded the picture, however, is that these claims have all been made against a background of conflicting intuitions regarding how best the standard Kantian project of specifying the necessary conditions of the possibility of experience is to be understood. There are, as we have seen, those conceptions that construe the transcendental strategy as exposing the relations of presupposition among our concepts showing the skeptic's notion of the world as being "parasitic" on the more conventional notions, and there are, on the other hand, those views which see it as being of a piece with such inferences as abduction or inference to the best explanation. How can we account for such conflicting intuitions? I propose to approach this question by reconsidering Korner's uniqueness objection.

Korner, we may recall, traces the defect of all transcendental arguments to their failure in providing a uniqueness proof. Kant's arguments, he says, only show that certain conditions are sufficient for the possibility of experience, not that they are uniquely sufficient or necessary. He further presents an argument claiming that there are only three ways of showing that a scheme is unique and none of them is effective. I do not think that his argument establishes its conclusion. But the point he raises does seem to be true of many of the well-known transcendental arguments that claim to have significant anti-skeptical implications, and which are the focus of our attention in this chapter.

The reason being that many of these arguments proceed to establish their necessity claims through the elimination of competing alternatives.

For example, when trying to establish the conclusion of his objectivity argument, Strawson does not proceed by means of a direct deduction but "by seeing how it stands up to attack" (Strawson 1976, p. 98). He examines, for example, the alternative sense datum hypothesis to see if it satisfies, what he takes to be, the desiderata of experience. And, in another place, arguing from the possibility of re-identification to the existence of material objects, his argument seems to yield no more than the conclusion that material objects are only one way of meeting his requirements of re-identification. For when considering and dismissing another alternative, process-things, he merely says that he is "concerned to investigate the relations of identifiability-dependence between the available major categories, the categories we actually possess; and the category of process-things is one we neither have nor need" (Strawson 1959, p. 57; cf. Harrison 1989). The problem with such attempts at proving the necessity claims is obvious. Once one proceeds to provide a uniqueness proof by eliminating alternatives, there is always the possibility that one has overlooked some others. Our imaginative powers need not necessarily reach out to all regions of the logical space. Let us highlight this feature of the transcendental arguments by labeling them as "K-type" transcendental arguments (after Korner).[6] It seems to me that with this species of transcendental arguments we are able to explain many of the conflicting intuitions regarding their structure. In particular, I wish to show how Rosenberg's "abductive" conception of transcendental arguments can be accounted for in the light of recognizing this feature of such arguments.

Rosenberg is inclined to view a transcendental deduction as some sort of practical reasoning, a justificatory argument legitimizing a particular set of concepts (Rosenberg 1975). This he describes as having the following structure: We shall achieve the epistemic end E; the best or the only way to achieve E is to adopt conceptual cores having certain features, F; it is C_s, rather than its predecessor C_p, which has the features F; hence, we may adopt the conceptual core C_s. This sounds very much like an inference to the best explanation where our belief in the legitimacy of C_s is justified on the ground that its adoption best explains the obtaining of E. Indeed, Rosenberg regards this reading of a transcendental deduction as "no different from a Peircean abduction" (Rosenberg 1975, p. 623). This analysis has been criticized by Stroud for failing to do justice to the Kantian insight (Stroud 1977). Kant was not concerned, he says, with uncovering the necessary conditions of the possibility of any *particular* experience; rather he sought to specify those which are necessary for *any* experience whatsoever. But I do not think that this is quite fair to Rosenberg. It is true that he concentrates on what legitimizes the transition from one conceptual core to another, but what he is really concerned with is what can bring about the epistemic end *E* which, for him, is what Kant in the Deduction took to be "the internal synthesis of experience in a single consciousness" (Rosenberg 1975, p. 622). Rosenberg's idea is that "the fact that espousal or adoption of a particular conceptual frame or system of representations eventuates in such an enhanced synthesis is necessarily a *reason* for us to espouse or adopt it" (Rosenberg 1979, p. 251).

I think there is a good deal of plausibility about this claim. Despite their different surface structures, the statement "the truth of *P* is a necessary condition for the possibility of experience" tends to remind one of the statement "the truth of *P* is the best explanation of the obtaining of experience." What *is* problematic about this association is that a transcendental argument seeks to identify a unique condition as that which is necessary for the obtaining of experience, whereas an abduction, being primarily a form of *explanation*, acknowledges alternative ways of bringing about an experience and appeals to such notions as simplicity, parsimony, etc that have no echo in transcendental arguments. It is, indeed, such disparities that keep the two types of reasoning poles apart, rather than, as Stroud suggests, their differences over the type of experience involved. But these differences, as I shall argue later, are only apparent. It seems to me that transcendental arguments of the K-type variety—which, as was emphasized, include most of the well-known examples of such arguments—do indeed collapse into abductive inferences.

To see this, let us first deliberate on how K-type transcendental arguments are best understood. Consider again Strawson's objectivity argument. He first enunciates a number of necessary conditions for the possibility of experience which include such features as unity, conceptualization, self-ascription, and so on. He then claims that only an experience of an objective realm meets these requirements, and backs it up by examining whether an experience consisting of a series of disconnected impressions (the sense datum hypothesis) can equally satisfy those requirements. He rejects the sense datum hypothesis on the ground that it fails to cohere with the rest of what we know about experience. Unlike the realist hypothesis, this particular conception of experience, he says, fails to exhibit the kind of unity that is a necessary feature of experience. What Strawson is then doing is to choose between the competing hypotheses by seeing how best they fit certain background assumptions or information, in this case, about the nature of experience. Strawson's transcendental reasoning may then be seen as an inference to the most coherent explanation, where a particular hypothesis is adopted depending on how coherent a picture it paints of the nature and the obtaining of experience.

This is actually the typical strategy adopted by coherentists (in epistemology) when spelling out their positions. Consider the following illustration of a coherence account of justification (Audi 1988, p. 88). We hear the leaves rustling, and come to form the belief that the wind is blowing. The reason why we adopt this belief rather than, say, the belief that children are shaking the tree is that it is the former belief that tells a more coherent story or explanation of the sounds we hear. It meshes better with the rest of our beliefs about the leaves' movements, the noise they typically produce and the like. We reject the "children hypothesis," for example, on the ground that the noise produced by shaking a tree is different from that produced by wind, which is similar to the whisper-like sound we hear at the moment. What we are then doing is to go through a series of steps expressing necessary conditions (in the nomological sense) for the possibility of leaves rustling (leaves rustle only if a distinct noise is produced, which is possible only if wind is blowing through them, etc.).[7] This is very much like the way Strawson's K-type objectivity argument seeks to justify the physical object hypothesis on the ground that it, rather than the sense datum hypothesis, tells a more coherent story about the obtaining of experience. Strawson himself comes very close to stating this point when saying of a transcendental deduction that it is not just an argument but also an explanation, a story.

> We have before us the materials of a transcendental drama; and we wish to know how the drama is played out. In the mind we have the pure forms of sensible intuition and the pure concepts of an object in general. Extraneous to the mind we have the unknown and unknowable source of the matter for these forms, the source of that out of which our contentful experience is made. Nature, the subject-matter of our objective judgments, is the outcome ... [W]e want to understand in particular how such disparate faculties can cooperate to make it. In the Transcendental Deduction the story is told, the explanation is given. (Strawson 1976, p. 86)

Having realized that K-type transcendental arguments can be construed as inferences to the most coherent explanation, we are now in a position to see how they connect to inferences to the best explanation (IBE). An inference to the best explanation is an argument where we pick out the hypothesis that best explains the evidence, from among observationally equivalent alternatives, as the one more likely to be true. At first glance, however, there does not seem to be much in common between these types of inferences. In an inference to the most coherent explanation our choice of the desired hypothesis is guided by such criteria as coherence, whereas in an inference to the best explanation this choice is based on such explanatory virtues as simplicity, and the like.

But these differences can be explained away once we call to mind the salient features of IBE as discussed in the previous chapter. One prominent question, we may recall, concerned the nature of the canons of theory choice used in the application of IBE standardly couched in terms of such (largely unanalyzed) notions as simplicity, parsimony, ad-hoc-ness, and others. We saw that simplicity is not a presuppositionless concept, rather, the use of simplicity must be seen as carrying with it substantial background assumptions. For instance, when pressed to give our reasons for claiming that the Sun will rise tomorrow, we usually proceed by invoking our well-confirmed theories of planetary motion. Or, to repeat an example already discussed, suppose we hear scratching in the wall when we go to sleep at night, and subsequently find our clothes torn and our cheese disappeared. We infer that there are mice, rather than, say, rabbits, frogs, and others, in the house since that seems to offer the best (simplest) explanation of our observations. Here our appeal to the simplicity of the "mouse hypothesis" is just a surrogate for stating a set of background assumptions that include our well-confirmed beliefs about the behavior of animals (forming the relevance class). Alternative hypotheses, such as rabbit/frog hypotheses, are rejected on the ground that the noise that rabbits or frogs produce is different from what we hear at nights. These hypotheses fail to cohere with the rest of our beliefs and assumptions. (Recall the example of opting for the belief that the wind is blowing rather than children shaking the tree as the best explanation of the rustling of leaves.)

Of course these assumptions can themselves be challenged. But the moral remains intact; when discharging their function, explanatory virtues embody background assumptions about the subject matter under discussion. When viewed in this light, an inference to the best explanation turns into an inference to the most coherent explanation where the credibility of the target hypothesis is assessed by seeing how well it coheres with the rest of our (independently justified) beliefs. But these latter inferences are, as we saw, what underpin K-type transcendental arguments. So K-type transcendental arguments eventually collapse into inferences to the best explanation. This way we can explain many of the conflicting intuitions that have been expressed about transcendental arguments, particularly the claim about their being abductive inferences.[8] Our conclusion has also the virtue of explaining the most salient feature of K-type transcendental arguments, namely, their impotence to provide a uniqueness proof. This is because the sort of abductive inferences into which they collapse are usually inferences to the best *available* explanations, rather then the best *potential* ones. We often choose from among available explanations, leaving the possibility of a better explanation coming along in future wide open, thus, making the notion of "best" a relative notion. It is the relative character of this species of inference to best explanation that is transformed into the uniqueness problem when the inference is seen in the mirror of (K-type) transcendental reasoning.

To conclude, we started by considering various conceptions of transcendental arguments, evaluating their potential in refuting Cartesian skepticism in the context of some of the standard objections raised against them. We then distinguished between the validity and (epistemic) effectiveness of such arguments, contending that some of these objections actually concern their effectiveness, that is, their *use* as an anti-skeptical tool. This led us to delineate the scope and limits of transcendental arguments seeking to uncover the necessary conditions of the possibility of language and experience respectively. The general conclusion was that transcendental arguments are ineffective in combating skeptical doubts. Finally, having identified a distinct class of such arguments, as K-type transcendental, we tried to show why some theorists have thought of transcendental arguments as being of a piece with such inferences as abduction, thus, accounting for some of the intuitions expressed in regard to their aim and structure.

Notes

1 Elements of a Theory of Justification

1. Appealing to our past perceptions in order to identify our evidence might be thought to raise the specter of the problem of circularity. We seem to be relying on sense experience (perception) to argue that perception is a reliable indicator of truth. But note that the perspective constraint only requires that we recognize or be aware of our reasons for our beliefs. It does not require that we should also be aware of (know) the adequacy of those reasons. Second, what is at issue is whether one is justified in holding a belief rather than whether one can show that one is so justified. Finally, there is nothing obviously wrong with relying on our faculties to find out whether those faculties are reliable. This is, however, a large issue that we cannot pursue here. See, for example, Alston (1993a). For criticism see Sosa (1994b) who thinks that epistemic circularity is ultimately unavoidable and that it does not undermine our knowing that our belief-forming processes are reliable. For other defenses of epistemically circular arguments see Cling (2002); Lemos (2004); and Bergman (forthcoming).
2. It is worth noting that although some theorists are inclined to use a statistical or propensity conception of probability in construing truth conducivity, the sense intended here is that of the (Keynesian) epistemic probability.
3. This example is from Cohen (1984) though he uses it for a different purpose.
4. On a standard deontological conception of epistemic justification, B's beliefs are not justified because they are formed in violation of certain epistemic obligations involving good reasoning.
5. While going along with Sosa's general strategy, John Greco (2000) has suggested that we should refrain from identifying perspectives with implicit meta-beliefs. Rather, they should be seen as *dispositions* that an agent manifests when thinking conscientiously. There are a number of problems with Greco's proposal. I focus only on the following. What the perspective problem seeks to highlight is that for a belief to be justified, the cognizer must have some sort of epistemic *access* to the grounds of that belief. This epistemic ingredient is completely lost in Greco's metaphysically oriented account which is couched in terms of the *ownership* of dispositions by epistemic agents. Ownership and epistemic access are entirely different concepts.

2 The Deontological Conception of Justification

1. Alston uses a propensity conception of probability to define what he intends by truth-conducive justification. As noted earlier however (Chapter 1, n.2) this is by no means mandatory. One might, as we did, opt for an epistemic sense of probability to define truth conductivity. Here though, for the sake of argument, I shall follow Alston's lead but argue that the phenomenon

he highlights leaves the truth conductivity of deontological justification intact.

2. Alston's remarks in the quoted paragraph and the examples he subsequently gives of cases involving beliefs on the basis of testimony, beliefs resulting from physiological or psychological malfunctioning, and so on, where, due to lack of time or resources, we fail to conduct an ideal epistemic inquiry, seem to suggest a different formulation of deontological justification. S is J_d (blameless) in believing that p iff S is blameless (J_d) in believing that he has adequate evidence for p. But, because of the obvious circularity, this can no longer be regarded as a *definition* of J_d. It also engenders an infinite regress of beliefs.

3. Incidentally, as we shall see, Alston's considered position is that deontological justification only requires that our beliefs be under our indirect voluntary control and so it does not really need to presuppose doxastic voluntarism.

3 The Internalism/Externalism Divide

1. For a persuasive discussion as to why probabilistic relations are not reflectively knowable by human agents see Goldman (1999).

2. By "self-knowledge," Boghossian does not mean just a true belief about one's thoughts, but a *justified* one. See Boghossian (1989, p. 6).

3. Boghossian's (strong) internalist constraints on justification might generate regresses of their own (see Alston 1989), but we are not here challenging the internalist conception of justification.

4. Justification externalists need not presuppose self-knowledge even in the case of the inferentially justified beliefs, for such a case would eventually rest on the case of non-inferentially justified beliefs where no self-knowledge seems necessary at all. It is true that in the case of inferentially justified beliefs an externalist must be *aware* of the contents of his thoughts. But recall that we are using "self-knowledge" not in the sense of having even a true belief in the contents of our thoughts, but, at least, having a *justified* belief in those contents.

5. For a thorough and convincing response to McKinsey-type arguments see McLaughlin and Tye (1998a), and the relevant articles in Ludlow (1998). For discussions of the slow switching argument see, for example, McLaughlin and Tye (1998b) and Vahid (2003).

4 The Problem of the Criterion

1. Cling also regards, what he calls, "the knowledge argument" as an important instance of the problem of the criterion, and this argument is clearly a lower-level version as this is made clear by its premise: We can know a proposition only if we have independent knowledge of a criterion of truth (Cling 1997, p. 112).

2. Van Cleve's formulation of the problem of the criterion is not ideally clear, especially in regard to the nature of the propositions from which epistemic principles are to be derived. However, my claim that it is (LPC) that he has in mind can be supported by the following observations. First, he says he regards the problem of the criterion as a generalized form of the Cartesian Circle, and the

propositions that play a similar role in the latter problem are of non-epistemic nature ("God exists and is not a deceiver"). Second, having being asked to clarify his position, he has responded thus: "I think (LPC) is all I had ever really meant to address. ... I agree, at least, in retrospect, that Chisholm's version of the problem of the criterion is (HPC) rather than (LPC). The 'other propositions' [mentioned in the formulation of the problem of the criterion] were not epistemic, and epistemic principles were not necessarily supposed to be derivable from them alone" (personal communication).

3. I have deliberately quoted from Chisholm's most recent writings on this topic to avoid exegetical worries over some of the ambiguous statements he makes in his earlier writings. Cling also thinks that "Chisholm poses the ... argument in terms of the higher-order reading of the questions 'what do we know?' and 'how are we to decide whether we know?' " (Cling 1994, p. 266). Steup (1992) also presents the problem of the criterion in terms of its higher-level version.

4. According to Chisholm there are two ways of escaping the circle created by the propositions constituting (HPC). We can be particularists and claim that we can determine the extent of our justified beliefs independently of any criteria of justification. This amounts to accepting (2) and rejecting (1) (in HPC). Or, we can be methodists by claiming that we can specify the criteria of justification independently of assuming any particular justified belief. This amounts to accepting (1) and rejecting (2). There is, however, a different solution currently in vogue in the literature which amounts to rejecting both (1) and (2) but accepting that we can have no independently justified beliefs and no independently specifiable criteria of justification. This is the method of the so-called "wide reflective equilibrium" which derives from the works of Nelson Goodman and John Rawls. All these "solutions" are problematic one way or another, though particularist approaches have struck many as being more plausible. I shall discuss one influential version of such solutions in the course of identifying the structure of the problem of the criterion.

5. Van Cleve confirms this interpretation of his position: "I agree that my approach is inconsistent with internalism. ... I make the externalist dimension explicit in a later paper, 'Can Atheists Know Anything?' " (personal communication).

5 Universalizability and Closure

1. I have renamed Adler's principle as (FUP) intending it to stand for "full-blooded universalizability principle" for reasons that will become clear later.

2. This would also dispose of an objection raised against the thesis of epistemic universalizability by Levin (Levin 1987, p. 69). As our discussion of the barn example illustrates the defeater environment can be much richer than Levine allows.

3. Hare (1963). Nagel says pretty much the same thing; "The bare universality of moral claims is relatively uncontroversial, and might well be called part of their meaning" (Nagel 1990, p. 102).

4. As will become clear later, my use of the term "context" has only superficial affinities with the way the term is used in the currently popular contextualist theory.

5. There is indeed an analogous principle in confirmation contexts which resembles the principle of closure. This is the so-called *special consequence condition* (Hempel 1965). It says that if an observation report confirms a hypothesis H, then it also confirms every consequence of H.

6. As will be made clear later my view of the principle of the closure has some affinities with Stine's although our background frameworks as well as some of our conclusions radically differ.

7. As explained earlier, since I am concerned with the possibility of the failure of the principle of closure, the sort of situations discussed are those that involve cases where the additional information has an undermining character. This is not to claim that any additional information in any situation will prevent justification from being transferred via entailment.

8. Cf. also Brueckner (1998) for a response to my position as well as his (1985).

6 Skepticism and Underdetermination

1. Not everybody agrees that the agent's evidence remains the same under these circumstances. See Williamson (1997) for a recent dissenting view. He identifies an agent's total evidence with what she knows. For our purposes here, I shall go along with the majority view.

2. This is a strong version of closure. Typical formulations of closure, as we have seen, take knowledge to be closed under *known* entailment. But Brueckner argues that a cognizer can have justification for believing v without actually believing it, thus, the principle (CJ).

3. It is worth noting that, as Cohen (1998) observes, we are not compelled to appeal to (UJ) in order to argue for the premise (2C). There are other ways of defending (2C), for example, by invoking the fact that if SK were true, it would explain the obtaining of our evidence. One may thus view the Cartesian skeptical argument, as Cohen suggests, as a paradox, a set of incompatible claims each of which enjoys intuitive appeal.

4. This is a somewhat qualified version of an example given in Swinburne (1973, pp. 90–1).

7 Argument from the Principle of Charity

1. In a recent article, Keith DeRose proposes a contextualist "nonheroic" response to the Cartesian skeptical argument according to which premise (2) and the conclusion of the argument are true if evaluated according to high, absolute standards for knowledge, but false when evaluated by the standards for knowledge in ordinary contexts. A nonheroic response is one, "which attempts not to show how to gain knowledge in the face of the skeptical argument, but rather to show how the skeptical argument never worked in the first place, by protecting the knowledge of the unsophisticated" (DeRose 2000, p. 129). Accordingly, the proposition "I am a BIV" is false when evaluated by ordinary standards for knowledge because "this is how my Mom would come to believe (and, according to me, know) that she is not a Brain in a Vat if the issue were presented to her: Immediately upon hearing the hypothesis that she is a BIV, she would reject it as silly" (DeRose 2000, fn. 26).

But this contextualist strategy can hardly be regarded as a serious response to the Cartesian challenge. For one can easily resolve almost all outstanding problems in philosophy by employing this strategy. Questions such as God's existence could easily be decided if one were to rely on the reactions of the "unsophisticated" under ordinary circumstances.

2. See, for example, Greco (2000) who, without offering any reason, rejects such attempts on the ground of failing to engage with skeptical arguments.

3. It is, I believe, useful to deal with these arguments separately both because of their order of appearance in Davidson's articles, and also because of the distinct responses they have prompted. The "omniscient interpreter" strategy was fully exploited against skepticism as early as Davidson (1977).

4. There are also responses that take a different direction. McGinn (1986) and Foley (1992), for example, have sought to show how one can make sense of the possibility of global error by reconstructing Davidson's method of radical interpretation. While Foley follows the Quinean line of attaching epistemic significance to sensory stimulations, McGinn opts for its mentalistic version by giving pride of place to experience and proposing a two-stage method whose salient feature is that the causal chain connecting the subject's belief-system to her environment passes through experience.

5. The gist of Malpas's argument actually derives from Davidson's remarks in his (1987b) paper (see also Burge 1988) which may be described as follows. The contents of our second-order thoughts are determined by the contents of our first-order thoughts, and since, according to externalism, the latter are environmentally determined, our second-order thoughts turn out to be about the very same objects and stuff that our first-order thoughts are. We cannot therefore be wrong about the contents of out thoughts. See Vahid (2003) for an extended discussion.

6. For an argument against this assumption see Kornblith (1989).

7. Davidson would probably prefer "*are* indistinguishable" rather than "*must* be indistinguishable" as he dislikes the sort of modal talk involved in the latter.

8. There are possible-world definitions of weak and strong supervenience besides the modal operator definitions. For a comprehensive study of the two types of definitions see McLaughlin (1995).

9. I have formulated the principle of charity in terms of sensory evidence to make the point that follows. The point can also be made by formulating the principle in terms of sensory experience. Davidson thinks that sensations are simply the causes of beliefs, not evidence for them. I shall shortly formulate a different version of charity that takes the Davidsonian attitude into account.

10. To avoid complications, let us focus only on the most basic and elementary cases of perceptual belief as when we form a belief as a result of seeing a rabbit running by.

11. (CHc) requires careful handling. As Davidson himself has recognized, if we go directly from facts about which sentences someone holds true under certain circumstances to conclusions about the interpretations of those sentences, then the principle of charity would be in danger of making it impossible for someone to be in error. For this reason Davidson changes the form of evidence that is needed for the theory of interpretation by focusing on languages and communal attitudes to the truth of sentences in order to

leave room for individual error. Principle of charity is, thus, recognized as a holistic constraint applying to systems of belief. Accordingly, (CHc) should not be understood as suggesting that the content of each particular belief is determined by *its* particular cause. What it actually says is that content supervenes on the *normal* cause of beliefs *of that type*.

12. Concepts are generally thought to constitute the content of a belief. Moreover, one can think of the concept expressed by a term as given by what it means. Now even if the meaning of a sentence is identical to the content of the belief expressed in accepting that sentence, we can still suppose that the meaning of the sentence supervenes on the content of the belief, because identity is sufficient for supervenience. (Compare: We can say of a pressure of a mole of gas that it supervenes on its temperature and volume since they are both determined by pressure itself. I take this example from Chalmers (1996, p. 36)). This is all I need for the use to which I am putting supervenience, that is, providing an alternative route to show how meanings can be thought of as supervening on appropriate environmental circumstances.

13. A prominent example is Dennett's intentional system theory. According to Dennett intentional ascription inevitably involves an element of interpretation. But Dennett's brand of interpretivism is not a constitutive one. He defends an instrumentalist account of commonsense psychology according to which, strictly speaking, no intentional ascriptions can be true. In Dennett, then, we find an example of someone who has no objections to subjecting intentional ascription to consistency constraints (in accordance with the principle of charity), but who also refuses (like Hare) to see it as committing him to a realist position. He can thus be seen as subscribing only to an ascriptive version of the principle of charity (as a supervenience constraint) on the basis of essentially similar (Davidsonian) considerations. See various articles in Dennett (1987). See Dennett (1991) for his somewhat modified views.

8 Argument from Epistemic Conservatism

1. Here, of course, I am referring to Quine's views in "Epistemology Naturalized." There have been other versions of naturalistic epistemology that recognize and try to incorporate the distinctive features of traditional epistemology. However, since it is Quine who is usually cited as one of the most prominent advocates of epistemic conservatism, I am focusing on his views. Other, more acceptable, versions of naturalistic epistemology usually distinguish themselves by taking causes of beliefs as being relevant to their justification. It would be interesting to note that another prominent advocate of conservatism, namely, Chisholm, rejects the causal approach in favor of erecting standards of justification for beliefs that have no place for their causes. Perhaps the more interesting question in the context of epistemic conservatism is what naturalism commits one to.

2. It might be suggested that one may have a background belief according to which most of what one remembers was learned in an epistemically proper manner. Would that be sufficient to justify the belief about India's population? As Goldman (1999) says, this evidence is not sufficient for justification, for if I had learnt the belief from, say, a local unreliable newspaper, then, even

given that background belief, I would not be justified in holding the belief. The way I learned the belief is still relevant and decisive.

3. This is, of course, equivalent to Goldman's non-undermining condition that he rightly thinks is necessary for a belief's justification. He mentions a number of ways in which a belief's permittedness may be undermined. See Goldman (1986, pp. 62–3).

4. When referring to the reliability of belief-forming mechanisms in elaborating the explanatory constraint, it is quite obvious that Lycan has Goldman-type reliability theories in mind. For he explicitly mentions Goldman's account and says that "[e]ven if my theory of the initial justification of ultimate explainees eventually fails, we could always fall back on a straightforward reliability account, since our ultimate explainees tend to be the very sorts of beliefs for which a reliability theory works well" (Lycan 1988, p. 172). This remark further supports my claim that, with the added constraints, Lycan's conservative norm looks increasingly like a variant of the familiar reliability norm.

9 Argument from Inference to the Best Explanation (IBE)

1. Aune (1991), Goldman (1988), and Vogel (1993), among others, represent the first group. The second group is represented by Lycan (1988). Vogel clearly recognises that IBE's legitimacy is at the heart of the problem saying that the truth-conduciveness of the explanatory virtues "must be addressed at some point by anyone who bases an answer to skepticism on explanatory considerations" (Vogel 1993, p. 111).

2. I am not denying that we have intuitions about rational and irrational theory choices. I am, rather, claiming that the analogy is not very close. For even among those who propound a rational model of theory change (e.g., Popper and Lakatos), there are heated controversies over the value of such properties as empirical content (simplicity), ad hocness, testability (confirmation), etc., for the assessment of the relative merits of rival theories.

3. One might construe Lycan's argument simply as an application of induction over a varied sample, rather than an instance of IBE. But this move is definitely not open to Lycan. He explicitly endorses Harman's thesis that induction itself is best seen as a particular instance of the more general practice of inferring to the best explanation, and devotes a chapter to showing how "each of the most prominent forms of inductive and statistical inference [can be reconstructed] as a type of explanatory inference" (Lycan 1988, p. 179). What underlie the cases of reasonable induction, he says and I am inclined to agree with him, are the explanatory virtues of the inferred hypotheses.

4. Lycan also provides an evolutionary account of why we use the customary set of virtues as criteria of theory-preference. This is because employing this specific set has explanatory advantages. He denies however that the adaptive utility of our habit of using them makes them epistemically justified.

5. See also Alston's recent discussion of IBE arguments – in the context of realism debate – which consists of only showing that none of the usual criteria of theory choice are able to identify the standard account as the best explanation of our sensory experience. He, too, seems to regard simplicity as a global and abstract feature of inductive inferences (Alston 1993a).

6. It is rather puzzling to say of IBEs that "they do not beg the question" in scientific contexts. This remark masks a confusion between the scientific uses of IBE to postulate theoretical entities, and the so-called "miracle argument" for scientific realism (the truth of the theories is the best explanation of their success). In making this remark the authors seem to have Fine's objection in mind, for in the preceding paragraph, having endorsed his attack on IBE arguments for realism, they go on to say that "[h]owever, these doubts about IBE lose their force when we switch [to scientific] contexts." But it is not IBE that, according to Fine, begs the question. It is rather the miracle argument that does the begging by assuming the legitimacy of IBE which, according to Fine, is what is actually at issue between realists and anti-realists.

7. David Lewis has noted that in any concrete conversation we are guided in what we say by certain relatively clear presuppositions which provide the context and which can shift with the course of that conversation (Lewis 1979). The idea is that the set of presuppositions we eventually come to share determine which alternatives are relevant. Having realized that these alternatives can be ruled out, we then go on to attribute knowledge to each other. The sharing of the same set of presuppositions may, thus, be said to create an epistemic community whose members can reach a consensus on the size of the relevance class.

10   The Epistemological Significance of Transcendental Arguments

1. Kant resumes his attack on skepticism about the external world in a section, added to the second edition of the *Crtique*, called "Refutation of Idealism." There he returns to the themes of self-consciousness and temporality, and restates his claim that intuition of spatial objects is a necessary condition of the possibility of experience. There are, however, a number of views about the significance of the argument in the Refutation. Some see it as an elaboration of some of Kant's contentions in the Deduction and a more detailed working out of their implications. Others, however, tend to view the Refutation as marking a new development in Kant's philosophy where he eventually frees himself from the grip of transcendental idealism. (It is suggested that, dissatisfied with the comparison of his position in the first edition of the *Critique* with Berkeley's idealism, Kant sought to distance himself from such views by inserting the Refutation in the second edition of the *Critique* which coincided with the elimination of the Fourth Paralogism.) For the purposes in this chapter, however, I shall continue to concentrate on Strawson's reconstruction of Kant's argument in the Deduction where transcendental idealism is ignored anyway.

2. Why did then Kant present his transcendental arguments within an idealist framework? Cassam traces Kant's motive in doing so to his belief that it should not be a mere accident that appearances happen to provide a basis for the unity of consciousness, for there would then be no guarantee that they would continue to do so in future. Continuity is ensured, however, if we take the "world" referred to in the argument to be the world of appearances. See Cassam (1987).

3. While endorsing this objection, Brueckner (1983) says that it does not apply to *Kantian* transcendental arguments where it is the possibility of experience rather than meaningful discourse that is in question, and he goes on to show how Strawson's and Rorty's reconstructions of Kant's anti-skeptical strategy also falls prey to this charge. But it seems to me that some version of the verification principle, for example, the version that Brueckner himself enunciates later in his paper to the effect that "a putative concept is genuine only if it is possible to know whether any entities fall under the concept," is clearly applicable to the Kantian argument provided, of course, that the Doxastic Hypothesis is true.

4. Davidson himself describes an argument of his against conceptual relativism, which exploits the principle of charity, as transcendental (Davidson 1974, p. 72). Others have seen it in the same way. See, for example, McGinn (1977) and Rorty (1979).

5. Exploiting a Davidsonian framework, Stroud has recently suggested that a less ambitious Kantian strategy might be possible. For an effective criticism see Brueckner (1996).

6. It is controversial to what extent Kant's own arguments fall prey to the uniqueness charge. Rorty, for example, thinks that "all the arguments of the 'Refutation' and 'Deduction' do is to rule out one alternative—the skeptical, Humean, 'sense-datum' alternative" (Rorty 1979, p. 82). In line with the general drift of this chapter, I shall refrain from considering this exegetical question, and instead concentrate on the transcendental arguments that are distinctively K-type. After all the interpretations that are the subject of investigation in this part of the chapter are not that close to Kant's intentions in the Deduction.

7. By citing this example, I am not necessarily endorsing a coherence theory of justification. We can choose to say that the belief about the wind blowing is justified because it coheres with the rest of our beliefs which are themselves *independently* justified (rather than in virtue of merely belonging to a coherent set).

8. It is true that the best explanation arguments play an essential role in scientific reasoning, and, thus, unlike Kantian transcendental arguments, involve empirical assumptions. But this should not make us oblivious to the role that they also play in philosophical thinking. As we saw in Chapter 9, in epistemology, metaphysics and elsewhere, such inferences have a basic role in explicating philosophical theories as well as substantiating them.

References

Adler, J. 1981, "Skepticism and Universalizability," *The Journal of Philosophy*, 78: 143–56.

———. 1990a, "Epistemic Universalizability: From Skepticism to Infallibility," in Roth and Glenn (eds), *Doubting*, The Netherlands: Kluwer.

———. 1990b, "Conservatism and Tacit Confirmation," *Mind*, 99: 559–70.

Alston, W. 1971, "Varieties of Privileged Access," repr. in Alston 1989, *Epistemic Justification*, Ithaca and London: Cornell University Press. pp. 249–85.

———. 1985, "Concepts of Epistemic Justification," repr. in Alston 1989, *Epistemic Justification*, Ithaca and London: Cornell University Press. pp. 81–115.

———. 1988, "The Deontological Conception of Epistemic Justification," repr. in Alston 1989, *Epistemic Justification*, Ithaca and London: Cornell University Press, pp. 115–53.

———. 1989, *Epistemic Justification*, Ithaca and London: Cornell University Press.

———. 1993a, *The Reliability of Sense Perception*, Ithaca and London: Cornell University Press.

———. 1993b, "Epistemic Desiderata," *Philosophy and Phenomenological Research*, LIII (3): 527–51.

———. 1996, *A Realist Conception of Truth*, Ithaca and London: Cornell University Press.

———. Forthcoming, "Doing Epistemology Without Justification," *Philosophical Topics*.

Armstrong, D. 1978, *Universals and Scientific Realism*, Cambridge: Cambridge University Press.

Audi, R. 1988, *Belief, Justification and Knowledge*, Belmont, California: Wadsworth Publishing Company.

Aune, B. 1991, *Knowledge of the External World*, London: Routledge.

Axtell, G. (ed.) 2000, *Knowledge, Belief, and Character*, Lanham: Rowman & Littlefield Publishing.

Bennett, J. 1979, "Analytic Transcendental Arguments," in Bieri *et al.* (eds), 1979, *Transcendental Arguments and Science*, Holland: Dordrecht.

Ben-Menahem, Y. 1990, "The Inference to the Best Explanation," *Erkenntnis*, 33: 319–44.

Bergman, M. Forthcoming, "Epistemic Circularity: Malignant and Benign." Available at http://philosophy.rutgers.edu/EVENTS/Epis2003/Bergmann.doc

Bieri, P. *et al.* (eds) 1979, *Transcendental Arguments and Science*, Holland: Dordrecht.

Boghossian, P. 1989, "Content and Self-knowledge," *Philosophical Topics*, 27: 5–26.

———. 1997, "What the Externalist Can Know A Priori," repr. in Wright, C. *et al.* (eds) 1998, *Knowing Our Own Minds*, Oxford: Clarendon Press.

BonJour, L. 1980, "Externalist Theories of Empirical Justification," repr. in Kornblith (ed.) 2001, *Epistemology: Internalism and Externalism*, Oxford: Blackwell Publishers.

———. 1985, *The structure of Empirical Knowledge*, Cambridge and Massachusetts: Harvard University Press.

BonJour, L. 1992, "Externalism/Internalism," in Dancy and Sosa (eds), *A Companion to Epistemology*, Oxford: Blackwell, pp. 132–6.

———. 2000, "Sosa on Knowledge, Justification and 'Aptness' " in Axtell (ed.) 2000, *Knowledge, Belief, and Character*, Lanham: Rowman & Littlefield Publishing.

Boyd, R. 1983, "On the Current Status of Scientific Realism," repr. in Boyd (ed.) 1992, *The Philosophy of Science*, Cambridge, MA: MIT Press.

Boyd, R. *et al.* (eds), 1992, *The Philosophy of Science*, Cambridge, MA: MIT Press.

Brueckner, A. 1983, "Transcendental Arguments I," *Nous*, 17: 551–75.

———. 1984a, "Epistemic Universalizability Principles," *Philosophical Studies*, 46: 297–305.

———. 1985, "Skepticism and Epistemic Closure," *Philosophical Topics*, 13: 89–117.

———. 1986, "Charity and Skepticism," *Pacific Philosophical Quarterly*, 67: 264–8.

———. 1994, "The Structure of the Skeptical Arguments," *Philosophy and Phenomenological Research, LIV*: 827–35.

———. 1996, "Modest Transcendental Arguments," in Temberlin, J. (ed.), *Philosophical Perspectives*, 10, Metaphysics, Oxford: Blackwell Publishers.

———. 1998, "Closure and Context," *Ratio*, XI: 78–82.

Burge, T. 1979, "Individualism and the Mental," in French, P. *et al.* (eds), *Midwest Studies in Philosophy*, 4: 73–121, Minneapolis: University of Minnesota Press.

———. 1988, "Individualism and Self-knowledge," *Journal of Philosophy*, 85(11): 649–63.

Cartwright, N. 1983, *How the Laws of Physics Lie*, Oxford: Clarendon Press.

Cassam, Q. 1987, "Transcendental Arguments, Transcendental Synthesis and Transcendental Idealism," *Philosophical Querterly*, 37(149): 355–78.

Chalmers, D. 1996, *The Conscious Mind*, New York: Oxford University Press.

Chase, J. 2001, "Is Internalism About Content Inconsistent With Internalism About Justification," *Australasian Journal of Philosophy*, 79: 227–46.

Cherniak, C. 1986, *Minimal Rationality*, Cambridge, MA: MIT Press.

Chisholm, R. 1973, *The Problem of the Criterion*, Milwaubee: Marquette University Press.

———. 1977, 1989, *Theory of Knowledge*, 2nd and 3rd edns, New Jersey: Prentice Hall.

———. 1980, "A Version of Foundationalism," in Wettstein *et al.* (eds), *Midwest Studies in Philosophy V*, Minneapolis: University of Minnesota Press.

———. 1988, "The Indispensability of Internal Justification," *Synthese*, 74: 285–96.

Christensen, D. 1994, "Conservatism in Epistemology," *Nous*, 28: 69–89.

Cling, A. 1994, "Posing the Problem of the Criterion," *Philosophical Studies*, 75: 261–92.

———. 1997, "Epistemic Levels and the Problem of the Criterion," *Philosophical Studies*, 88: 109–40.

———. 2002, "Justification affording Circular Arguments," *Philosophical Studies*, 111: 251–75.

Cohen, S. 1984, "Justification and Truth," *Philosophical Studies*, 46: 279–95.

———. 1998, "Two Kinds of Skeptical Arguments," *Philosophy and Phenomenological Research*, LVIII: 143–59.

Conee, E. and Feldman, R. 2001, "Internalism Defended," repr. in Kornblith (ed.) 2001, *Epistemology: Internalism and Externalism*, Oxford: Blackwell Publishers.

Craig, E. 1990, "Davidson and the Skeptic: The Thumbnail Version," *Analysis*, 50: 213–14.

David, M. 1996, "Review of Foley's *Working Without a Net*," *Philosophy and Phenomenological Research*, LVI(4): 943–52.

———. 2001, "Truth as the Epistemic Goal," in Steup (ed.) 2001, *Knowledge, Truth and Duty*, New York: Oxford University Press, pp. 151–70.

Davidson, D. 1973, "Radical Interpretation," repr. in Davidson 1984, *Truth and Interpretation*, Oxford: Clarendon Press.

———. 1974, "On the Very Idea of a Conceptual Scheme," repr. in Davidson 1984, *Truth and Interpretation*, Oxford: Clarendon Press.

———. 1977, "The Method of Truth in Metaphysics," repr. in Davidson 1984, *Truth and Interpretation*, Oxford: Clarendon Press.

———. 1981, "A Coherence Theory of Truth and Knowledge," repr. in LePore (ed.) 1986, *Truth and Interpretation*, Oxford: Basil Blackwell.

———. 1982, "Empirical Content," repr. in LePore (ed.) 1986, *Truth and Interpretation*, Oxford: Basil Blackwell.

———. 1984, *Truth and Interpretation*, Oxford: Clarendon Press.

———. 1985, "Replies to Essays X-XII," in Vermazen, B. and Hintikka, J. (eds) *Essays on Davidson: Actions and Events*, Oxford: Clarendon Press.

———. 1987a, "Afterthoughts," in Malachowski, A. (ed) *Reading Rorty*, Oxford: Basil Blackwell.

———. 1987b, "Knowing One's Own Mind," *Proceedings and Addresses of the American Philosophical Association*, 441–58.

Day, T. and Kincaid, H. 1994, "Putting the Inference to the Best Explanation in its Place," *Synthese*, 98: 271–95.

Dennett, D. 1987, *The Intentional Stance*, Cambridge, MA: MIT Press.

———. 1991, "Real Patterns," *Journal of Philosophy*, 88: 27–51.

DePaul, M. 2001, "Value Monism in Epistemology," in Steup (ed.) 2001, *Knowledge, Truth and Duty*, New York: Oxford University Press.

DeRose, K. 2000, "How Can We Know That We're Not Brians in Vats?," *The Southern Journal of Philosophy*, XXXVIII (Supplement): 121–48.

Donnellan, K. 1966, "Reference and Definite Descriptions," *Philosophical Review*, 75: 281–304.

Dretske, F. 1970, "Epistemic Operators," *Journal of Philosophy*, 70: 1007–23.

Dretske, Fred. 1981, "The Pragmatic Dimension of Knowledge," *Philosophical Studies*, 40: 363–78.

Feldman, R. 1988a, "Subjective and Objective Justification in Ethics and Epistemology," *The Monist*, 71: 403–19.

———. 1988b, "Epistemic Obligations," in Tomberlin (1988), *Philosophical Perspectives*, 2, California: Ridgeview Publishing Company.

Field, H. 1989, *Realism, Mathematics & Modality*, Oxford: Basil Blackwell.

Fine, A. 1984, "The Natural Ontological Attitude," repr. in Boyd (ed.) 1992, *The Philosophy of Science*, Cambridge, MA: MIT press.

Foley, R. 1979, "Justified Inconsistent Beliefs," *American Philosophical Quarterly*, 16: 247–57.

———. 1982, "Epistemic Conservatism," *Philosophical Studies*, 43: 165–82.

Foley, R. 1987, *The Theory of Epistemic Rationality*, Cambridge, MA: Harvard University Press.

———. 1992, "Can Metaphysics Solve the Problem of Skepticism?," *Philosophical Issues*, 2: 131–47.

———. 1993, *Working Without a Net*, New York: Oxford University Press.

———. 1994, "The Epistemology of Sosa," in Villanueva (1994), *Philosophical Issues 5: Truth and Rationality*, Atascadero, CA: Ridgeview Publishing Company.

Foley, R. and Fumerton, R. 1985, "Davidson's Theism?," *Philosophical Studies*, 48: 83–9.

Forster, E. 1989, "How are Transcendental Arguments Possible?," in Schaper, E., *et al.* (eds) 1989, *Reading Kant*, Oxford: Basic Blackwell.

Fumerton, R. 1994, "Sosa's Epistemology," in Villanueva (1994), *Philosophical Issues 5: Truth and Rationality*, Atascadero, CA: Ridgeview Publishing Company.

Genova, A. 1984, "Good Transcendental Arguments," *Kant Studien*, 75: 469–95.

Ginet, C. 1975, *Knowledge, Perception, and Memory*, Dordrecht: D. Reidel.

Goldman, Alan. 1988, *Empirical Knowledge*, California: University of California Press.

Goldman, A. 1976, "Discrimination and Perceptual Knowledge," repr. in Goldman (ed.) 1992, *Liaisons*, Cambridge, MA: MIT Press.

———. 1979, "Varieties of Epistemic Appraisal," *Nous*, 13: 23–38.

———. 1986, *Epistemology and Cognition*, Harvard University Press.

———. 1988, "Strong and Weak Justification," repr. in Goldman (ed.) 1992, *Liaisons*, Cambridge, MA: MIT Press.

———. 1992, *Liaisons*, Cambridge, MA: MIT Press.

———. 1999, "Internalism Exposed," repr. in Kornblith (ed.) 2001, *Epistemology: Internalism and Externalism*, Oxford: Blackwell Publishers.

———. 2001, "The Unity of Epistemic Virtues," repr. in Goldman (ed.) *Pathways to Knowledge*, 2002, New York: Oxford University Press.

Goldstick, D. 1971, "Methodological Conservatism," *American Philosophical Quarterly*, 8: 186–91.

Goodman, N. 1973, *Fact, Fiction and Forecast*, Indianapolis, IN: Bobbs-Merril.

Greco, J. 2000, *Putting Skeptics in Their Place*, Cambridge: Cambridge University Press.

Grice, P. 1961, "The Causal Theory of Perception," *Proceedings of the Aristotelian Society*, supp. vol. 35: 121–68.

Haack, S. 1991, "What is 'the Problem of the Empirical Basis', and does Johnny Wideawake Solve it?," *British Journal for the Philosophy of Science*, 42: 369–89.

Hare, R. 1952, *The Language of Morals*, Oxford: Clarendon Press.

———. 1963, *Freedom and Reason*, Oxford: Oxford University Press.

Harman, G. 1965, "Inference to the Best Explanation," *The Philosophical Review*, 74: 88–95.

———. 1986, *Change in View*, Cambridge, MA: MIT Press.

Harrison, R. 1989, "Atemporal Necessities of Thought: or, How not to bury Philosophy by History," in Schaper, E. *et al.* (eds) 1989, *Reading Kant*, Oxford: Basil Blackwell.

Hempel, C. 1965, *Aspects of Scientific Explanation*, New York: Free Press.

Hookway, C. 1988, *Quine*, Oxford: Polity Press.

Kant, I. 1933, *Critique of Pure Reason*, 2nd edn. transl. N. Kemp Smith. London: Macmillan and Co.

Kim, J. 1993, " 'Strong' and 'Global' Supervenience Revisited," in Kim, *Supervenience and Mind*, Cambridge: Cambridge University Press.

Klagge, J. 1988, "Supervenience: Ontological and Ascriptive," *Australasian Journal of Philosophy*, 66: 461–9.

Klein, P. 1981, *Certainty,* Minneapolis, MN: University of Minnesota Press.

———. 1986, "Radical Interpretation and Global Skepticism," in LePore (ed.) 1986, *Truth and Interpretation*, Oxford: Basil Blackwell.

Korcz, K. 1997. "Recent Work on Basing Relation," *American Philosophical Quarterly*, 34: 171–91.

Kornblith, H. 1989, "The Unattainability of Coherence," in Bender, J. (ed.), *The Current State of Coherence Theory*, The Netherlands: Kluwer Publishers.

Kornblith, H. (ed.). 2001, *Epistemology: Internalism and Externalism*, Oxford: Blackwell Publishers.

Korner, S. 1971, *Fundamental Questions in Philosophy*, London: Penguin.

Kripke, S. 1977, "Speaker's Reference and Semantic Reference," in French *et al.* (eds), *Midwest Studies in Philosophy*, Minneapolis: University of Minnesota Press.

———. 1980, *Naming and Necessity*, Oxford: Blackwell.

Laudan and Leplin. 1991, "Empirical Equivalence and Underdetermination," *The Journal of Philosophy*, LXXXVIII: 269–85.

Lehrer, K. 1990, *Knowledge*, London: Routledge.

Lemos, N. 2004, "Epistemic Circularity Again," *Philosophical Issues*, 14: 254–71.

LePore, E. (ed.). 1986, *Truth and Interpretation*, Oxford: Basil Blackwell.

Levin, J. 1987, "Skepticism, Objectivity, and the Invulnerability of Knowledge," *Philosophy and Phenomenological Research*, XLVIII(1): 63–78.

Lewis, D. 1979, "Scorekeeping in a Language Game," *Journal of Philosophical Logic*, 8: 339–59.

Lipton, P. 1991, *Inference to the Best Explanation*, London: Routledge.

Ludlow, P (ed.). 1998, *Externalism and Self-Knowledge*, Stanford, CA: CSLI.

Lycan, W. 1988, *Judgement and Justification*, Cambridge: Cambridge University Press.

Mackie, J. 1963, "The Paradox of Confirmation," *British Journal for the Philosophy of Science*, 13: 265–77.

———. 1983, *Ethics*, England: Penguin Books.

———. 1974, *The Cement of the Universe*, Oxford: Oxford University Press.

Maitzen, S. 1995, "Our Errant Epistemic Aim," *Philosophy and Phenomenological Research*, 55: 869–76.

Malpas, J. 1992, *Donald Davidson and the Mirror of Meaning*, Cambridge: Cambridge University Press.

———. 1994, "Self-knowledge and Skepticism," *Erkenntnis*, 40: 165–84.

McGinn, C. 1977, "Charity, Interpretation and Belief," *The Journal of Philosophy*, LXXIV: 521–35.

———. 1984, "The Concept of Knowledge," in French, P. *et al.* (eds), *Midwest Studies in Philosophy*, Vol. 9, Minneapolis: University of Minnesota Press.

———. 1986, "Radical Interpretation and Epistemology," in LePore (ed.) 1986, *Truth and Interpretotion*. Oxford: Basil Blackwell.

———. 1989, *Mental Content*, Oxford: Basil Blackwell.

McKinsey, M. 1991, "Anti-individualism and Privileged Access," *Analysis*, 51: 9–16.

McLaughlin, B. 1995, "Varieties of Supervenience," in Savellos (ed.), *Supervenience: New Essays*, Cambridge: Cambridge University Press.

McLaughlin, B. and Tye, M. 1998a, "Externalism, Twin Earth, and Self-knowledge," in Wright, C. *et al.* (eds) 1988, *Knowing Our Own Minds*, Oxford: Clarendon Press.

McLaughlin, B. and Tye, M. 1998b, "Is Content-Externalism Compatible with Privileged Acess?," *The Philosophical Review*, 107(3): 349–80.

Moltke, S. 1971, "Transcendental Arguments," *Nous*, 5: 15–26.

Moser, P.K. 1991, *Knowledge and Evidence*, Cambridge: Cambridge University Press.

Nagel, T. 1976, "Moral Luck," *Proceedings of the Aristotelian Society*, supp. vol. L.

———. 1990, "The Foundations of Impartiality," in Seanor and Fotion (eds) 1990, *Hare and Critics*, Oxford: Clarendon Press.

Nozick, R. 1981, *Philosophical Explanations*, Cambridge MA: Harvard University Press.

Plantinga, A. 1993, *Warrant: The Current Debate*, Oxford, New York: Oxford University Press.

Pollock, J. 1974, *Knowledge and Justification*, Princeton, NJ: Princeton University Press.

Popper, K. 1977, *The Logic of Scientific Discovery*, London: Hutchinson.

Pryor, J. 2001, "Highlights of Recent Epistemology," *British Journal for the Philosophy of Science*, 52: 95–124.

Putnam, H. 1975, "The Meaning of 'Meaning', " in Putnam (ed.) *Mind, Language, and Reality: Philosophical Papers*, Vol. 2, Cambridge: Cambridge University Press.

Quine, W.V.O. 1951, "Two Dogmas of Empiricism," in *From a Logical Point of View*, 2nd edn, New York: Harper & Row.

Railton, P. 1989, "Explanation and Metaphysical Controversy," in Kitcher, P. and Salmon, W. (eds) 1989, *Minnesota Studies in the Philosophy of Science*, Vol. XIII, Minneapolis.

Rorty, R. 1971, "Verificationism and Transcendental Arguments," *Nous*, 5: 3–14.

———. 1979, "Transcendental Arguments, Self-reference, and Pragmatism," in Bieri, P. *et al.* (eds) 1979, *Transcendental Arguments and Science*, Holland: Dordrecht.

Rosenberg, J. 1975, "Transcendental Arguments Revisited," *The Journal of Philosophy*, October 23: 611–24.

———. 1979, "Transcendental Arguments and Pragmatic Epistemology," in Bieri, P. *et al.* (eds) 1979, *Transcendental Arguments and Science*, Holland: Dordrecht.

Salmon, N. 1982, *Reference & Essence*, Oxford: Basil Blackwell.

Schaper, E. *et al.* (eds) 1989, *Reading Kant*, Oxford: Basil Blackwell.

Schaffler, I. 1963, *The Anatomy of Inquiry*, New York: Knopf.

Sklar, L. 1975, "Methodological Conservatism," *Philosophical Review*, LXXIV: 374–400.

Sober, E. 1988, *Reconstructing the Past*, Cambridge MA: MIT Press.

———. 1994, *From a Biological Point of View*, Cambridge: Cambridge University Press.

Sosa, E. 1986, " 'Circular' Coherence and 'Absurd' Foundations', " in LePore (ed.) 1986, *Truth and Interpretation*, Oxford: Basil Blackwell.

———. 1988, "Knowledge in Context, Skepticism in Doubt," repr. in Sosa (ed.) 1991, *Knowledge in Perspective*, New York: Cambridge University Press.

———. 1991, *Knowledge in Perspective*, New York: Cambridge University Press.

———. 1994a, "Virtue Perspectivism: A Response to Foley and Fumerton," in Villanueva (ed.) 1994, *Philosophical Issues 5: Truth and Rationality*, Atascadero, CA: Ridgeview Publishing Company.

———. 1994b, "Philosophical Scepticism and Epistemic Circularity," *Aristotelian Society Supplementary Volume*, 68: 263–90.

———. 2000, "Perspectivism in Virtue Epistemology: A Response to Dancy and BonJour," in Axtell (ed.) 2000, *Knowledge, Belief and Character*, Lanham: Raonnan & Littlefield Publishing.

Steup, M. 1988, "The Deontic Conception of Epistemic justification," *Philosophical Studies*, 53.

———. 1992, "Problem of the Criterion," in Dancy and Sosa (eds), *A Companion to Epistemology*, Oxford: Basil Blackwell.

———. 1999, "A Defense of Internalism," in Pojman, L. (ed.), *The Theory of Knowledge*, California: Wadworth.

———. 2001, *Knowledge, Truth and Duty*, New York: Oxford University Press.

Stine, G. 1976, "Skepticism, Relevant Alternatives, Deductive Closure," *Philosophical Studies*, 29: 249–60.

Strawson, P.F: 1959, *Individuals*, London: Methuen.

———. 1976, *The Bounds of Sense*, London: Methuen & Co Ltd.

———. 1985, *Skepticism and Naturalism: Some Varieties*, London: Columbia University Press and Methuen.

Stroud, B. 1968, "Transcendental Arguments," repr. in Walker, R. (ed.) 1982, *Kant on Pure Reason*, Oxford: Oxford University Press.

———. 1977, "Transcendental Arguments and 'Epistemological Naturalism'," *Philosophical Studies*, 31: 105–15.

———. 1984, *The Significance of Philosophical Skepticism*, Oxford: Clarendon Press.

———. 1994, "Scepticism, 'Externalism', and the Goal of Epistemology," *Aristotelian Society*, suppl. vol. 68: 291–307.

———. 2000, *Understanding Human Knowledge* Oxford: Oxford University Press.

Swinburne, R: 1973, *An Introduction to Confirmation Theory*, London: Methuen.

Tomberlin, J. 1988, *Philosophical Perspectives*, 2, California: Ridgeview Publishing Company.

Vahid, H. 2003, "Externalism, Slow Switching and Privileged Self-Knowledge," *Philosophy and Phenomenological Research*, LXVI(2): 370–89.

Van Cleve, J. 1979, "Foundationalism, Epistemic Principles, and the Cartesian Circle," *The Philosophical Review*, 88: 55–91.

———. 1985, "Epistemic Supervenience and the Circle of Belief," *The Monist*, 68: 90–104.

Van Fraassen, B. 1980, *The Scientific Image*, Oxford: Clarendon Press.

Villanueva, E. (ed.), 1994. *Philosophical Issues 5: Truth and Rationality*, Atascadero, CA: Ridgeview Publishing Company.

Vogel, J. 1990, "Cartesian Skepticism and Inference to the Best Explanation," repr. in Williams, M. (ed.) 1993, *Skepticism*, England: Dartmouth Publishing Company.

———. 1992, "Sklar on Methodological Conservatism," *Philosophy and Phenomenological Research*, 52: 125–31.

———. 2004, "Varieties of Skepticism," *Philosophical Issues*, 14: 426–55.

Walker, R. 1989, "Transcendental Arguments and Skepticism," in Schaper, E. *et al.* (eds) 1989, *Reading Kant*, Oxford: Basil Blackwell.

White, J. 1991, "Knowledge and Deductive Closure," *Synthese*, 86: 409–23.
———. 1976, "Moral Luck," *Proceedings of the Aristotelian Society*, supp. vol. L.
Williamson, T. 1997, "Knowledge as Evidence," *Mind*, 106: 717–41.
———. 2000, *Knowledge and its Limits*, Oxford: Oxford University Press.
Wright, C. *et al* (eds). 1998, *Knowing Our Own Minds*, Oxford: Clarendon Press.
Yalcin, U. 1992, "Skeptical Arguments from Underdetermination," *Philosophical Studies*, 68: 1–34.

Index